Number and Pattern
in the Eighteenth-century Novel

Number and Pattern in the Eighteenth-century Novel

Defoe, Fielding, Smollett and Sterne

Douglas Brooks

Department of English, University of Manchester

Routledge & Kegan Paul

London and Boston

First published in 1973
by Routledge & Kegan Paul Ltd
Broadway House, 68–74 Carter Lane,
London EC4V 5EL and
9 Park Street,
Boston, Mass. 02108 U.S.A.

Printed in Great Britain by
Western Printing Services Ltd,
Bristol

ISBN 0 7100 7598 7

Library of Congress Catalog Card No. 72–97944

For my parents, in gratitude

Contents

Preface

I began the present study as an exploration of repetitive patterns in the eighteenth-century novel. But it soon became apparent that what I had at first taken to be random repetitions which held a given work together by conveying a loose impression of unity were, in fact, ordered symmetries of a numerological kind. In order that the reader ignorant of number symbolism may view my arguments against their historical background, therefore, I supply in chapter i a brief account of the origins and continuity of the numerological tradition in Western European—and particularly English—thought as it affected literary structures. The rest of the book is devoted to analyses of the major novels of Defoe, Fielding, Smollett, and Sterne, respectively. I omit discussion of Richardson's novels because to have included an account of them would have made the book too unwieldy. That a detailed structural examination would be worth while, however, has already been well demonstrated by F. W. Hilles's perceptive 'The Plan of *Clarissa*', *Philological Quarterly*, 45 (1966).

The first part of chapter iii is a slightly expanded version of '*Moll Flanders*: An Interpretation', which originally appeared in *Essays in Criticism*, 19 (1969); and chapter iv is a complete reworking of 'Symbolic Numbers in Fielding's *Joseph Andrews*', an essay published in Alastair Fowler (ed.), *Silent Poetry: Essays in Numerological Analysis* (1970).

I would like to thank Martin Battestin, Damian Grant, Douglas Jefferson, and Edwin Webb, for help and suggestions. My greatest debt, however, is to Alastair Fowler, who read parts of this book in draft: the frequency with which he is mentioned in the notes gives some indication of how much I owe to him. Finally, my thanks to my mother for her patient typing of the manuscript.

Where no place of publication is stated for a book it may be assumed to be London.

The highest beauty of form must be taken from nature; but it is an art of long deduction, and great experience, to know how to find it. We must not content ourselves with merely admiring and relishing; we must enter into the principles on which the work is wrought: these do not swim on the superficies, and consequently are not open to superficial observers.

Sir Joshua Reynolds, Discourse VI, 10 December 1774

The common end of all *narrative,* nay, of *all,* Poems is to convert a *series* into a *Whole*: to make those events, which in real or imagined History move on in a *strait* Line, assume to our Under-standings a *circular* motion—the snake with it's Tail in it's mouth. Hence indeed the almost flattering and yet appropriate Term, Poesy—i.e. poiēsis=*making*. Doubtless, to *his* eye, which alone comprehends all Past and all Future in one eternal Present, what to our short sight appears strait is but a part of the great Cycle—just as the calm Sea to us *appears* level, tho' it be indeed only a part of a *globe*. Now what the Globe is in Geography, *miniaturing* in order to *manifest* the Truth, such is a Poem to that Image of God, which we were created with, and which still seeks that Unity, or Revelation of the *One* in and by the *Many*, which reminds it, that tho' in order to be an individual Being it must go forth *from* God, yet as the *receding from him* is to *proceed* towards Nothingness and Privation, it must still at every step turn back toward him in order to *be* at all—Now, a straight Line, continuously retracted forms of necessity a circular orbit.

Coleridge to Joseph Cottle, 7 March 1815 (in E. L. Griggs, ed.,
Unpublished Letters of Samuel Taylor Coleridge (1932), II. 128–9)

i Introduction:
The Numerological Background

The English novel as we know it emerged in the early to middle
eighteenth century. Defoe's first novel, *Robinson Crusoe*, was published
in 1719, his last, *Roxana*, in 1724; the novels of Richardson and Fielding
were all published between 1740 and the early 1750s, as were Smollett's
Roderick Random (1748) and *Peregrine Pickle* (1751). The emergence of the
novel thus coincides with the hey-day of English Augustanism.

It is only within the past twenty or thirty years that we have come
to appreciate the peculiar difficulties and subtleties of Augustan
literature, both verse and prose, though the critical emphasis has
tended to be on the former. These difficulties reside largely in its
allusiveness—the habit, easily nurtured in a period of considerable
intellectual and social cohesion when writer and reader shared the
same cultural outlook, of embodying in one's satire, poetical epistle,
or whatever, references to that common background: the classics,
the emblem books, and so forth. For the early eighteenth century,
near enough to appear deceptively modern, is, in many respects, so
alien (as many an undergraduate reader struggling with the *Tale of a
Tub* or *The Dunciad* has discovered) that to come to terms with its art
requires a considerable effort of historical awareness and understanding: a readiness, among other things, to accept that the intellectual, ethical, and artistic concerns of Renaissance humanism lived on
well into the eighteenth century, and that English Augustanism saw
their last flowering and death-throes.

Critical interest in the novel, too, bears witness to growing sympathy with the historical and intellectual climate in which it was
fostered. Instead of seeing the works of Defoe, Fielding, and others, as
nineteenth-century novels *manqués*, we are, as our knowledge in-
creases, gradually becoming less arrogant about what used to be
regarded as their inadequacies. In short, we are beginning to realize

1

that they share in the complexities of the poetry of the period. But much research remains to be done, and the present book is an attempt to clear away some existing misconceptions about just one element in these novels, their formal structure. For structure, in the eighteenth century as in earlier centuries, could carry symbolic weight and contribute to a work's meaning. It is my contention that our early novelists conceived of structure in what we would now call numerological terms. And at this point, perhaps, I should offer definitions, and sketch in the essentials of the numerological background to show how it was handed down to the eighteenth century.

I

By the term 'numerology', as it is used in modern literary criticism, is meant (1) the structural exploitation in the literary artifact of symbolic numbers and (2) any kind of arithmetical patterning. Sometimes both forms appear in the same work; sometimes only the one or the other. In literature, music, and the visual arts numerology was a dominant compositional mode up to, and including, the eighteenth century. Occasionally the patterns thus created were wilfully esoteric (because number symbolism was still in the Renaissance regarded as a 'mystery' reserved only for the initiated); but many others were simpler and would have been accessible even to the fairly casual observer.

The tradition with which the present book is concerned originates with the Pythagorean and Platonic belief that the cosmos was definable in terms of number, and that its structure was both mathematical and musical. For when, as the story goes, Pythagoras discovered the mathematical principles governing musical intervals—that the ratio 1:2 yields the *diapason* or octave, 3:2 the *diapente* or fifth, 4:3 the *diatesseron* or fourth, and 8:9 the tone—he thought that he had revealed a fundamental truth not only about the universe itself, but also about the microcosm, man, who, in order to contemplate and respond to the universe and music as he does, must also possess number within him. Aristotle expressed the notion thus in his *Politics*:[1] 'we seem to have a certain affinity with tunes and rhythms; owing to which many wise men say either that the soul is a harmony or that it has harmony.' In addition, the Pythagoreans regarded individual numbers symbolically: 1, or the monad, at the head of the numerical series, came to stand for the creative principle; 2, the dyad, because it breaks away

2

from the integrity of the monad, was identified with evil, and so forth. Numbers were also designated male (if they were odd) or female (even).

Plato's view of the cosmos as it appears in the *Timaeus* is essentially Pythagorean in origin. Plato regarded it as an elaborate mathematical structure which, in sections 35-6, he describes as consisting of a numerical series that became known as the *lambda* diagram because later commentators arranged the numbers involved in the following fashion, after the form of the Greek lower-case *lambda*:

The series contains both female (even) and male (odd) numbers, since from these everything is generated; and it stops with the cube of 2 and 3 because the cube takes us to the third dimension. Moreover, these are the numbers not only of Plato's World Soul but also of the individual soul: numbers and morality become one; for it is only the well-tempered soul that echoes the harmonies of the cosmos:[2]

> The vision of day and night and of months and circling years has created the art of number and has given us not only the notion of Time but also means of research into the nature of the Universe. From these we have procured Philosophy in all its range, than which no greater boon ever has come or will come, by divine bestowal, unto the race of mortals. This I affirm to be the greatest good of eyesight ... the cause and purpose of that best good, as we must maintain, is this,—that God devised and bestowed upon us vision to the end that we might behold the revolutions of Reason in the Heaven and use them for the revolvings of the reasoning that is within us, these being akin to those, the perturbable to the imperturbable; and that, through learning and sharing in calculations which are correct by their nature, by imitation of the absolutely unvarying revolutions of the God we might stabilize the variable revolutions within ourselves.

Similarly, it is the function of music 'to assist in restoring [the soul] to order and concord with itself' (47D). Needless to say, this also had

3

aesthetic implications. For if the soul responds to music, and music is number, then beauty itself must be objectively definable; that is, definable in musico-mathematical terms. This is the Pythagorean-Platonic view that was still being voiced for the English eighteenth century by Lord Shaftesbury in his *Characteristics* (1711):[3] 'What is beautiful is harmonious and proportionable; what is harmonious and proportionable is true; and what is at once both beautiful and true is, of consequence, agreeable and good.'

The Renaissance inherited its neo-Platonism via the Church Fathers, who, attempting to reconcile the Pythagorean-Platonic view of creation with the account in Genesis, and observing similarities between them, decided that the great Greek philosophers had been influenced by the Mosaic Pentateuch. Wisdom 11: 21—'Thou hast ordered all things in measure, and number, and weight'—now became a key Biblical text, and to St Augustine (for example) the mysteries in the Bible were often of a numerical nature: numbers mentioned substantively had to be explained (a celebrated instance is the 153 fishes of John 21: 11),[4] the placing of the tree of knowledge in the centre of the Garden of Eden (Genesis 3: 3) was regarded as being symbolically significant,[5] and so on.

Renaissance numerology, Pythagorean-Platonic and Biblical in origin, also reveals a preoccupation with astronomical, temporal, and calendrical numbers. So common are they in sixteenth-century literary structures, indeed, that one must attribute their efflorescence, at least in part, to the contemporary obsession with time and mutability.[6] Moreover, number symbolism received additional impetus from the humanist revival[7] and was, inevitably, essential to contemporary speculations about the plan of the universe. In this respect the Preface to John Dee's *Euclid* (1570) is typical:[8]

> By *Numbers* propertie therefore, of us, by all possible meanes (to the perfection of the Science) learned, we may both winde and draw ourselves into the inward and deepe search and vew, of all creatures distinct vertues, natures, properties, and *Formes*: And also farder, arise, clime, ascend, and mount up (with Speculative winges) in spirit, to behold in the Glas of Creation, the *Forme* of *Formes*, the *Exemplar Number* of all *thinges Numerable*: both visible and invisible, mortall and immortall, Corporall and Spirituall.

At this point mention should be made of Henry Cornelius Agrippa (1486–1535), whose *De occulta philosophia* was published in 1531. Agrippa is perhaps the best-known representative of Renaissance occultism,[9] but alongside the more obscure diagrams and beliefs in his treatise we find orthodox Christian humanist attitudes, including, in Book II, a straightforward enough account of number symbolism with a chapter for each of the first 10 digits and less detailed discussion of other numbers. As Agrippa explains, the study of number is important because:[10] '*Severinus Boethius* saith, that all things which were first made by the nature of things in its first Age, seem to be formed by the proportion of numbers, for this was the principall pattern in the mind of the Creator.' He continues: 'Harmony also, and voices have their power by, and consist of numbers, and their proportions, and the proportion arising from numbers, do by lines, and points make Characters, and figures.'

Agrippa also includes in Book II an elaboration of the familiar notion of man as microcosm, the proportions of whose body and soul reflect those of the cosmos.[11] I quote from chapter 27: 'Seeing man is the most beautiful and perfectest work of God, and his Image, and also the lesser world; therefore he by a more perfect composition, and sweet Harmony, and more sublime dignity doth contain and maintain in himself all numbers, measures, weights, motions, Elements and all other things which are of his composition. . . .' When he gets down to details, he produces the following:

> The thumb is to the wrest in a circular Measure in a double proportion and half; For it contains it twice and a half as five is to two; But the proportion of the same to the brawn of the Arm neer the shoulder is triple; The greatnesse of the leg is to that of the Arm, a proportion half so much again as of three to two. . . . These are those measures which are everywhere found; by which the members of mans body according to the length, bredth, height, and circumference thereof agree amongst themselves, and also with the Celestials themselves: all which measures are divided by manifold proportions either upon them that divide, or are mixed, from whence there results a manifold Harmony. For a double proportion makes thrice a Diapason; four times double, twice a Diapason, and Diapente.

And so on. My illustrative quotation from the next chapter (28)—'*Of the Composition and Harmony of the humane soul*'—can be briefer. The chapter begins with this Pythagorean analysis:

5

As the Consonancy of the body consists of a due measure and
proportion of the members: so the consonancy of the minde of
a due temperament, and proportion of its vertues and operations
which are concupiscible, irascible, and reason, which are so
proportioned together. For Reason to Concupiscence hath the
proportion *Diapason*; but to anger *Diatessaron*: and Irascible to
Concupiscible hath the proportion *Diapente*. . . .

And in case we should think that this kind of thing had been forgotten
by the eighteenth century, it is worth noting that Hogarth, discussing
proportion in chapter 11 of his *Analysis of Beauty* (1753), could allude to
(if only to reject) the idea that the divisions of the body 'are govern'd
by the laws of music.' After mentioning Albrecht Dürer's *Four Books of
Human Proportion* and G. P. Lommazzo's sixteenth-century *Trattato
dell'arte della pittura*, Hogarth comments:[12]

'The length of the foot, say they, in respect to the breadth, makes
a *double suprabipartient*, a *diapason* and a *diatesseron*:' which, in my
opinion, would have been full as applicable to the ear, or to a
plant, or to a tree, or any other form whatsoever; yet these sort
of *notions* have so far prevail'd by time, that the words, *harmony
of parts*, seem as applicable to form, as to music.

It is significant that the first, and only, English translation of
Agrippa's *Three Books* was published in London in 1651; for this is clear
evidence of the continuity of the tradition it represents (right down
to planetary magic squares)[13] well into the century of the new science
and of what E. J. Dijksterhuis has called[14] 'the mechanization of the
world picture'. Number, of course, remained the basis of this new
world-view; but attitudes towards number and the universe slowly
changed: speculative numerology yielded to a mathematics to which
Pythagorean and theological symbolism was no longer relevant. And
this in turn entailed the discrediting of that unconsciously analogical
way of thinking about man and the universe so characteristic of the
medieval period and the Renaissance, of which the numerological
tradition was so essential a part. That the tradition, in fact, lived on it
is the purpose of the present book to suggest. But it was, inevitably,
regarded with increasing scepticism by the majority.

Thus, Swift's hack in *A Tale of a Tub* (1704) is satirized for his numerological inclinations:[15]

Now among all the rest, the profound Number *THREE* is that which hath most employ'd my sublimest Speculations, nor ever without wonderful Delight. There is now in the Press, (and will be publish'd next Term) a Panegyrical Essay of mine upon this Number, wherein I have by most convincing Proofs, not only reduced the *Senses* and the *Elements* under its Banner, but brought over several Deserters from its two great Rivals *SEVEN* and *NINE*.

And yet, as a careful reading of the *Tale* will show, Swift, on the side of the ancients in the ancients versus moderns controversy, is not satirizing that inherited view of the world to which theories of proportion and symbolic numbers belong, but, rather, an undiscriminating type of mind which, over-zealous, pedantic, and full of misconceptions and preconceptions, twists the evidence to fit its theories against common sense and reason. Hence, towards the end of Section X there is an even more elaborate attack on esoteric numerological extremism:[16]

And First, I have couched a very profound Mystery in the Number of O's multiply'd by *Seven*, and divided by *Nine*. Also, if a devout Brother of the *Rosy Cross* will pray fervently for sixty three Mornings, with a lively Faith, and then transpose certain Letters and Syllables according to Prescription, in the second and fifth Section; they will certainly reveal into a full Receit of the *Opus Magnum*. Lastly, Whoever will be at the Pains to calculate the whole Number of each Letter in this Treatise, and sum up the Difference exactly between the several Numbers, assigning the true natural Cause for every such Difference; the Discoveries in the Product, will plentifully reward his Labour.

But, as I have said, to satirize extremism is not to satirize the essentials of the tradition itself. And if Swift's exact meaning is difficult to unravel, then Dr George Cheyne—friend of Richardson and Fielding —was explicit enough about his belief in the principle of analogy, even taking it to the mystical extreme, familiar enough in earlier centuries, of seeking out[17] 'tripartite divisions of the physical world [to] confirm the unity of the Trinity' while at the same time seeing gravitation as an analogue of 'man's impulse to reunite with God'. To Cheyne the old (the search for 3s) coexisted happily with the new (gravitation), and the universe was still a divine hieroglyph, at every point yielding symbolic meanings.

Even in the mid-eighteenth century John Upton, another friend of Fielding, found no difficulty in interpreting symbolic numbers when he came to annotate his edition of *The Faerie Queene* (1758), identifying Spenser[18] as 'our Pythagorean poet' who 'use[s] mathematics as a kind of mean between sensible and intellectual objects'. Since I quote below, in chapter v, from his reading of the numerological twenty-second stanza in *The Faerie Queene*, II. 9, I offer here another example of his method from st. 12 of the same canto, in which Guyon is told that the castle of Alma (that is, says Upton, 'the human body') has been besieged for seven years. Upton explains the number as follows:[19] 'He says *seven years*, perhaps, in allusion to the seven ages of the world. . . . Or perhaps the number *Seven* has a particular reference to the various stages of mans life.' And in support of his last suggestion he cites two of the ancient authorities on number symbolism, Censorinus's *De die natali*, chapters 7 and 14, and Macrobius's *Commentary on the Dream of Scipio*, I. 6. The latter was one of the most influential neo-Platonic treatises in the medieval period and beyond. It is indeed significant, then, that as late as 1758 Upton could advise his reader[20] that 'this whole chapter of Macrobius should be red over, to understand well this Canto of Spenser: for our poet plainly had it in view, as well as the *Timaeus* of Plato': and this, it should be recalled, a year after Edmund Burke's *Philosophical Enquiry into the Origin of our Ideas of the Sublime and Beautiful* (1757) had rejected completely Pythagorean-Platonic proportional theories, as Hogarth had also rejected them in his *Analysis of Beauty*.[21] The new voice may be represented by the following quotation,[22] with its sceptical dismissal of the familiar Vitruvian idea:[23]

> I know that it has been said long since, and echoed backward and forward from one writer to another a thousand times, that the proportions of building have been taken from those of the human body. To make this forced analogy complete, they represent a man with his arms raised and extended at full length, and then describe a sort of square, and it is formed by passing lines along the extremities of this strange figure. But it appears very clearly to me, that the human figure never supplied the architect with any of his ideas.

To sum up: this rejection of the Pythagorean-Platonic tradition in the 1750s is no surprise. What does provide food for thought is its survival, in a relatively pure form, so late in the English artistic and philosophical consciousness. Although the occult accretions—represented, for example, by the more obscure sections of Agrippa's *Three Books*—seem largely to have disappeared during the later seventeenth century, familiarity with the principles of number symbolism, as the *Tale of a Tub* attests, and some at least of the symbolic meanings themselves, remained common until the middle of the eighteenth century, particularly among those writers who perpetuated Christian humanism: Dryden, Swift, Pope, Fielding, Gray, and so forth. For them numerology, gradually undermined by the empiricism of the preceding few generations, still retained the validity of poetic truth, representing a stable way of knowing nature which they could hark back to with an understandable enough mixture of half-belief, scepticism, and nostalgia.

II

How, then, does all this affect literary structures? The eighteenth century inherited from the Renaissance the doctrine of poetry as mimesis, or imitation of nature. In the Renaissance, and deriving from St Augustine, the view of the world as 'God's poem' took on increasing authority. It is repeated concisely and explicitly by Abraham Cowley in the first book of his unfinished Biblical epic, the *Davideis* (1668), in a passage which usefully includes the further correlative and traditional assumption that if the world is a poem, and God therefore a poet, then the poet must also be a god, and his poem another world, or heterocosm, echoing (or miming) formally the harmonies of the macrocosm:[24]

> As first a various unform'd *Hint* we find
> Rise in some god-like *Poets* fertile *Mind*,
> Till all the parts and words their places take,
> And with just marches *verse* and *musick* make;
> Such was *Gods Poem*, this *Worlds* new *Essay*;
> So wild and rude in its first draught it lay;
> Th'ungovern'd parts no *Correspondence* knew,
> An artless *war* from thwarting *Motions* grew;
> Till they to *Number* and fixt Rules were brought
> By the *eternal Minds Poetique Thought*.

Rudolf Wittkower has shown how, on the authority of Vitruvius's *De architectura*—and *pace* Burke!—this analogical mode of thought

9

affected architecture, by tracing examples in the work of Palladio and other theorists and practitioners. He devotes an appendix to a translation of the neo-Platonist Francesco Giorgi's memorandum of 1 April 1535 for the church of S. Francesco della Vigna which is so explicit a declaration of numerological intent that it must be quoted from here:[25]

> I should like the width of the nave to be 9 paces . . . which is the square of three, the first and divine number. The length of the nave, which will be 27, will have a triple proportion which makes a diapason and a diapente. And this mysterious harmony is such that when Plato in the *Timaeus* wished to describe the wonderful consonance of the parts and fabric of the world, he took this as the first foundation of his description, multiplying as far as necessary these same proportions and figures according to the fitting rules and consonances until he had included the whole world and each of its members and parts. We, being desirous of building the church, have thought it necessary, and most appropriate to follow that order of which God, the greatest architect, is the master and author.

Ten years earlier, in 1525, Giorgi had published his *De harmonia mundi totius*, a syncretistic treatise on the harmony of the universe offering a fusion of Christian and Platonic ideas which itself attempts, structurally, to mime those harmonies that are its subject-matter. As Giorgi's French translator, Guy le Fevre de la Boderie, pointed out in the introductory epistle to his translation (1579),[26] 'our author, imitating the order of the world and, as nearly as he could, its Creator and Architect, first of all has divided up this harmony of the world into three Cantos'; and so he goes on, explaining the symbolism of the book- and chapter-totals.

We can now see how numerology influenced both architecture and literature. We can also now appreciate that when a poet used the analogy of the poem as world model he might well intend it in a way that far transcended mere metaphor and the vaguely suggestive; and that, as often as not, he tried to express the analogy in structural terms. In doing so, as I have said, he would draw on the Christianized Pythagorean-Platonic tradition, occasionally on occult numbers, and on temporal and astronomical numbers.

The familiar and related metaphor of 'the book of nature' or 'book of the world'—examples of which have been traced by E. R. Curtius from the twelfth century on[27]—confirms, clearly enough, the heterocosmic analogy. This, too, was a notion still alive in the eighteenth century, as Addison's *Spectator* 166 (10 September 1711) attests:[28] 'As the supreme Being has expressed, and as it were printed his Ideas in the Creation, Men express their Ideas in Books, which by this great Invention of these latter Ages may last as long as the Sun and Moon, and perish only in the general Wreck of Nature.'

In literature number symbolism is, broadly speaking, either substantive (i.e., numbers are mentioned explicitly in the text) or formal. Well-known instances of substantive numerology are Donne's poem 'The Primrose' and *The Faerie Queene*, II. 9. 22, with its reference to 7 and 9. Here the critic's interpretative task is the relatively simple one of establishing the likely significance of the numbers as they appear in their context, by checking in contemporary treatises or sources known to have been available at the time. In the Renaissance, of course, there is no shortage of these, though special mention should be made of Pietro Bongo's *De mystica numerorum significatione* (1583, and reprinted several times under slightly differing titles), a work unsurpassed in the thoroughness of its analyses of Pythagorean-Biblical number lore.

Formal numerology—the concern of the present book—is at once a more challenging and exciting matter. This involves the description of numerically-based spatial patterns which, as I said at the beginning, either may or may not draw on traditions of number symbolism. For example, in chapter vi I discuss examples of numerical patterning in Smollett's *Roderick Random*, but the numbers in themselves do not possess a symbolic significance. Fielding and Sterne, on the other hand, do appear to be aware of, and to exploit, traditional symbolic meanings. Numerological analysis of poetry might reveal that the total number of lines in a work, the number of stanzas, the number of lines in a stanza, or all three, are symbolically significant. In eighteenth-century prose fiction, similarly, book-totals and chapter-totals (or, in the case of *Humphry Clinker*, letter-totals) sometimes prove to be symbolic. Again, the critic substantiates his case by citing reliable authorities for all meanings adduced and showing convincingly how they relate to the verbal meaning of the work under consideration.

Until recently it was believed that the practice of numerical composition in literature was restricted to the medieval period. Pioneering studies here were Vincent F. Hopper's *Medieval Number Symbolism* (New York, 1938) and Excursus xv (on 'Numerical Composition') in E. R.

Curtius's *European Literature and the Latin Middle Ages*. The publication, in 1960, of A. Kent Hieatt's *Short Time's Endless Monument: The Symbolism of the Numbers in Edmund Spenser's 'Epithalamion'*, however, revealed for the first time complex formal numerology, temporal in kind, in a Renaissance poem: *Epithalamion*'s twenty-four stanzas were shown to represent the hours of the wedding-day therein celebrated (with the actual time at which darkness fell structurally expressed) and the 365 long lines to symbolize the number of days in the year. These, it must be said, are only the basic elements of a remarkably elaborate cosmic model whose temporal structure at once complements and extends the poem's themes: marriage, generation, and mutability.[29]

Hieatt failed to persuade some readers largely, one suspects, because he was unable to locate precedents and to place Spenser's achievement within its formal, numerological, tradition. Almost immediately, however, his discovery began to receive implicit confirmation: in 1961 Gunnar Qvarnström published a book including an account of numerological patterns in *Paradise Lost* which demonstrated that the poem is symmetrically balanced about its arithmetical centre and that the line-totals of some of the speeches are symbolically significant (these findings appeared in English in 1967 under the title *The Enchanted Palace: Some Structural Aspects of 'Paradise Lost'*). Two years later, in her essay 'The Hidden Sense' (1963), Maren-Sofie Røstvig published the results of her researches into the numerological structures of some poems of Milton and Spenser and the works of Henry More. But it was not until 1964 that numerological criticism made its biggest advance yet, with Alastair Fowler's analysis of Pythagorean and astronomical number symbolisms in *The Faerie Queene* in *Spenser and the Numbers of Time*. Fowler also included a general section on numerology —its place in Renaissance thought; the types found in sixteenth- and seventeenth-century poetry (Pythagorean-Platonic; Biblical; astronomical); and suggestions and warnings for the critic. Here, among other points, Fowler emphasized (a) that the critic must restrict his count to clearly defined sections in a work, so that the numbers on which he is basing his argument can be in no way open to dispute (*Epithalamion does* possess twenty-four stanzas and 365 long lines, for example) and (b) that the numbers must complement the work's substantive meaning.

More recently the background has been further clarified by Christopher Butler's *Number Symbolism* (1970)—a brief but important history of numerology in Europe and its aesthetic implications from its Pythagorean beginnings to the present day—and by *Silent Poetry: Essays in Numerological Analysis* (1970), edited by Fowler, which contains contributions by various critics on a large variety of works from the medieval period on. Maren-Sofie Røstvig's essay 'Structure as Prophecy: The Influence of Biblical Exegesis upon Theories of Literary Structure' deserves particular mention as a valuable and suggestive guide to the importance of the numerological (largely Augustinian) tradition for Biblical exegesis, and hence for the use of numerology in religious poetry.

This brief survey of the growth of numerological criticism within the past decade or so fittingly concludes with another book of Fowler's, *Triumphal Forms: Structural Patterns in Elizabethan Poetry*. Fowler fills in yet more of the historical background (especially the association of numerology with the humanist revival) and, in the many individual analyses he offers, concentrates on two main patterns: the temporal, and what he calls the 'triumphal form', in which there is a firm emphasis on the arithmetical centre in a given work. Fowler traces many examples of such central emphasis, noting that the mid-point is generally marked by substantive references to elevation, sovereignty, or balance. He sees this particular form as deriving ultimately from the iconography of cosmic kingship (the expression of the earthly monarch's pre-eminence through solar metaphors; in the Ptolemaic system the sun is the central—fourth—of the seven planets) and the Christian notion of the *Sol iustitiae* or Sun of justice (Christ come in judgment described in terms of the midday sun) via the triumphal pageant and triumphal arch, where the sovereign or an image of sovereignty was often enthroned at the centre.

Fowler has here, by all appearances, uncovered what is probably the predominant single formal pattern in English Renaissance and seventeenth-century poetry, one which, moreover, survived well into the next century, not only in poetry, but, as I hope to show, in the novel and the visual arts—Hogarth's engravings, for example, some of which I discuss in chapter iv.

Emphasis on the centre invites not only elementary symmetry of the A B A type but, in addition, more complex, chiastic, schemes: A B C D C B A. And this, to a large extent, is what the present work is about: the symbolic centre and chiastic structures in the eighteenth-century novel together with the circular form inevitable with the chiasmus, and the use of symbolic numbers themselves. It will be understood that I believe these patterns to be consciously contrived and to have been intended by their authors to function meaningfully: in the first half of the eighteenth century at least, and in some cases beyond, the literary artifact was still viewed as an imitation of nature and therefore as a cosmic model. From early on, as we have seen, number had been indispensable to this view of literature and its function. And if, as I think is the case, numerological patterning is more common in the novel than in the poetry of the period, then this must be because any new form looks to old models (in this case literary, but also in the visual arts): it would appear that the more artistically aware of our early novelists, seeking ways of ordering a long prose fiction, found part of their answer in inherited, numerological, structures. This in turn raises questions about, in Ian Watt's phrase, 'the rise of the novel' that I cannot begin to go into here. What I offer, then, is an exploratory essay in support of those critics who stress the religious element in the eighteenth-century novel; except that instead of restricting myself to the preoccupation with Providence as expressed at the level of plot and verbal commentary,[30] I concentrate largely on formal structure. As I see it, the presence of symmetries and number symbolisms indicates that for these novelists aesthetic order was still the universal order in little: for them as for Pope,[31] 'All Nature is but Art . . .; All Chance, Direction . . .; All Discord, Harmony, not understood.' But I also trace the break-down of this belief and practice, particularly in the cases of Defoe and Fielding's *Amelia*.

It is appropriate now, I think, to offer further reminders of the average eighteenth-century reader's acquaintance with, and attitude to, number symbolism. He was, as I have said, sceptical; and yet it would be a mistake to underestimate his familiarity with it, a familiarity mixed with affectionate understanding. In *Spectator* 58 (7 May 1711), for example, under the motto *Ut pictura poesis erit*, Addison is moved to write, in part, on numerology. He analyses several pattern-poems from Ralph Winterton's *Poetae minores graeci* (1677 edn), one of which is in the shape of 'a Shepherd's Pipe'. The following description is one of the neatest pieces of numerological criticism yet penned:[32] 'The Shepherd's Pipe may be said to be full of Musick, for it is composed of nine different Kinds of Verses, which by their several Lengths resemble the nine Stops of the old musical Instrument, that is likewise the Subject of the Poem.' Again, in *Spectator* 221 (13 November 1711) Addison gently satirizes the Pythagorean *tetractys* (10 as the sum of the first four numbers);[33] and finally, in *Spectator* 632 (13 December 1714),

14

Thomas Tickell—in a paper Fielding might have had in mind when he wrote the first chapter of *Joseph Andrews*, Book II—demonstrates how 'The Love of Symmetry and Order, which is natural to the Mind of Man, betrays him sometimes into very whimsical Fancies', citing the example of '*Gregorio Leti* who had published as many Books as he was Years old; which was a Rule he had laid down and punctually observed to the Year of his Death', associating the twenty-four books of the Homeric epics with the number of letters in the Greek alphabet,[34] and going on to mention[35] the case of his

> Bookseller, who occasioned this Eighth Volume of *Spectators*, because, as he said, he thought Seven a very Odd Number. On the other Side, several grave Reasons were urged on this important Subject; as in particular, that Seven was the precise Number of the Wise Men, and that the most beautiful Constellation in the Heavens was composed of Seven Stars.

It seems from the following analyses that the Christianized Pythagorean-Platonic tradition survived longest, and that other, more obscure, types of numerological patterning—for example, those based on games[36]—belonged more to the sixteenth and earlier seventeenth centuries. I should also stress at this point that I am not concerned with private, idiosyncratic, number symbolisms: the notion of attributing arbitrary meanings to numbers and basing literary or musical structures on them belongs rather to the last century and our own than to earlier centuries. It coincides with the final loss of any kind of general awareness of the historical and philosophical significance of the tradition that I have outlined in this Introduction.

But we need to know much more about sources, particularly in the later seventeenth and eighteenth centuries. I can, in conclusion, only echo Alastair Fowler's suggestion that what is now required is a dictionary of number symbolism organized on historical principles.[37] Lacking such a dictionary I have, in the following pages, quoted from Pietro Bongo's treatise because of its comprehensiveness (though, of course, this does not mean that I think Fielding, Smollett, and Sterne had necessarily read copies of the work or even heard of it); from Agrippa's *Three Books* (the last numerological handbook to be published in England, apparently, and certainly available in the eighteenth century), and from classical and Biblical sources. In discussing Sterne I also refer to Rabelais's *Gargantua and Pantagruel*, an important influence on *Tristram Shandy*, which contains many references to number

15

symbolism—some of them as explicit and as elaborate as the most dedicated numerologist could wish for.

NOTES

1 *Politics*, 1340B; tr. H. Rackham, Loeb edn (1950), p. 661.

2 *Timaeus*, 47A-C; tr. R. G. Bury, Loeb edn (1929), pp. 107–9.

3 *Miscellany* III. 2, in *Characteristics of Men, Manners, Opinions, Times*, ed. J. M. Robertson, 2 vols (1900), II. 268–9.

4 On Augustine's interpretation of 153, see Christopher Butler, *Number Symbolism* (1970), p. 27 and refs.

5 See Alastair Fowler, *Triumphal Forms: Structural Patterns in Elizabethan Poetry* (Cambridge, 1970), p. 25.

6 Fowler, ibid., chaps 6 to 9, discusses many instances.

7 Butler, op. cit., p. 48.

8 Ibid., p. 47.

9 On Agrippa, see Raymond Klibansky, Erwin Panofsky, and Fritz Saxl, *Saturn and Melancholy: Studies in the History of Natural Philosophy, Religion, and Art* (1964), pp. 351ff.

10 *Three Books of Occult Philosophy*, tr. J. F. (1651), II. 2 (pp. 170–1).

11 On bodily proportion, see Erwin Panofsky, *Meaning in the Visual Arts: Papers in and on Art History* (Garden City, N.Y., 1955), ch. 2, 'The History of the Theory of Human Proportions as a Reflection of the History of Styles'.

12 William Hogarth, *The Analysis of Beauty*, ed. Joseph Burke (Oxford, 1955), p. 91.

13 In a magic square a series of numbers is arranged in a square so that 'the sum of each row and column and of both the corner diagonals shall be the same amount': W. S. Andrews et al., *Magic Squares and Cubes* (New York, 1960), p. 1. The planetary magic squares, current in Europe from at least the fourteenth century (Klibansky et al., *Saturn and Melancholy*, pp. 325–7), are illustrated by Agrippa, Book II, ch. 22 (pp. 244–52).

14 E. J. Dijksterhuis, *The Mechanization of the World Picture*, tr. C. Dikshoorn (1969).

15 *A Tale of a Tub*, ed. A. C. Guthkelch and D. Nichol Smith (Oxford, 1958), pp. 57–8.

16 Ibid., pp. 186–7. In a footnote on the opening sentence of this passage Swift further locates the object of his satire by remarking '*This is what the* Cabbalists *among the* Jews *have done with the* Bible, *and pretend to find wonderful Mysteries by it*' (ibid., p. 186n).

17 Earl R. Wasserman, 'Nature Moralized: The Divine Analogy in the Eighteenth Century', *ELH; A Journal of English Literary History*, 20 (1953), 44, referring to Cheyne's *Philosophical Principles of Religion* (1715) and *An Essay on Regimen* (1740). On the search for 3s see, for example, Donne's Sermon 'Preached at Lincolns Inne upon Trinity-Sunday. 1620'; in *The Sermons of John Donne*, ed. G. R. Potter and E. M. Simpson, 10 vols (Berkeley and Los Angeles, Calif., 1953–62), III (1957), 144–5.

18 John Upton, *Spenser's 'Faerie Queene'. A New Edition with a Glossary, and Notes Explanatory and Critical*, 2 vols (1758), II. 480.

19 Ibid., II. 478.

20 Ibid., II. 479. Later still, in his *General History of the Science and Practice of Music* (1776), Sir John Hawkins was interested in linking Newton and Pythagorean-Platonic

number symbolism: see Lawrence Lipking, *The Ordering of the Arts in Eighteenth-Century England* (Princeton, N.J., 1970), pp. 258–9.

21 On this shift in taste and outlook, see the Introd. to J. T. Boulton's edn of the *Enquiry* (1958), pp. lx–lxxvi, and Rudolf Wittkower, *Architectural Principles in the Age of Humanism* (1962), IV. 7.

22 *Philosophical Enquiry*, III. 4, ed. Boulton, p. 100.

23 See Vitruvius, *De architectura*, III. 1. 3.

24 Abraham Cowley, *Poems*, ed. A. R. Waller (Cambridge, 1905), p. 253. Part of a note on this passage reads: 'And the *Scripture* witnesses, that the World was made in *Number, Weight*, and *Measure*; which are all qualities of a good *Poem*' (p. 276).

25 *Architectural Principles*, p. 155.

26 On Giorgi, see Butler, *Number Symbolism*, pp. 56–61, and Maren-Sofie Røstvig, 'The Hidden Sense: Milton and the Neoplatonic Method of Numerical Composition', pp. 27ff., in *The Hidden Sense*, Norwegian Studies in English, 9 (1963).

27 *European Literature and the Latin Middle Ages*, tr. Willard R. Trask, Bollingen Series, 36 (Princeton, N.J., 1967), ch. 16, esp. pp. 319–26.

28 *The Spectator*, ed. Donald F. Bond, 5 vols (Oxford, 1965), II. 154. The metaphor is important for Pope's *Dunciad*, as William Kinsley has shown in his 'The *Dunciad* as Mock-Book', *Huntington Library Quarterly* (*HLQ*), 35 (1971–2), 29–47.

29 In fact, the poem's structure is more complex than Hieatt thought: see Alastair Fowler, *Triumphal Forms*, pp. 161–73, and J. C. Eade, 'The Pattern in the Astronomy of Spenser's *Epithalamion*', *Review of English Studies* (*RES*), n.s. 23 (1972), 173–8, for modifications and additions to his analysis.

30 As, for example, does Aubrey Williams in his 'Poetical Justice, the Contrivances of Providence, and The Works of William Congreve', *ELH*, 35 (1968), 540–65, and his 'Interpositions of Providence and the Design of Fielding's Novels', *South Atlantic Quarterly*, 70 (1971), 265–86.

31 *An Essay on Man*, I. 289–91.

32 Ed. Bond, I. 245–6.

33 Ibid., II. 361.

34 See below, p. 73.

35 Ibid., V. 159–60.

36 See Fowler's discussion in *Triumphal Forms*, pp. 175ff., of Adrian Benjamin's suggestion that Sidney's *Astrophil and Stella* is based on an ancient game known as Penelope.

37 *Triumphal Forms*, p. 203.

ii Defoe: *Robinson Crusoe, Captain Singleton, Colonel Jack*

I *Robinson Crusoe*

Recent years have seen an increasing critical emphasis on the spiritual significance of *Robinson Crusoe* rather than on its economic implications. Ian Watt's reading of the novel, for instance, which sees Crusoe almost exclusively as 'an embodiment of economic individualism' and describes his urge to leave home and that 'middle State, or what might be called the upper Station of *Low Life*'[1] in which he has been brought up[2] as 'really the dynamic tendency of capitalism itself' has now found a corrective in two important studies, G. A. Starr's *Defoe and Spiritual Autobiography* (1965), and J. Paul Hunter's *The Reluctant Pilgrim: Defoe's Emblematic Method and Quest for Form in 'Robinson Crusoe'* (1966). Both works assume that Defoe's novels, and especially *Crusoe*, can be fully understood only if we take account of their religious background. Professor Starr shows that Crusoe's conversion conforms to the pattern traditionally followed in seventeenth-century spiritual autobiographies; while Professor Hunter discusses the novel in terms of such sub-literary forms as contemporary guide literature, the 'providence tradition' (writings concerned with pointing to God's manifest intervention in human affairs, often in connection with shipwrecks), and spiritual biography, and offers a sensitive interpretation which takes careful note of metaphorical and allusive patterns.[3] It seems to me that the findings of both critics take us close to Defoe's primary intention in the novel: accepting it at its face value, as I think we must, as a fictional autobiography about sin, repentance, and conversion, I want to suggest that the work's structural organization, too, has an essential part to play in justifying, to quote the Preface, '*the Wisdom of Providence*'.

Put simply, Crusoe's conversion means that he can detect the governing hand of Providence where previously he had experienced

18

only aimlessness and disorder. As Hunter notes,[4] Crusoe's life after conversion becomes explicitly ordered: 'I bestirr'd my self to ... make my Way of living as regular as I could' (114), for example. And the order here is, clearly enough, a reflection of that order which was traditionally synonymous with Divine Providence. But, in addition, substantive references to Providence (too numerous to list) are supported by a symmetrical structural patterning which is itself Providential: Defoe is working within that mimetic tradition I have described in the Introduction, in which formal structure inevitably has an emblematic significance. We must not forget, either, that even as late as the first half of the eighteenth century the book itself, as a physical object, was still, potentially at least, a cosmic model, as the continued currency of such phrases as 'the book of nature' attests.[5]

Even a cursory reading of *Crusoe* reveals that it is divided into three distinct parts: Crusoe's adventures before being shipwrecked; his stay on the island; and his adventures after leaving it. On closer inspection, however, it emerges that the first and last parts are connected by various cross-references. E. M. W. Tillyard[6] was the first to notice the connection, pointing out how the wolves encountered in the Pyrenees recall the animal noises heard on the coast of Africa (26–7), and noting that Defoe makes the cross-reference explicit: 'the Howling of Wolves run much in my Head; and indeed, except the Noise I once heard on the Shore of *Africa*, of which I have said something already, I never heard any thing that filled me with so much Horrour' (352–3). Tillyard's insight has been developed by Frank H. Ellis,[7] who shows that the cross-references between the two framing sections are more numerous than Tillyard thought, and that they are arranged in symmetrical fashion to produce a large-scale chiasmus (that is, they follow the scheme A B C C B A). The parallels observed by Ellis are as follows: after his escape with the boy Xury from Sallee, Crusoe sails 'southward to the truly *Barbarian* Coast, ... where we could ne'er once go on shoar but we should be devour'd by savage Beasts, or more merciless Savages of humane kind' (26), thus anticipating the encounter in the Pyrenees with 'the Carcass of [a] Horse, and of two Men, devour'd by [wolves]' (356); following this we have the parallel isolated by Tillyard (the 'hideous Howlings and Yellings' of p. 27 answered by 'the Howling and Yelling' of the wolves on p. 355); and finally, on p. 28, the black boy Xury expresses his fear to Crusoe that '*If wild Mans come, they eat me*', just as Friday (Xury's counterpart in the second half of the novel) fears that the cannibals on the island 'were come to look for him, and would cut him in Pieces, and eat him' (273).

An additional structural feature is the way Defoe anticipates Crusoe's isolation on the island by what we might call two proleptic epitomes: as a prisoner of the Moors he has to look after his Master's 'little Garden' (21), which is both a foreshadowing of the moment after Crusoe's conversion when he finds his island[8] 'like a planted Garden' (117) and also a more immediate anticipation of his experiences as a planter in Brazil, experiences which are themselves a hint to Crusoe of what might lie in store for him, as Defoe is again at pains to make clear: 'I liv'd just like a Man cast away upon some desolate Island, that had no body there but himself' (40). Significantly, although his first action after leaving the island is a brief visit to England to see the widow to whom he had entrusted his money (330, see p. 41 for the original incident), Crusoe next goes to Lisbon to find out about his Brazilian plantation and renew his acquaintance with the Portuguese captain who had taken him there in the first place. Such a prudential concern for his effects is, of course, characteristic of Defoe's hero; but this action also reinforces the chiastic arrangement of the first and third parts of the novel: Adventures with Xury / Brazil // Island // Brazil / Adventures with Friday. The symmetry becomes more exact when we notice that the amount of space devoted to these events in each part is approximately the same: Crusoe as prisoner of Moors and his adventures with Xury, nineteen pages; crossing of the Pyrenees with Friday, fifteen pages; Brazil in Part I, nine pages; Brazil in Part III, eleven pages.[9]

The events which form the framework of the novel are patterned with considerable care. We must now turn to the central section—the island—to see if the same structural precision is evident there.

An elementary symmetry is immediately apparent: the first part of Crusoe's isolation traces his own spiritual regeneration; the second part complements the first in that Crusoe now has to put his hard-won Christianity into practice by converting Friday and confronting the cannibals, so that it becomes social in its emphasis rather than remaining merely personal and individual.[10] The transition begins with the appearance of the footprint, which also functions as a telling test of the strength of Crusoe's religious faith. But the footprint is not only thematically central: it is structurally central as well, appearing as it does exactly halfway through the novel, that is, in the first edition, on pp. 181–2 out of a total of 364 (its centrality holds good for any edition, and the symmetry is particularly striking when we consider that Defoe gave himself no external divisions to work to, like Richardson's letters and Fielding's books and chapters). The reader does not have to indulge in arithmetical calculation—of however simple a kind—to discover the footprint's centrality. For Defoe underlines it in several ways: firstly, by the time of day (midday) at which Crusoe notices it: 'It happen'd one Day about Noon going towards my Boat, I was exceedingly surpriz'd with the Print of a Man's naked Foot on the Shore ...'; secondly, by immediately having Crusoe go 'up to a rising Ground to look farther'; and thirdly, by an explicit reference to the mid-point at the beginning of the paragraph preceding that in which Crusoe discovers the footprint: 'As this was also about half Way between my other Habitation, and the Place where I had laid up my Boat, I generally stay'd, and lay here in my Way thither ...' (where the statement seems to be structurally self-referring—to allude to the topography of the book as well as of Crusoe's island).

That Crusoe should mount the 'rising Ground' marks the novel out as being indebted to the iconographical tradition of elevation at the centre which I have discussed in the Introduction.[11] This is important in itself, but it becomes even more important in connection with the temporal directive (noon); for there can be little doubt that Defoe alludes to the identification of the midday sun with the *Sol iustitiae* and the consequent interpretation of noon as a time of trial and judgment (as in *Paradise Lost*, where Eve is tempted and falls at noon).[12] It is also worth reminding ourselves of the symbolism—involving emphasis on the centre—surrounding the cult of the sun king, a cult which utilized the Christian idea of the *Sol iustitiae* and received its most elaborate and extravagant expression at the court of Louis XIV (Louis died only four years before the publication of *Crusoe*);[13] and that Crusoe's observations on sun worship in the *Serious Reflections during the Life and Surprising Adventures of Robinson Crusoe* (1720) include a fifty-six-line verse meditation on that subject which structurally affirms the sun's sovereignty in the following, centrally placed, triplet (ll. 27–9):[14]

> thou [the sun]
> Govern'st the moon and stars by different ray, ⎫
> She queen of night, thee monarch of the day, ⎬
> The moon, and stars, and earth, and plants obey. ⎭

Of no less significance is the interest taken by Biblical commentators in centrality, when justified substantively by the text (e.g., the tree of knowledge 'in the midst of the garden', Genesis 3: 3), and as an aspect of their examination of the Bible's physical structure.[15] I have traced a typical example of the latter dated as late as 1793,[16] and in view of all this it is difficult to accept that the allusions in *Crusoe* can be read in any other than a symbolic way. (The centre of *The Farther Adventures* (also 1719) is similarly accented, marked as it is by the baptism of the penitent Will Atkins's wife, and the Christian marriage ceremony of the two; pp. 159–60 out of a total of 319 in Aitken's edition (1895).)

The footprint is clearly a trial of Crusoe's spiritual strength: perhaps, bearing in mind the temporal symbolism, even his vagueness as to the time—'about Noon'—suggests his lack of spiritual preparedness. Equally clearly it initiates a new stage in the novel's development. To take the first point first: Crusoe's immediate reaction is one of fear; he undergoes bestial degradation ('never frighted Hare fled to cover, or Fox to Earth, with more Terror of Mind than I to this Retreat' (182)), and in his 'dismal Imaginations' he thinks 'it must be the Devil' (ibid.).[17] He has failed his trial ('thus my Fear banish'd all my religious Hope' (184)), and when he looks again at the footprint he '[shakes] with cold, like one in an Ague' (188). The echo is unmistakable: for a moment he has relapsed into his former moral condition, which had been symbolized by his feeling 'cold and shivering' and having an 'Ague very violent' (101); it announces unequivocally—and this brings me to the second point—that Crusoe's subsequent experiences on the island will be a complement to the first part of his stay. The first part narrates, in detail that it would be tedious as well as unnecessary to recapitulate here, Crusoe's coming to terms not only with God and His Providence but also with the island itself; ontogeny repeats phylogeny as his dwellings become more elaborate and his technology more sophisticated[18] ('I arriv'd at an unexpected Perfection in my Earthen Ware.... In my Wicker Ware also I improved much' (170), etc.). Here the very fact of progress is at once obvious and important; and it is answered in Part II by the careful charting of the progress of Crusoe's social re-education. The footprint, test of Crusoe's spiritual strength, is also a mysterious reminder of the outside world and thus marks the beginning of his re-education. The next stage comes when he thinks he sees 'a Boat upon the Sea, at a great Distance' and the remains of a cannibal feast ('Skulls, Hands, Feet, and other Bones of humane Bodies' (194)). Then he actually sees the cannibals, albeit at a distance ('no less than nine naked Savages, sitting round a small Fire' (216)), an event which is soon followed by the wreck of the

European ship and his first real contact with humanity—but (the irony is bitter) dead humanity in the shape of the 'drownded Boy' (223) and the two dead seamen (226). The progression culminates in the arrival of Friday and the subsequent rapid increase in the population of the island (the arrival of the Spaniard and of Crusoe's father, pp. 278ff., etc.).[19] Defoe's point is, presumably, that before Crusoe can be reunited with Europeans he has to overcome the greater challenge of converting Friday (and thereby, as we have seen, strengthening his own faith) and of confronting and rationalizing the psychological shock represented by the cannibals and manifested in his obsessive desire to kill them (for example, dreaming 'often of killing the Savages, and of the Reasons why I might justify the doing of it' (218–19)).[20]

The pattern, as I have indicated, is readily apparent and essentially simple. It becomes more satisfying when we notice that Defoe has consciously incorporated cross-references between the two halves of Crusoe's life on the island; for Defoe, like any Christian, is constantly aware of pattern in art as in life. Thus, the wrecked European ship just alluded to, in which Crusoe finds liquor, powder, clothing, and so forth, recalls Crusoe's own shipwreck and the supplies he retrieved from his vessel. He even finds a dog to replace the one he had in the first part of his stay on the island. It is when he comes across money in the ship, however, that the parallel with the first wreck (Crusoe's taking away of the money on p. 66) is made explicit: 'Well, however, I lugg'd this Money home to my Cave, and laid it up, as I had done that before which I had brought from our own Ship' (229). But the parallel between the two shipwreck episodes is not intended merely to give aesthetic satisfaction. Defoe is concerned with charting Crusoe's moral progress, and so, in contrast to the random trips to the earlier wreck, we have the more arduous voyage to the wreck of the Spanish vessel which Crusoe now prays 'to God to direct', and which is made the less hazardous by his prudent noting of the directions of the currents (224–5). There is, furthermore, a moral significance to another equally obvious parallel between the two halves of Crusoe's stay on the island, the making of a canoe. In the first part Crusoe decides to make 'a Canoe, or Periagua' and sets about the task 'the most like a Fool, that ever Man did, who had any of his Senses awake' (148–9), considering neither the size nor how he is going to get it into the water (he remarks on the 'Want of Hands to move it'). Later, and this time with the help of Friday, Crusoe makes another 'large Periagua or Canoe'; and he is again careful to draw the analogy with the first canoe and make the moral explicit: 'But the main Thing I look'd at, was to get [a tree] so near the Water that we might launch it when it was made, to avoid the Mistake I committed at first' (269).

It is not long after this that the battle with the cannibals takes place in which the Spaniard and Friday's father are rescued. Crusoe then comments: 'My Island was now peopled, and I thought my self very rich in Subjects; and it was a merry Reflection which I frequently made, How like a King I look'd' (286). Once more we detect the echo— not only of Crusoe's remark, 'I might call my self King, or Emperor over the whole Country which I had Possession of' (151), but, more specifically, of a remark some twenty pages later: 'Then to see how like a King I din'd too all alone, attended by my Servants, *Poll*, as if he had been my Favourite, was the only Person permitted to talk to me. My Dog . . . sat always at my Right Hand, and the two Cats, one on one Side the Table, and one on the other' (175).

I should like to notice one final example of repetitive patterning in the novel, this time involving Crusoe's dream of the 'Man . . . all over as bright as a Flame' whose descent makes the earth appear to tremble and the air to fill 'with Flashes of Fire' (102). This dream initiates Crusoe's repentance and conversion; and so it is significant that he and the converted Friday should themselves become avenging angels as they attack the cannibals and rescue their prisoners. For we are told that it is Friday's father's

> Opinion that they were so dreadfully frighted with the Manner of their being attack'd, the Noise and the Fire, that he believed they would tell their People, they were all kill'd by Thunder and Lightning, not by the Hand of Man, and that the two which appear'd, (*viz.*) *Friday* and me, were two Heavenly Spirits or Furies, come down to destroy them. . . . (287–8)

The pattern is completed when Crusoe meditates on the three men who have been abandoned by the English mutineers: he tells us that they 'look'd like Men in Despair. This put me in Mind of the first Time when I came on Shore, and began to look about me; How I gave my self over for lost: How wildly I look'd round me: What dreadful Apprehensions I had . . .' (298–9). Thus does the end of Crusoe's stay on his island echo its beginning;[21] and just as he was awakened to spiritual salvation by the angel in his dream, so now can Crusoe himself fulfil a Providential role by appearing to the castaways as 'a *Spectre-*

like Figure . . . sent directly from Heaven', so that one of them asks: '*Is it a real Man, or an Angel!*', and Crusoe replies: 'Be in no fear about that, Sir, . . . if God had sent an Angel to relieve you, he would have come better Cloath'd, and Arm'd after another manner than you see me in . . .' (301–2).[22]

Two structural schemes, both built on cross-reference and repetition, have thus emerged. The first is chiastic: the mysterious footprint is placed firmly in the centre of the novel, and the opening and closing sections which frame the island adventures answer each other in recessed-symmetrical fashion. The second is the two-part division of the island section itself (again marked by the footprint), the second part being a formal replica of the first (i.e., A B C; A B C), with the one concentrating on Crusoe's isolated confrontation of himself and his environment, and the other on his social re-education. There can be no doubt, from Defoe's own pointers in the text, that the patterning is deliberate: in imposing order on his material he has also produced a paradigm of the ordered workings of Providence. And to these structurally functional cross-references should be added other verbal echoes which contribute in a general way to our sense of the novel's balance and symmetry: Crusoe's cry, '*Can God spread a Table in the Wilderness*' (110), for instance, which receives its affirmative response after his conversion: 'I frequently sat down to my Meat with Thankfulness, and admir'd the Hand of God's Providence, which had thus spread my Table in the Wilderness' (153). The technique of verbal repetition may well have its origins in Biblical exegetical method,[23] and this particular instance also explicitly involves the question of typology, a favourite Puritan device and one which obviously encourages the search for a repetitive order (the Old Testament fulfilled in the New Testament), as well as dictating a cyclical view of individual and racial history.[24] Of special relevance in this connection is Hunter's suggestion[25] that the twenty-eight years of Crusoe's 'isolation and suffering' (a typological re-enactment of the exile of the Israelites) 'parallel the Puritan alienation between the Restoration and accession of William and Mary'. If we accept this instance of numerical allusiveness, then it lends support to my numerological interpretation of the centre of the novel, as well as to Martin Greif's suggestion that Crusoe is shipwrecked eight years after his initial act of rebellion because 8 is traditionally associated with regeneration.[26] Finally, in view of the precision of the novel's chronology[27] and the Puritan habit of regarding the date of one's conversion as one's new birthday,[28] we are surely justified in interpreting the nine months which elapse from the moment of Crusoe's being cast away to that of his recovery from his illness and his spiritual conversion (30 September to 30 June) as a symbolic gestation period,[29] the more so, perhaps, as at the beginning of his recovery, immediately after his dream of the 'Man . . . in a bright Flame of Fire' (102), Crusoe reminds us of the regenerative 8 by referring to his '8 Years, of Seafaring Wickedness' (103).

Crusoe—and this applies to a greater or lesser degree to Defoe's other novels—emphasizes pattern because his narrative is retrospective. Looking back on his life as a penitent who now admits God's Providence with the intention of edifying himself and others, he cannot but detect pattern and correspondence. Hunter's comments[30] on the Puritan habit of keeping a diary are relevant here:

> Because all events were actively willed by God, and because a proper understanding of divine intention depended upon correct interpretation of the pattern of events, every individual was obliged to observe carefully all those events which impinged on his life. But because the meaningful pattern of events was not always immediately self-evident, one needed to keep an event-by-event record so that he could later contemplate from a distance the interrelation of these events and comprehend God's total meaning in them.

And in case we should still be sceptical of elaborate and/or imposed structures in such a context, it is worth recalling that among the various patternings he has found in spiritual biographies, Starr traces one specifically—albeit elementary—numerological device—that of organization by septenaries, in accordance with the traditional division of man's life into seven-year periods.[31]

II *Captain Singleton*

Like *Robinson Crusoe*, *Captain Singleton* is a retrospective narrative, following, as Shiv K. Kumar has suggested, the redemptive scheme that is apparent in Defoe's first novel.[32] But it is not so insistent here as in *Crusoe*, and John J. Richetti seems nearer the spirit of the work as a whole when he insists[33] on Singleton as 'a compromise between the compelling egoism of the pirate-adventurer and the self-effacement and submission of the repentant sinner'. Consequently, the structural symmetries apparent in this novel remain curiously extrinsic.

Doubtless Defoe intended them to function as a paradigm of the ordered workings of Providence, as they do in *Crusoe*; but this is not how they strike the reader. Indeed, it now seems that Defoe's secular interests are to the fore: while paying lip-service to the formal conventions that had shaped *Crusoe* (repetition, the mid-point, and so forth), his main concern in *Singleton* is with utilizing those conventions to solve the purely practical and artistic difficulties of organizing an extended prose fiction.

Such a change in emphasis, far from being unexpected, is characteristic of the period: in music, polyphony, with its symbolic implications, was yielding to homophony; in architecture, proportional theories based on Pythagorean/Platonic formulae were being abandoned.[34] A similar shift was occurring in poetry, as the objective (iconographical) significance of structural divisions and the view of poetry and its function to which this belonged gave way to subjectivism and the poetry of process. What is in fact surprising is that the novel, the eighteenth century's 'new form', as it were, should, structurally speaking, have been so conservative—one might almost say archaic. As I have already hinted, though, the answer is simple enough: its creators inevitably brought to it conventions with which they were already familiar from other genres and art forms. To take a simple example: the seventeenth-century poetic tradition of the numerology of the centre obviously played a large part in dictating the emphasis on the mid-point that I trace in this and subsequent chapters.

In *Singleton*, then, as also in *Colonel Jack*, we can actually feel the move away from symbolic form taking place: if structural analysis of these works is not so rewarding as it was in the case of *Crusoe*, at least it shows that Defoe kept a constant eye on the formal aspects of his fiction and was not, in this respect, the careless writer that he is often thought to be.

Singleton falls into two equal halves. The first half contains Singleton's adventures in Madagascar and Africa, the second his adventures as a pirate; and the second half begins at the exact mid-point, on p. 138 out of a total of 277. The centre thus retains the emphasis it received in *Crusoe*, but lacks real iconographical import.

In Part I, the events in Madagascar (bartering with the natives, building encampments, and so forth) anticipate, on a smaller scale, Singleton's travels in Africa as a whole, in the same way that Crusoe's experiences in Brazil anticipate those on the island; while there are, in addition, internal patterns created by encounters with natives, and the discovery of gold, etc.[35] It is only with the second part of the novel, however, that Defoe's concern for the artistic unity of his work becomes fully apparent. For Part II begins with Singleton setting off 'in an evil Hour to be sure, on a Voyage to *Cadiz*' (138). The ship has 'to put in to the *Groyn*' because of a strong wind, and here Singleton is persuaded to join a group of mutineers led by Wilmot (138–9). The parallel is clear: Singleton has seen 'the Bay of *Cadiz*' right at the beginning of the novel (3) and a short while later has been involved in a mutiny which resulted in his being cast away on Madagascar (10–11).

Part II also sees the introduction of William the Quaker. He makes an early appearance (143), and by the end of the novel he has become Singleton's 'Ghostly Father', urging repentance (268ff.). But he starts giving advice to Singleton soon after his arrival on the scene (for example, pp. 147ff., about a ship they are chasing), and it is apparent that his role is intended to complement that of the gunner in Part I who instructs Singleton in astronomy and geography and tells him that 'Knowledge was the first Step to Preferment' in the world (56), just as it also complements that of the Englishman whom Singleton discovers in Africa and who leads them to the large amounts of gold (120ff.):[36] the Englishman becomes the guide and leader of Singleton and his men at this stage in the first part of the novel; William becomes their effective guide in Part II.

Other echoes and parallels remind us of Defoe's constant awareness of the first part of his novel when writing the second. There are, for instance, geographical affinities with Part I other than that of Cadiz, which I have already mentioned: 'the Bay of *All-Saints*' (148) (compare p. 5), the Cape of Good Hope (168; also on p. 5), and the central role played by Singleton's 'old Acquaintance the Isle of *Madagascar*' (171). When Singleton and his men return to Madagascar in Part II after cruising for booty they find a wrecked ship (in fact it turns out to be Wilmot's), and we are told that the crew 'had made a Launch, and a little Yard, and were all hard at Work building another little Ship, as I may call it, to go to Sea in...' (180). This is a deliberate echo of Singleton's earlier discovery, in Part I and again in Madagascar, of 'the Wreck of an *European* Ship' (40). He narrates how he and his companions had gone ashore, and: 'It was a very pleasant Sight to us, when coming on Shore, we saw all the Marks and Tokens of a Ship-Carpenter's Yard; as a Launch Block and Craddles, Scaffolds and Planks, and Pieces of Planks, the Remains of the Building a Ship or Vessel...' (41).

Later in Part II Singleton's hearing of the thirteen Englishmen who are reputed to have been cast away on the coast of North Japan (201–2) seems to be a faint reminder of the discovery of the Englishman in Africa who, I have suggested, is to some extent an anticipation of William. But the reminder—if, indeed, it is intended as one—is deliberately muted, and we realize why when Singleton and his men run aground off the coast of Ceylon (at which point, over the matter of peace signals and doubtless to affirm the structural parallel, Singleton refers to his '*African* Travels' (222)). For the natives have as their prisoner 'an old *Dutchman*' (225) whom they eventually rescue; and it is he, more even than William, who functions as the real structural counterpart to the Englishman of Part I. In addition, the Englishman's story, which 'would indeed be in it self the Subject of an agreeable History, and would be as long and as diverting as our own, having in it many strange and extraordinary Incidents' (123), and which is summarized for us on pp. 123–4, is matched by the longer story of Robert Knox in Part II (238–49), in position if not in substance.

But before they reach Ceylon they plan a voyage 'over the great *Indian* Ocean. This was indeed at first a monstrous Voyage in its Appearance, and the Want of Provisions threaten'd us. *William* told us in so many Words, that it was impossible we could carry Provisions enough to subsist us for such a Voyage. . .' (204). They sail down to New Guinea, 'thence, sailing still Southward, we left all behind us that any of our Charts or Maps take any Notice of' (205); on p. 214 William asks Wilmot 'what Occasion hast thou to run the Venture of starving, merely for the Pleasure of saying, thou hast been where no Body ever was before. . . .' The echo—this time of Singleton's African travels, and specifically the journey over the desert which faces him and his companions in the centre of the continent—is again unequivocal: here there had, predictably, again been difficulties over provisions, and once more they had been in completely uncharted territory: 'I firmly believe, that never Man, nor a Body of Men, passed this Desart since the Flood . . .' (86).

The end of Part II recalls, as we would expect, the end of the first part, the important difference being that Singleton is now ready for repentance, so that instead of squandering his money (and, as he reminds us on p. 257, being 'cheated and imposed upon'), he sends it to William's sister, whom he eventually marries. One final parallel is perhaps worth noting: namely, that William and Singleton part from their comrades and the Dutchman (271) just as Singleton and his two negroes had parted with their comrades and the Englishman on p. 137.

There is clearly a broad contrast between Singleton's 'ill-gotten Wealth' (263) of Part II and the wealth obtained by barter in Part I; and between his repentance at the end of Part II and the 'all Kinds of Folly and Wickedness' (138) with which he ends the first part. But, apart from this instance of moral opposition, the parallelism between the two halves seems, as I have said, rather a manifestation of Defoe's desire to impose pattern on a narrative that would otherwise appear merely loosely episodic, than of anything else. The reader is not convinced, as he is by *Crusoe*, that *Singleton* implies and exposes a Providential pattern through formal structure. The Providential paradigm has largely lost its significance to become mere scaffolding—a convenient method of structural organization.[37]

III *Colonel Jack*

Colonel Jack is largely about the quest for gentility. This concern is consistently evident, from the opening page, when Jack reports his father[38] as having instructed his nurse that 'she should always take care to bid me *remember, that I was a Gentleman*', through Jack's exploits as a thief ('I had a strange original Notion, as I have mentioned in its Place, of my being a Gentleman' (60)), his life in Virginia, where he is clothed at his master's expense and told to go into the warehouse 'a Slave, and come out a Gentleman' (127), his eventual realization, despite material prosperity, that the New World is not for him ('Now, I look'd upon my self as one Buried alive, in a remote Part of the World . . . and in a Word, the old Reproach often came in my way; Namely, that even this was not yet, the Life of a Gentleman' (172)), to his final disguise as 'a *Spaniard* of the better sort' (301). As W. H. McBurney has remarked,[39] 'the question, "Is this the life of a gentleman?" runs through the novel as a dominant *motif*.'[39]

And yet *Colonel Jack* also manifests a concern with the workings of Providence, a concern which coincides, inevitably, with its hero's admissions of guilt or stirrings of repentance. Sold into slavery in Virginia, Jack observes:

> DURING this Scene of Life, I had time to reflect on my past
> Hours, and upon what I had done in the World, and tho' I had
> no great Capacity of making a clear Judgment, and very little
> reflections from Conscience, yet it made some impressions upon

me; and particularly that I was brought into this miserable
Condition of a Slave by some strange directing Power, as a
Punishment for the Wickedness of my younger Years. . . . (119)

On p. 165 Jack's tutor, the penitent scholar-highwayman, instructs his
master in 'the Wonders of . . . merciful Providence', and a few pages
later Jack tells us that he did not as yet understand that the 'Turns of
Life were . . . all directed by a Sovereign God, that Governs the World,
and all the Creatures it had made' (168).

But the most important passage in this vein occurs at the end: its
importance lies in its explicit identification of literary structure with
Providence. Jack comments 'how in collecting the various Changes,
and Turns of my Affairs, I saw clearer than ever I had done before,
how an invisible over-ruling Power, a Hand influenced from above,
Governs all our Actions of every Kind, limits all our Designs, and
orders the Events of every Thing relating to us' (307–8). The Providential ordering of events is mirrored in the ordering of Jack's retrospective narrative: structure—if we are to believe the author—once
again has a symbolic function.

For one thing, Defoe has given the novel a clearly-defined circularity: we notice how Jack's end, like Crusoe's, echoes his beginning
when, as his autobiography draws to a close, Jack explains that he has
now had 'leisure to reflect, and to repent, to call to mind things pass'd,
and with a just Detestation, learn as *Job* says, *to abhor my self in Dust and
Ashes*' (308), thus recalling his boyhood and the novel's opening: 'As
for my Person, while I was a dirty Glass-Bottle House Boy, sleeping in
the Ashes, and dealing always in the Street Dirt, it cannot be expected
but that I look'd like what I was . . .' (7). The penitent interprets and
takes upon himself symbolically what he had once endured as a
physical fact.[40] As confirmation of the novel's circularity we might
also note that Jack's justification for writing his autobiography in the
first paragraph ('I think my History may find a place in the World, as
well as some . . .') is paralleled by the more elaborate justification on
pp. 307–8.

But it is when we turn to the centre—the section dealing with Jack
in Virginia—that Defoe's preoccupation with precise structural details
becomes fully apparent. On his arrival in Virginia, Jack is bought as a
slave and, as we have seen, 'had time to reflect on [his] past Hours'
(119). We are next told of the buying of some new servants, one of
whom is 'a young Fellow not above 17 or 18 Years of Age . . . an

incorrigible Pick-pocket'. Jack's master 'talk'd mighty Religiously to this Boy', and Jack 'was exceedingly mov'd at this Discourse' since it is 'directed to such a young Rogue, born a Thief, and bred up a Pick-pocket like my self'. He continues: 'I thought all my Master said was spoken to me, and sometimes it came into my Head, that sure my Master was some extraordinary Man, and that he knew all things that ever I had done in my Life' (120–1).

The pickpocket, Jack explains, is clearly a reflection of his former self, which is sloughed off as he 'begin[s] the World again' (120); and complementing this pickpocket in the first half of the Virginia episode is the transported scholar-highwayman in the second half, whom Jack, by now a wealthy planter, employs to educate him (157ff.). For the scholar's history, which he alludes to on p. 161, again reminds Jack of his own:[41] 'I was so sensible of the Truth of what he said, *knowing it by my own Case*, that I could not enter any farther upon the Discourse . . .' (161–2). But it is also his role to educate Jack not so much in Latin as in matters spiritual. What Jack should see in this second reflection of his past is a monitory emblem, urging repentance. Jack has, after all, already confessed to 'a secret Horror at things pass'd, when I look'd back upon my former Life' (155), though it is, by his own admission, a horror inspired rather by his innate gentility than by other-worldly concerns: compare and contrast the scholar who, 'look[ing] back upon his past life . . . with horror' (161), points out that, as a servant, 'my Body is punish'd, but my Conscience is not loaded; and as I us'd to say, that I had no Leisure to look in, but I would begin when I had some Recess, sometime to spare; now God has found me Leisure to Repent . . .' (162).

This, of course, is the state of spiritual awareness that Jack reaches (or claims to have reached) only at the end of the novel. At this earlier stage of his development all he is aware of is 'a heaviness on my Soul without being able to describe it, or to say, what ailed me' (165). And despite the scholar's affirmation of 'the Wonders of . . . merciful Providence', which had saved him from hanging so that he might repent, Jack finally informs us that his 'Thoughts were [not] yet Ripen'd' for conversion (171) and turns his attentions once more to the pursuit of gentility.

Looking back on this period of his life from the comfort of his disguise as a Spanish don, however, Jack is able to diagnose his spiritual blindness at this point, in a passage that I have already alluded to:

it was impossible for me to conceal the Disorder I was in, as often as he talk'd of these things; I had hitherto gone on upon a Notion of things founded only in their appearance, as they affected me with Good, or Evil; esteeming, the happy and unhappy Part of Life to be those that gave me Ease, or Sorrow, without regarding, or indeed much understanding how far those Turns of Life were influenced by the giver of Life; or how far they were all directed by a Sovereign God, that Governs the World, and all the Creatures it had made. (168)

But what Jack did not realize at the time is that he had already been instructed by example in the gratitude he should manifest to a merciful God.[42] The example had been the behaviour of the negro Mouchat, whom Jack, instead of punishing for 'a notorious Offence' (136), had treated mercifully as an experiment 'to trye whether as *Negroes* have all the other Faculties of reasonable Creatures, they had not also some Sense of Kindness, some Principles of natural Generosity, which in short, is the Foundation of Gratitude; for Gratitude is the Product of generous Principles' (ibid.). The experiment had worked. Jack had fulfilled a Providential (redemptive) role towards Mouchat, as his own master, frequently referred to as Jack's 'benefactor', had fulfilled a similar role towards Jack. Later on, Jack does the same for the scholar ('I made him one of my Overseers, and thereby rais'd him gradually to a Prospect of living in the same manner, and by the like steps that my good Benefactor rais'd me' (173)), yet is incapable of recognizing that there is a benefactor greater than himself and his master—God, the 'Benefactor' of p. 166, to whom Jack as well as the scholar owes a 'Sense of Mercy'. Indeed, Jack makes the point explicitly:

THIS Article of Gratitude struck deep, and lay heavy upon my Mind; I remembered that I was Grateful to the last degree to my old Master, who had rais'd me from my low Condition . . . ; but I had not so much as once thought of any higher obligation; no, nor, so much as like the Pharisee had said, one *God I thank thee*, to him, for all the Influence which his Providence must have had in my whole Affair. (170)

Only in retrospect can he detect the spiritual implications of this juxtaposition of negro and scholar—implications which become apparent as he orders his life in narrative form, carefully observing the pattern of events and seeing the one as an adumbration of the other. Very near the novel's centre Jack is given his liberty by his master and sets up as a planter in his own right (149ff.). It is here that he traces for us, in brief retrospect, his progress from pickpocket to master-planter (151–2). As a planter he is—perhaps symbolically—given the 'grateful Negro *Mouchat*' as a slave (153). Now starting life anew (in the first half of the Virginia episode he is a servant, in the second half a free man), and having already been confronted by his former self in the figure of the young pickpocket, he must sever all material connection with his former, criminal, existence. And this is what does occur in the exact centre of the novel, on p. 154 out of a total of 309, with the sinking of the ship bringing goods bought with his earlier ill-gotten wealth. Despite the initial shock occasioned by the loss, Jack is eventually able to feel

> a kind of Pleasure in the Dissaster that was upon me about the Ship, and that tho' it was a loss I could not but be glad, that those ill gotten Goods were gone, and that I had lost what I had stolen; for I look'd on it as none of mine, and that it would be fire in my Flax if I should mingle it with what I had now, which was come honestly by, and was as it were sent from Heaven, to lay the Foundation of my prosperity, which the other would be only as a Moth to consume. (157)

The mid-point, as in *Crusoe*, has a manifest symbolic function, and is observed with minute particularity.

Here also Jack performs another symbolic act, in reviewing his past life once more ('I had . . . a secret Horror at things pass'd, when I look'd back upon my former Life') and then anticipating the future ('BUT to look forward, to Reflect, how things were Chang'd'). Coming as it does again in the centre of the novel (pp. 155–6), this is perhaps intended as a structural directive, reminding us that half of the novel is past, and half yet to come. (Compare the explicitness of the foot-print on Crusoe's island in the middle of the book at midday.)[43]

The middle section of the novel, then, falls into two complemen-tary halves: Jack as slave, Jack as planter. Moreover, negro gratitude for mercy in the first half is answered by the scholar's gratitude to a merciful Providence in the second, and dividing them, at the novel's mid-point, is the obviously Providential sinking of the ship.

In addition, the Virginia episode as a whole is framed in a manner that accents its climactic position. Jack goes there, it will be recalled, only because he has been lured on board ship and kidnapped;[44] and this is after he has joined the army and deserted (104ff.). The first thing that happens when he leaves Virginia is that he is captured by a French privateer (176), after which he makes his way to the Spanish Netherlands and becomes a volunteer in the army, reminding us as he does so that 'this was my second Essay at the Trade of Soldiering' (184). The pattern produced is, in fact, a chiastic one: Army / Kidnapping // Virginia // Captured by French / Army.

Although this chiasmus, taken together with the opening and concluding references to ashes, seems to be the full extent of the novel's symmetrical patterning, however, there remains a considerable element of simple repetitive structuring, a few examples of which are worth examining. Thus, the theme of gratitude and mercy, so crucial to the middle of the novel, is also important when Jack returns to his Virginia plantations after his various marriages. Soon after his arrival he discovers his first wife employed as one of his own slaves, and describes her as 'falling down on her Knees just before [him]' and begging mercy (255). He asks the scholar (now his overseer) to go to the warehouse to bring clothes for her just as, earlier, his master had ordered an overseer to call him over 'in the ordinary Habit of a poor half naked Slave' and have him clothed as 'a Gentleman' in a warehouse (126-7). Initially, as the wife seeks mercy, we are reminded of Mouchat. But when she narrates her history after leaving Jack ('her Life was . . . a Collection of various Fortunes, up and down, in Plenty, and in Misery; in Prison, and at Liberty'), declares that she is 'sincerely Penitent', and compares herself to the prodigal son (258), we see that her role is closer to that of the scholar. Indeed, Jack announces twice within a few pages (259, 262) that 'Providence had, as it were cast her upon me again', which implies that even he recognizes her monitory role. In practice, though, her potential in this respect is not developed: she is concerned less with the spirit than with such practical matters as preventing her husband (they marry again on p. 263) from being identified as one of the Jacobite rebels (266ff.).

It is she who is finally able to inform him that the rebels have been granted a general pardon by George I, 'a Secret, and right Notion of the Clemency, and merciful Disposition' of which monarch Jack claims to have sensed as early as p. 268, especially after his wife has mentioned the possibility of a pardon. The pardon, when it does arrive, has the following effect on Jack:

> AND here let me hint, that having now as it were receiv'd my
> Life at the Hands of King *GEORGE*, and in a manner so satisfying

as it was to me, it made a generous Convert of me, and I became
sincerely given in to the Interest of King *GEORGE*; and this from
a Principle of Gratitude, and a Sense of my Obligation to his
Majesty for my Life. . . . (276)

Jack himself is now cast in the part of the grateful Mouchat. But
McBurney[45] is not completely right in describing this as 'climax[ing]
a series of mercy-gratitude scenes'; for the climax surely comes at the
end of the novel, with Jack's final recognition 'that we should pay the
homage of all Events to [God]' (308). McBurney[46] justly calls Jack's
gratitude to George I 'a quasi-religious experience': the genuine
religious experience, prepared for by the scholar and Jack's penitent
wife, is placed, as we would expect, at the close of his narrative. This,
at least, would seem to be how Defoe intended the sequence to be
read. One remains unconvinced, however, that Jack's gratitude to
God is as profound as his gratitude to his king.

Among other repetitions we might note that Will's role as Jack's
'Master and Tutor in Wickedness' (81) complements that of the
scholar; that the sinking of the ship in the centre is anticipated by the
wetting and spoiling of Captain Jack's stolen goods at Lauderdale
(99),[47] and echoed on p. 276 when a sloop, which had been sent to
Jack at Antigua, arrives 'empty, and gutted of all her Cargo'; and
that the questioning of Jack by his master (122ff.) recalls the episode
when Jack had returned the letter-case to the gentleman in the
custom-house and the man had catechized him (36ff.): Jack entrusts
his reward money to the man (39) as, later, he entrusts his bill for £94
to his master (125). Moreover, a footnote emphasizes the parallel:
'*NOTE*. He did not now talk quite so blindly, and Childishly, as when
he was a Boy, and when the Custom-House Gentleman talked to him
about his Names' (123).

There can, then, be little doubt from the directives in the text that
the symmetrical and repetitive patterning in *Colonel Jack* is conscious
and that it is intended to function symbolically by affirming the
presence of 'an invisible over-ruling Power' (308). And yet, as I suggested in connection with *Singleton*, this is not the impression of even
the most observant and sympathetic reader. The trouble is, I think,
that once more we have an instance of meaningful inherited techniques turning into mere scaffolding. There is, as there was potentially
in *Crusoe* and in practice in *Singleton*, a conflict in *Colonel Jack* between
the secular (the gentility theme) and the spiritual, and it is with the

latter that the structure as I have outlined it really belongs. True, the implications of the centre, for example, are handled more sensitively than in *Singleton*, but that is about all one can say. Defoe's unease in *Colonel Jack* is, on the face of it, the more surprising when we recall that it was written after *Moll Flanders*; for in *Moll*, as I argue in the next chapter, the old symmetries are transformed into organic and subtle means of psychological exploration. But it is perhaps a fair assumption that in *Moll* Defoe was writing with an imaginative intensity that he was unable to sustain through either the *Journal of the Plague Year* (also 1722) or *Colonel Jack*.

NOTES

1 *Robinson Crusoe*, p. 3. Quotations are from the facsimile of the first edn (1 vol., 1719), introd. Austin Dobson (1883). Future page references will be included in my text.

2 *The Rise of the Novel* (1963 edn), pp. 65, 68.

3 Among other works offering not dissimilar accounts of the novel are Edwin B. Benjamin, 'Symbolic Elements in *Robinson Crusoe*', *Philological Quarterly* (*PQ*), 30 (1951), 206–11; Martin J. Greif, 'The Conversion of Robinson Crusoe', *Studies in English Literature* (*SEL*), 6 (1966), 551–74, and Robert W. Ayers, '*Robinson Crusoe*: "Allusive Allegorick History" ', *Publications of the Modern Language Association of America* (*PMLA*), 82 (1967), 399–407.

4 *The Reluctant Pilgrim* (Baltimore, Md., 1966), pp. 172–4.

5 See above, Introduction, pp. 10–11.

6 *The Epic Strain in the English Novel* (1958), p. 32.

7 Introd. to *Twentieth Century Interpretations of 'Robinson Crusoe'* (Englewood Cliffs, N.J., 1969), pp. 12–13.

8 Crusoe's comment on the coincidence of dates confirms the parallel: he leaves the island 'the same Day of the Month, that I first made my Escape in the *Barco-Longo*, from among the *Moors* of *Sallee*' (330).

9 I.e., pp. 20–38 and 346–60; 38–46 and 332–42 respectively.

10 See Hunter, p. 182, and Starr, *Defoe and Spiritual Autobiography* (Princeton, N.J., 1965), pp. 121–2. Maximillian E. Novak emphasizes the civilizing process that is also going on here in *Defoe and the Nature of Man* (1963), pp. 48–9.

11 Hunter, pp. 194ff., comments on the series of 'prospects' in *Robinson Crusoe* (referring to Moses on Pisgah), but fails to notice their structural implications: e.g., 'the Top of a little Mountain' on which Crusoe stands in the hope of seeing a ship shortly after his arrival on the island (80), is answered by his 'climbing up to the Top of the Hill' to see the ship which finally rescues him (323). The 'rising Ground' of p. 181 comes, of course, exactly between them.

12 *Paradise Lost*, IX. 739; and see Fowler's note (in *The Poems of John Milton*, ed. John Carey and Alastair Fowler (1968)), and also IV. 30n, deriving the concept of the *Sol iustitiae* from Malachi 4: 2 and citing Erwin Panofsky, *Meaning in the Visual Arts*, pp. 259ff.

37

13 See Fowler, *Triumphal Forms*, pp. 23ff., and Ernst H. Kantorowicz, 'Oriens Augusti —Lever du Roi', *Dumbarton Oaks Papers*, 17 (1963), 117–77 and particularly 162ff.

14 *Romances and Narratives by Daniel Defoe*, ed. G. A. Aitken, 16 vols (1895), III. 127–8.

15 *Triumphal Forms*, p. 25.

16 Reproduced in the Appendix.

17 So that the Sun of righteousness is displaced in his mind (for however brief a period) by its infernal antitype. Crusoe also ignores the Providential Ps. 104: 20–2 ('Thou makest darkness, and it is night: wherein all the beasts of the forest do creep forth. The young lions roar after their prey, and seek their meat from God. The sun ariseth, they gather themselves together, and lay them down in their dens'), which affirms the power of the sun over the beasts of darkness. See Kantorowicz, p. 171, for a discussion of this psalm in connection with a medallion of Louis XIV, and an apposite quotation from *Richard II*, III. ii. 36ff. In Christian iconography the foot symbolizes humility and human fallibility: e.g., Ps. 94: 18: 'When I said, My foot slippeth; thy mercy, O Lord, held me up.' In other words, the footprint should be understood by Crusoe as a warning against self-sufficiency and a reminder of God's Providence.

18 As John J. Richetti remarks: '[Crusoe] has to re-experience the conquest of nature through technology, to examine natural phenomena from the secular, utilitarian viewpoint with the same precision employed in finding their divine configurations'; *Popular Fiction Before Richardson: Narrative Patterns 1700–1739* (Oxford, 1969), pp. 94–5.

19 Swift seems to have borrowed the idea of gradual re-education in *Gulliver's Travels*, IV. 11: after leaving the Houyhnhnms Gulliver first lands on a bare rock, then voyages 'to the *South-East* Point of *New-Holland*' which at first seems deserted and where he eats shell-fish and drinks water. He then encounters natives (who possess fire), is picked up by European seamen and meets their captain, Pedro de Mendez, who offers him chicken and wine, etc.

20 For a brilliant discussion of this section of the novel, and the novel as a whole, in terms of Crusoe's problems about identity, see Homer O. Brown, 'The Displaced Self in the Novels of Daniel Defoe', *ELH*, 38 (1971), 562–90. Brown's findings complement my own, but are pursued in greater detail.

21 There is even a numerical correspondence: after the shipwreck, Crusoe says that he and his companions 'committed our selves being Eleven in Number, to God's Mercy, and the wild Sea' (49); and 'eleven Men' arrive on the island from the ship in which Crusoe eventually makes his escape (297). In the first instance 11 possibly symbolizes transgression (a meaning which goes back to St Augustine, *Civ. Dei*, XV. 20) and penitence (Cornelius Agrippa, *Three Books of Occult Philosophy*, II. 14 (p. 216), glossing Exodus 26: 7).

22 Later on Crusoe sees the ship's captain 'as a Man sent from Heaven to deliver me', and comments on the 'secret Hand of Providence governing the World' (324).

23 Christopher Butler, *Number Symbolism*, p. 26, comments on the traditional (Augustinian) view of the Bible as 'a huge harmonic structure of verbal echoes', citing Peter Brown's *Augustine of Hippo* (1967), p. 254.

24 The circularity of the Christian story, in which the sin of the first Adam is atoned for by Christ, the second Adam, is mimed in the circular structure of *Paradise Lost* (see J. R. Watson, 'Divine Providence and the Structure of *Paradise*

Lost', *Essays in Criticism* (*EC*), 14 (1964), 148–55). Maren-Sofie Røstvig discusses the circular structure of the Bible in her 'Structure as Prophecy', in Alastair Fowler (ed.), *Silent Poetry*, pp. 51–2. The essay as a whole is relevant to my argument. And Hunter comments on the importance of typology for Puritanism, identifying it in part with 'the cyclical pattern of history' (*The Reluctant Pilgrim*, p. 99).

25 Hunter, p. 204.

26 Martin J. Greif, 'The Conversion of Robinson Crusoe', *SEL*, 6 (1966), p. 556n. Crusoe states: 'I went on Board in an evil Hour, . . . the same Day eight Year that I went from my Father and Mother at *Hull*' (46). A Biblical source for this interpretation of 8 is I Peter 3: 20–1. But doubtless the 'terrible Storm' which blows in the Yarmouth roads 'the eighth Day in the Morning' (10) alludes to 8 as the number of Divine judgment ('the end of the world', Agrippa, *Three Books of Occult Philosophy*, II. 11 (p. 202)), since the storm is itself a familiar emblem of such judgment. Dryden's use of the symbolism is discussed by Alastair Fowler and the present author in 'The Structure of Dryden's *A Song for St. Cecilia's Day, 1687*', in Fowler (ed.), *Silent Poetry*, pp. 197–8.

27 On this topic see Dewey Ganzel's thorough analysis in 'Chronology in *Robinson Crusoe*', *PQ*, 40 (1961), 495–512. Also important for the patterning of the novel is Crusoe's emphasis on the coincidence of dates, as in the eight years of p. 46. But see especially p. 157: 'The same Day of the Year that I escaped out of the Wreck of that Ship in *Yarmouth* Rodes, that same Day-Year afterwards I made my escape from *Sallee* in the Boat', etc. This habit also derives from a commonplace of Biblical exegesis (Røstvig, 'Structure as Prophecy', pp. 47–8), and is treated as a Providential emblem in the *Serious Reflections*, where Exodus 12: 41 is cited as well as various seventeenth-century historical examples of such coincidences. Crusoe here remarks 'how Providence causes the revolutions of days to form a concurrence between the actions of men, which it does not approve, or does approve, and the reward of these actions in this world . . .' (ed. Aitken, p. 189).

28 Discussed by Starr, p. 61 and n., who refers to John 3: 3–7.

29 Again noticed by Swift, perhaps: Gulliver wakes up to his new life in Book I, ch. 1 after a sleep of 'above Nine Hours' (see W. B. Carnochan, *Lemuel Gulliver's Mirror for Man* (Berkeley and Los Angeles, Calif., 1968), p. 133 and n); a gestation period of fittingly Lilliputian duration!

30 *The Reluctant Pilgrim*, pp. 82–3.

31 *Defoe and Spiritual Autobiography*, pp. 36–7 and n.

32 Shiv K. Kumar, Introd. to Oxford English Novels (OEN) *Captain Singleton* (1969), p. ix. All subsequent references are to this edn, which is a reprint of the first edn (1 vol., 1720).

33 *Popular Fiction Before Richardson*, p. 84.

34 On the former, see Manfred F. Bukofzer, *Music in the Baroque Era* (1948), pp. 365–9 (discussing 'audible form and inaudible order'), and Edward E. Lowinsky, 'Taste, Style, and Ideology in Eighteenth-Century Music', in Earl R. Wasserman (ed.), *Aspects of the Eighteenth Century* (Baltimore, Md., 1965), pp. 163–205; on the latter, see Rudolf Wittkower, *Architectural Principles in the Age of Humanism*, pp. 142–54.

35 There are complementary battles with natives on, for example, pp. 51ff. and 75ff., and gold is discovered on pp. 94ff. and 129ff. Gary J. Scrimgeour, 'The Problem of Realism in Defoe's *Captain Singleton*', *HLQ*, 27 (1963–4), 21–37, notes

that 'the largest single group of incidents' is formed by encounters with wild beasts (p. 31): yet another contribution to the internal patterning of Part I. He discusses gold as a theme on pp. 32ff.

36 For the Englishman's basis in fact, see Scrimgeour, p. 36.

37 Of the religious and Providential passages in the novel, the following are worth listing: Singleton's first 'religious Thought' on p. 61; the 'Clap of Thunder' which Singleton sees as a sign of Divine vengeance (194–5); and William's comments on Providence and repentance on pp. 266ff.

38 Quotations are from the OEN *Colonel Jack*, ed. S. H. Monk (1965), which reproduces the text of the first edn, 1 vol., 1722.

39 W. H. McBurney, '*Colonel Jacque*: Defoe's Definition of the Complete English Gentleman', *SEL*, 2 (1962), 325. Michael Shinagel also discusses this aspect of the novel in *Daniel Defoe and Middle-Class Gentility* (Cambridge, Mass., 1968), ch. 8.

40 The ashes reappear when Jack's life starts anew on p. 186: 'I was a meer Boy in the Affair of Love, and knew the least of what belong'd to a Woman, of any Man in *Europe* of my Age; . . . and I had been till now as perfectly unacquainted with the Sex, and as unconcern'd about them, as I was when I was ten Year old, and lay in a Heap of Ashes at the *Glass-House*', where the echo reinforces the notion of Jack's new beginning at this point of the narrative.

41 S. H. Monk, Introd. to *Colonel Jack*, p. xii, comments on the parallel between Jack and his tutor.

42 On the importance of gratitude in general for Defoe, see M. E. Novak, *Defoe and the Nature of Man*, ch. 5.

43 Cf. also what happens in the centre of *Tom Jones*: discussed below, pp. 98–9.

44 M. E. Novak remarks that the kidnapping of Jack and Captain Jack looks back to the captain's earlier kidnapping of small children; *Economics and the Fiction of Daniel Defoe* (Berkeley and Los Angeles, Calif., 1962), p. 90.

45 '*Colonel Jacque*: Defoe's Definition of the Complete English Gentleman', p. 335, listing Mouchat, the scholar-highwayman, and the first wife.

46 Ibid.

47 Both instances have been noticed by McBurney, ibid., p. 330 and n.

iii Defoe: *Moll Flanders* and *Roxana*

I *Moll Flanders*

I have departed from chronological order in discussing *Colonel Jack* (December 1722) before *Moll Flanders* (January 1722) because, as I hope to show, there is a strong imaginative affinity between *Moll* and *Roxana*, whereas the less fully realized *Jack* belongs, for the purposes of my argument at least, with the tentative *Singleton*. Certainly, in *Jack* Defoe did not write with the creative energy manifested in either of the novels now under consideration, where we see Defoe developing techniques for exploring the darker recesses of the psyche as a necessary consequence of his moral determination to demonstrate, as he does with an almost compulsive urgency, the inescapable omnipresence of a guilt-ridden past, once exceptional (and in both cases sexual) guilt has been incurred. The structural patterns discussed in the preceding chapter—chiasmus, the central accent, and the element of repetition—are modified, as I have said, to become subtle instruments of psychological penetration. I make no apology, by the way, for concentrating on structure and psychology rather than, with most recent critics, on the question of irony (is it conscious? does it explain the inconsistencies in the novel? and so forth), because the problems thus raised about *Moll* and Defoe's artistic self-awareness, although they have been the subject of undeniably valuable discussions, seem to me to be somehow peripheral. At least, they don't account for the novel as I, and, I suspect, many others read it: while making Defoe perhaps too clever and complex in one direction, they underestimate his achievement in another.[1]

As a preliminary, it must be noted that *Moll* again—like *Singleton*—has a basically bipartite structure, the first part containing Moll's sexual adventures, the second her life as a thief, her imprisonment, and her transportation to America. The difference here, however, is that Defoe has effected an organic rather than merely schematic relationship between the two halves. I begin with the episode of the two brothers, an episode which is crucial to our understanding of the novel.

Moll, it will be recalled, is seduced by the elder brother of the family in which she is a maid, then is persuaded by him to marry Robin, the younger brother, who loves her and has proposed to her. She is a bewildered, passive object in the centre of a family dispute: her position is no sooner established as the elder brother's mistress (it is stressed that she is virtually his wife, pp. 45, 57),[2] than he suggests that she should accept Robin's offer of marriage, thus becoming his sister where formerly she was his whore (45), later affirming: 'I shall always be your sincere friend, without any inclination to nearer intimacy, when you become my sister' (64). He presses her hard, and the traumatic effect the affair has on Moll is symbolized in her near-fatal illness (48ff.). Not surprisingly, after her marriage she succumbs to incestuous fantasies: 'I was never in bed with my husband but I wished myself in the arms of his brother; . . . I committed adultery and incest with him every day in my desires, which, without doubt, was as effectually criminal in the nature of the guilt as if I had actually done it' (68).

Robin dies after five years, and there is an interval consisting of two main episodes, in one of which Moll marries a gentleman-tradesman who, faced with financial ruin, leaves her 'a widow bewitched; I had a husband and no husband' (74); and in the second of which Moll helps a young lady avenge herself on a captain who regarded her as too easy a conquest (78–88). The notion of revenge on the male, and the fact that it is Moll who is taking the initiative, and not members of the opposite sex, are indicative of a radical change of character. It is indeed ironic, then, that by taking the initiative Moll should soon land herself in a situation which strongly resembles her earlier one with the two brothers: she now courts and marries her own brother.[3]

She discovers the truth only when she is on her husband's plantation in Virginia and his mother narrates her life story. As she listens to it, Moll gradually gathers 'that this was certainly no more or less than my own mother, and I had now had two children, and was big with another by my own brother' (102), following this with a declaration which echoes the one quoted above from p. 68: 'I lived therefore in open avowed incest and whoredom, and all under the appearance of an honest wife; and though I was not much touched with the crime of it, yet the action had something in it shocking to nature, and made my husband, as he thought himself, even nauseous to me' (103).

At first she conceals the situation from her husband, merely telling him that their union is not a lawful one. This alone has a strong effect on him: 'he turned pale as death, and stood mute as one thunderstruck, and once or twice I thought he would have fainted' (108). He recovers, but when Moll decides at last that the full truth must be told—'that I am your own sister, and you my own brother' (119)—his reaction is even more severe: 'I saw him turn pale and look wild' and nearly faint away, says Moll; then 'he became pensive and melancholy', 'a little distempered in his head', eventually falling 'into a long, lingering consumption' (119–20).

Each detail here matches one in the first episode. Just as Moll's brother 'turned pale as death' and nearly fainted, so does Moll when the elder brother begins to suggest that she might marry Robin ('turning pale as death' she nearly sinks down out of her chair (44)); and just as Moll's brother becomes ill when he hears of his incest so, we recall, does Moll when the elder brother, on another visit, tries to persuade her to accept Robin's proposal. Anticipating her brother's illness almost exactly, Moll becomes melancholy, it is feared that she will 'go into a consumption; and which vexed me most, they gave it as their opinion that my mind was oppressed' (49).

I have just described the parallel as an ironic one, and of course it is ironic that Moll should carefully court her own brother, thus unwittingly depriving herself of the secure marriage she was seeking. There is, however, more to it than this. For the most important thing to emerge is the contrast with what happened the first time. It is not really Moll who suffers at all—she does not become ill; her brother does. She has treated her brother as the elder brother treated her, so that in causing his illness by revealing their incestuous relationship she has had her revenge. A man must suffer as she suffered; and the only man who can so suffer is her own brother.

But the achieving of revenge through this almost ritualistic re-enactment of the first episode is not enough. Far from atoning for the guilt she incurred by loving and dreaming of the elder brother while sleeping with Robin, Moll has in fact worsened her situation by increasing her guilt—imaginary incest is now real incest. She has placed herself in some kind of hall of mirrors, as it were: in the remainder of Part I she faces mocking, fragmented, parodies of her dilemma; in Part II she moves towards a solution of it.[4]

Since the episode of the two brothers is so important to my reading of the novel, it is worth pausing at this point to see whether Defoe himself is likely to have attributed to it the traumatic implications that I see it as possessing. An indispensable aid here is provided by his treatise *Conjugal Lewdness; or, Matrimonial Whoredom*, published in 1727 but which, Defoe states in the Preface, he had been working on for '*almost thirty Years*'.[5] The subject of chapter 6, the heading declares, is '*Of being Over-rul'd by Perswasion, Interest, Influence of Friends, Force, and the like, to take the Person they have no Love for, and forsake the Person they really lov'd*'. The relevance of this to the case of Moll and the two brothers is evident enough and is supported to some extent by a repeated (though common) proverbial image: Moll goes to church with Robin 'like a bear to the stake' (66); in *Conjugal Lewdness*, chapter 6, the lady goes to church with the man she doesn't love 'like a Bear haul'd to a Stake . . .' (175). The subject is continued in chapter 7, which is entitled '*Of Marrying one Person, and at the same time owning themselves to be in Love with another*', and the second paragraph merits quotation in full:

> But to marry one Woman and love another, to marry one Man and be in love with another, this is yet worse, tenfold worse [than to marry a person one does not love], if that be possible! 'tis, in its kind, a meer Piece of Witchcraft; it is a kind of civil, legal *Adultery*, nay, it makes the Man or Woman be committing Adultery in their Hearts every Day of their lives; and can I be wrong therefore to say, that it may be very well called a Matrimonial Whoredom? if I may judge, it is one of the worst Kinds of it too.

The heinousness of the matter in Defoe's eyes could not be clearer; neither could its similarity to Moll's 'in short, I committed adultery and incest with him every day in my desires. . .'. Defoe's psychological insight is acute. He realizes—and the whole long Providential tradition of 'Truth unveiled by Time' in which he is working in both *Moll* and *Roxana* confirms this—that a guilty secret cannot remain concealed:[6] 'How many times . . . does the Secret come out afterwards, either unawares by themselves, or in delirious Fits, extremities of Distempers, Dreams, talking in the Sleep, and such other Ways, which prove however fatal to the Peace of the Family, yet unavoidable?' (ch. 7, 183). And yet to this 'Matrimonial Whoredom' Moll has added—as she admits herself—the further crime of incest (in chapter 13, Defoe refers to the case of a man who had intercourse with, and then wanted to marry, his own daughter. He calls this 'not Matrimonial Whoredom only, but Matrimonial Incest', and 'the last is a superlative in Wickedness' (353)).[7] Moll has committed this 'superlative in Wickedness' in marrying Robin and indulging in mental 'adultery and incest' with his brother, and so she must, in the inevitable scheme of things, be punished for it; or (and this is really the same thing) punish herself. As Defoe remarks in the Conclusion to *Conjugal Lewdness*: 'Let the Offenders, the guilty Persons, consider, Heaven can find out Ways to punish them, tho' we cannot find out Words to reprove them' (388). Sometimes the punishment will manifest itself in physical infirmity; sometimes, I suggest, the punishment will be more horrifying: it will be mental rather than physical, so that the world of objective fact will be coloured by the knowledge of one's guilt, reflecting it wherever one turns. This is what happens in *Moll* and *Roxana*: hinted at in the somewhat stilted allegory of *The Pilgrim's Progress*, where the characters encountered are projections of Christian's own doubts, fears, and inadequacies, there will be nothing quite like it in English fiction—not even in Richardson—until the mature Dickens of *Great Expectations*, where Pip, like Moll and Roxana, lives in a world of mocking alter egos and *doppel-gängers*.[8] Such is the power of the Puritan literary imagination at its greatest.

If we return to the novel itself, the pattern that emerges, and the reasons for it, should now be apparent. Moll arrives back in England from Virginia, and goes to Bath. She has no sooner arrived there than a gentleman indicates his affection and regard for her. He has a wife, but tells Moll 'that the lady was distempered in her head' (126), thus immediately forging a link between him and Moll, whose brother-husband, we recall, is 'a little distempered in his head'.[9] The link is strengthened when we are told that 'he had no wife, that is to say, she was as no wife to him' (138), since this is probably an echo of the 'husband and no husband' phrase already quoted (74).

Hence the two are virtually identified, and the similarities appear to hint that Moll might at last have found, in this reflection of herself, someone with whom she can establish a happy, normal, untainted relationship. Ominous signs begin to appear, however. The man visits her while she is in bed—'yet he never offered anything ... further than a kiss' (126)—and, after enquiring about her financial circumstances, makes her 'take a whole handful' of gold from him (130). I say 'ominous' because this is an approximate repetition of the scheme adopted by the elder brother—he kissed and caressed Moll (though without

45

seeking 'the last favour') and 'put almost a handful of gold in [her] hand' (29). Again she appears to be reliving—however faintly—that first episode. Confirmation comes when Moll travels to Gloucester with the man. They stop at an inn where only one room is available, and Moll's companion tells the landlord 'very readily' that 'these beds will do, and as for the rest, we are too near akin to lie together, though we may lodge near one another' (133). Moll becomes a sister once more, then; and although the significance of this remark escapes her at the time, even she becomes suspicious when, slipping into bed with her, 'he took me in his arms, and so I lay all night with him, but he had no more to do with me, or offered anything to me, other than embracing me . . . in his arms', for she comments, with superb understatement and scarcely-concealed disappointment: 'This was a surprising thing to me, and perhaps may be so to others, who know how the laws of nature work' (133).

This strange, unnatural relationship, with its fleeting echoes of what has gone before, lasts for 'near two years' (134), until Moll at last seduces the man and 'exchange[s] the place of friend for that unmusical, harsh-sounding title of whore', thus reversing her original metamorphosis from whore to sister-friend of the elder brother. The two part when the man falls ill and repents of his adultery, leaving Moll with 'the world to begin again' (147).

The new beginning is, however, illusory. Moll now becomes acquainted with a bank official and then with Jemmy (later her Lancashire husband); the two episodes are closely bound together in an alternating pattern,[10] and in each, once again, Moll finds herself confronted by the past.

The echoes are obtrusive and insistent. Thus, almost as soon as Moll has met the bank official (with the intention of entrusting her money to him while she travels to Lancashire), they start talking of personal matters, and he reveals to her that 'he had a wife, and no wife' (153; repeated 155). The analogy with Moll's Bath lover is clear and does not escape her (153), though another echo, which appears a few pages later, does: 'you came to ask advice of me', the bank official says to her, 'and I will serve you as faithfully as if you were my own sister' (157).

When he has obtained a divorce Moll marries him, thinking that she has at last found security. But the echoes previously noted are a warning to the reader if not to Moll, and Moll is herself jolted into awareness when her husband dies suddenly as the result of financial worry after they have been married five years and have had two children (218–19). This last marriage has taken her back exactly where she began: her first marriage, to Robin, lasted five years (until his death), and by it she had two children (67).

Maximillian Novak has recently noted[11] that the marriage to the bank official (described as a period of stasis, as 'a safe harbour, after the stormy voyage of life past was at an end' (217)) offers Moll 'Defoe's ideal—the private life of a contented family'. The ideal cannot last for Moll since she is working her way through an elaborate ritual pattern of purgation which can terminate only in a confrontation with her brother in Virginia. But because it is an ideal, it is significant that this episode should mark the end of the first part of the novel (Part II begins after the bank official's death), occurring approximately at its centre, which thus, as we see, still receives structural and thematic emphasis. (The exact centre, excluding the Preface, is at pp. 201–2; Moll's marriage is on p. 212.)

Interestingly, to support his suggestion as to the importance of the family in Defoe's thinking, Novak quotes a tabular representation of human happiness as a mean (or median) state between the extremes of madness and poverty from his *Condoling Letter to the Tatler* (1710). I reproduce the table below; for its symmetrical (specifically, chiastic) structure tells us a great deal about Defoe's schematic way of thinking, particularly on moral matters, and so should go some way towards confirming the structural patterns in the novels outlined in this and the preceding chapter:[12]

Madness,
Poverty,
Extravagence,
Excess or Profusion,
Waste,
Generous Liberality,
Plenty,
FAMILY
Frugality,
Parsimony,
Niggardliness,
Covetousness,
Sordidly Covetous,
Wretchedness or Rich Poverty,
Madness

Here is the Word *FAMILY* in the Centre, which signifies the Man,
let his Circumstances be what it will, for every Man is a Family
to himself. He is plac'd between *Plenty* and *Frugality*; a Blessed,
Happy Medium, which makes Men beloved of all, respected of
the Rich, blessed by the Poor, useful to themselves, to their
Country, and to their Posterity.

But in spite of its structural prominence, it must be reaffirmed that
the bank-official episode merely frames what I regard as a far more
important one both structurally and thematically—Moll's marriage
to her Lancashire husband. For once more a familiar pattern emerges:
Moll's relationship with Jemmy recalls in detail her relationship with
her brother-husband. On the first occasion Moll had passed for a
fortune of £1,500; on the second, she is reputed to be worth £15,000
(89, 165). In the former case rumour's instrument is the captain's wife
with whom Moll is lodging; in the latter, it is the man's sister, who
had stayed in the same lodging-house as Moll. Furthermore, the
moment when Moll has to disclose the true state of her finances is
similar in both cases (95ff.; 168ff.), while an additional parallel
appears with the discussion between Moll and Jemmy as to whether
or not they should travel across to Virginia (181–3): although Jemmy
decides against it and leaves Moll, this obviously recalls Moll's
actual voyage to Virginia undertaken after her marriage to her
brother.

Here the episode ends, though it is worth noting that it too has its
hint of the incest motif when Jemmy tells Moll that the woman who
introduced her to him 'was none of his sister, but had been his whore
for two years before' (170). This alludes to a sentence in the two
brothers episode ('you shall be my dear sister, as now you are my dear
[whore]' (45)), but there is a difference: this is the first time (except for
the short marriage to the linen-draper) that Moll herself has not been
involved in an actually or apparently incestuous relationship. By
introducing the motif at this point Defoe is implicitly contrasting
Jemmy's attitude to Moll with the elder brother's (who literally
created a sister out of her), and the Bath gentleman's (who imagined
her as his sister, and indulged in a peculiar relationship with her
before becoming her lover proper); while the combined echoes of the
Bath-gentleman episode and the 'incestuous' marriage to Robin
which accompany the bank official again mock Moll, and serve as an
indication that here again she has achieved only a false resolution, and

that she is still involved in the labyrinth she was led into by the elder brother.[13]

The marriage with Jemmy is, as I have said, different, despite its inauspicious beginning and apparent rapid end; for it is unique in its normality and in the fact that Moll loves her husband (note the unusual expressions of emotion on p. 177—of no other man does Moll even hint that she would be prepared to 'beg' and 'starve' with him). It is in this marriage that the solution to Moll's dilemma lies; through it she will leave the labyrinth. And so the reason for the alternation of the bank-official episode and the Jemmy episode becomes clear: Defoe has juxtaposed false with true, repeated the problem and suggested the answer. When the two are really ready for each other Moll is reunited with Jemmy in Part II,[14] this time actually accomplishing the voyage to Virginia mooted after their marriage.

This, however, is to anticipate. Left a widow by the death of the bank official Moll must work her way back to Jemmy and the end of her dilemma; and as she does so her life is once more governed and shaped by the past.

Paralleling her initiation into the world in Part I is her initiation into a more limited world—that of theft—in Part II. One of her early crimes is the theft of two rings, 'one a small diamond ring, and the other a plain gold ring' (226)—fairly obviously, I think, recalling the diamond and wedding rings given to her by the bank official (209) which echo in their turn the 'small diamond ring' and 'plain gold ring' given by Jemmy (177).[15] Almost immediately after this Moll finds herself 'at a loss for a market for [her] goods' (227) because of her inexperience in these matters, and contacts her 'old governess', the woman who looked after her while she had Jemmy's baby (186ff.). In so doing she relives her situation at the beginning of the novel when she was in the care of the nurse at Colchester. At first, before she starts stealing again and is educated in the niceties of the trade by 'a schoolmistress' introduced to her by the governess (232), Moll lives by her needle while staying with her (229); in Part I Moll's nurse is her schoolmistress: she brings her and the other children up 'very religiously', and 'as mannerly and as genteelly as if we had been at the dancing-school'. In addition, Moll tells us 'she had taught me to work with my needle' (12).

The parallel illustrates Moll's decline since the period of her youthful aspirations and shows the extent to which her life reflects the image of the past despite its apparent change of direction. But simultaneously it hints implicitly at the solution to Moll's problem, for there is a strong link with Jemmy. The system of echoes and repetitions is by now sufficiently well established to arouse expectations in the reader, and the logic of this structural method runs as follows: the woman to whom Moll went when Jemmy left her and she was expecting his baby will be the one who, when Moll seeks her out again, will lead her to a reunion with Jemmy.[16] And this is precisely what does happen: the avarice of the one and the other ends in Moll's arrest and meeting with Jemmy in Newgate—which results in the visit to Virginia and the expiation of Moll's guilt.[17] (Thus we can also detect the logic behind the recapitulation of the first nurse–episode in the second: it is only fitting that the moment when Moll begins to move towards Jemmy and expiation should echo the moment which led directly to her entering the family of the two brothers where her guilt was incurred.)

As if to insist on this structural logic, Defoe makes Moll's first sight of Jemmy in Newgate recall the time she saw him at Brickhill. She narrates how, hearing that three highwaymen had been captured, 'we that were women placed ourselves in the way, that we would be sure to see them. . . '. To Moll's 'amazement and surprise' she recognized one of them as her Lancashire husband, was 'struck dumb at the sight', and 'quitted [her] company, and retired' (322–3). At Brickhill, Moll, very recently married, had looked out of the window of her room in an inn and seen three men on horseback, one of whom was her Lancashire husband. She had been 'frighted to death' at the discovery but, concealing herself, 'could not keep from peeping at them' (214). Moll remembers the Brickhill incident as soon as she sees Jemmy (323): it is almost as if she prevented his arrest then that they might be reunited now.

Moll does not actually speak to Jemmy for some time, the interval being occupied with her trial and sentence, her confessions to a minister, and the commuting of her sentence from death to transportation. When she does speak to him it is to persuade him, after hearing his story, to submit to transportation too, and she reminds him 'that he could not but call to mind that it was what I had recommended to him many years before' (349). Again our attention has been drawn to the parallel: the discussion here corresponds to the one between Jemmy and Moll after their marriage.

With the general scheme of Moll's return in mind, we can consider additional cross-references which make it a more complicated matter than it has so far seemed. The most important of these concerns the governess. On pp. 245–6 she briefly narrates her life history as pick-pocket, midwife and procuress. Immediately after this, Moll, afraid of being impeached by other thieves, decides to lie low for a while, but is persuaded by the governess to continue her trade disguised as a man—a disguise described by Moll as being 'contrary to nature' (247–8). She is paired with 'a young fellow' as a partner: 'And as we kept always together, so we grew very intimate, yet he never knew that I was not a man, nay, though I several times went home with him to his lodgings, according as our business directed, and four or five times lay with him all night' (248).

In the following paragraph she indicates that she is 'sick of' this partnership, and that her 'good fortune' soon ended it with the young man's arrest. What she is 'sick of' is its unnaturalness—she sleeps with a man but there is no love-making.

The echo sounds clearly, recalling the first Virginia episode and what followed. On pp. 100ff. Moll's mother tells her life story which, because of what Moll discovers from it, leads directly to her return to England, where she becomes acquainted with the Bath gentleman—a man who sleeps with her and yet refuses to indulge in sexual inter-course, 'a surprising thing' to those 'who know how the laws of nature work'.

Thus the governess is a reflection of Moll's own mother here[18] (she acts as 'a true mother to me' (325)), though a reflection with a difference. The two women have similar histories, but whereas the one is the cause of trouble, the other is the means of ending it, driving Moll back to Jemmy. This becomes apparent when the young fellow is caught and a search is set on foot for Moll: she decides it is best to leave London for a while, 'but not knowing whither to wander, I took a maid-servant with me, and took the stage-coach to Dunstable, to my old landlord and landlady, where I had lived so handsomely with my Lancashire husband. Here I told her a formal story, that I expected my husband every day from Ireland . . .' (252).

It is, of course, the governess who has occasioned the visit by per-suading Moll to steal in disguise. The notion of a return to Jemmy is explicit; implicit is the suggestion of a return to Virginia—for it was at Dunstable that Moll and Jemmy had discussed travelling there to better their financial position (181ff.).

Another echo sounds some forty pages later when Moll, disguised as a beggar and 'standing near a tavern door', is given a gentleman's horse to hold. She walks off with it, but then realizes that she has no means of disposing of it and so arranges its return. Her verdict on this affair is that it 'was a robbery and no robbery, for little was lost by it, and nothing was got by it' (293)—recalling a phrase which, though it occurs more than once in Part I, first appears only a short time after Robin's death ('a husband and no husband' (74)).[19]

In case the import of this suggestive hovering over the early part of Moll's life here should escape the reader, Defoe makes things explicit with an actual return to Colchester (308), where Moll inquires 'after the good old friends I had once had there, but could make little out; they were all dead or removed'. The relationship that was the source of all her trouble is spelled out for us—lover/brother-in-law ('the young gentleman my first lover, and afterwards my brother-in-law, was dead'). The man might be dead, but the guilt he left Moll with, concretized in the marriage to her own brother, is not. With the final posing of the problem only one thing remains—its solution. And so Moll is almost immediately arrested (314-15), to be joined by Jemmy and to make her return to Virginia.

Her guilt is to be lifted by confrontation. Moll must face again her brother and the offspring of their incestuous union, must relive momentarily that part of her life which was an unsuccessful attempt at revenge for the injuries caused by the elder brother, and which forced her into physical incest. The first obstacle to peace of mind is passed when Moll meets her son and he not only fails to upbraid her for her incestuous marriage, but reveals a genuine affection for her, approaching her 'not as a stranger, but as a son to a mother' (384). The second, and last, passes with the death of her brother who, alive, is the very embodiment of Moll's guilt. As she finds him he is a symbolic figure, already 'half dead' (388), 'very fretful and passionate, almost blind, and capable of nothing' (384), and with his death her guilt, and life of deception, vanish. She is free to confess. Accepted by her son, she must now be accepted by her husband for what she is, and, far more important, for what she has been.

He is surprisingly amiable and 'perfectly easy in the account' (393). Where the first Virginia episode (so intimately bound up with the affair of the two brothers) failed, the second, its re-enactment, succeeds. Through Jemmy the discordant notes of incest that have sounded through Moll's life achieve resolution; and when 'all these difficulties [have been] made easy' (394) Moll can return to England, and the novel come to an end.

II *Roxana*

Even more than *Moll Flanders*, *Roxana* conveys the horror of being pursued by guilt. In the whole of the long final section of the novel the
wealthy Roxana, now a baronet's wife and a countess, suddenly finds
that her money and position mean nothing. Like Jack when confronted
by the Preston rebels, she is forced into hiding and compelled to
disguise her identity.[20] But, as we saw with Moll, one can't escape the
consequences of one's past, and so it is—inevitably—Roxana's greatest
and most dramatic disguise, as a Turkish dancer, that haunts the last
pages of her narrative, becoming a persistent motif that at last con-
vinces her daughter Susan of her real identity.

Providential justice demands of a life like Roxana's that the moment
of triumph shall, ultimately if not immediately, be the cause of downfall. Thus, as the prince's mistress in France, and straight after catching
a glimpse of the French king, Roxana suddenly sees her first husband,
whom she thought to be dead (85);[21] and thus, as soon as she has
married the Dutch merchant and received the titles of lady and
countess, the daughter of her first marriage re-enters her life, to
remain haunting her even after the daughter has been murdered by
Amy, in a passage more terrifying than anything in *Moll Flanders* and
yet one for which the earlier novel has been an imaginative prepara-
tion: 'As for the poor Girl herself, she was ever before my Eyes; I saw
her by-Night, and by-Day; she haunted my Imagination, if she did not
haunt the House; my Fancy show'd her me in a hundred Shapes and
Postures; sleeping or waking she was with me . . .' (325).

It is significant that the girl should bear Roxana's own real name, as
Roxana has earlier made clear;[22] for this makes her an obvious and
vivid embodiment of her mother's past, which is as inescapable in her
case as it was in Moll's. Like Moll's life, too, Roxana's has an inexorable
circularity to it: with Susan—herself a projection of Roxana's guilt—
dead,[23] we leave her mother at the end of the novel confronting her
'other Daughter', who is again an alter ego and, in being so, once more
insists on the unavoidable omnipresence of the past: 'the Girl was the
very Counterpart of myself, only much handsomer' (328–9).

Character recurrence is as important a structural and thematic
device here as in *Moll Flanders*; and if we attend closely to the pattern
created by the appearance and disappearance of certain key figures a
perhaps not unexpected chiasmus emerges; a chiasmus hinted at in
the metaphor Roxana uses to describe her affair with the prince:[24]

53

'But the highest Tide has its Ebb; and in all things of this Kind, there is a Reflux which sometimes also is more impetuously violent than the first Aggression' (107).

I shall keep the mere tedious summary of events as brief as possible. An element of summary is, however, unavoidable if a convincing case for the patterning of the novel is to be established. Roxana's first husband, the brewer who runs off and leaves her (causing her to farm out her children) reappears in Paris, as we have seen, when she is with the prince. Later, just before her affair with the Dutch merchant (135ff.), she is assured by Amy that the brewer is now dead (132), though later still she finds that this is untrue (197) and his death is not finally confirmed until p. 232, at which point Roxana also hears that her former lover, the prince, is searching for her (231). The prince is wounded on a boar hunt, and his illness makes him penitent (237), just as, earlier, he had cast Roxana off when his wife's illness, then death, had also made him repent his carnality (109). The sequence is completed by Roxana's second 'husband', the jewel merchant who was also her landlord and with whom Roxana put Amy to bed (46–7) —an event that Roxana recalls with horror in the storm off Harwich (126), and that is echoed in her affair with the peer on p. 187: 'he fell foul of poor *Amy*, and indeed, I thought once he wou'd have carry'd the jest on before my Face, as was once done in a like Case. . . .'

Roxana's affairs involve her, obviously enough, in a rapid ascent of the social ladder—brewer, jewel merchant, foreign prince—an ascent which reaches its climax with her involvement with the English king.[25] This in itself imposes a vertical pattern on the narrative. But if we look now, in diagrammatic form, at the sequence of events in the first third of the novel as outlined above (up to Roxana's hearing of the supposed death of her first husband on p. 132), in relation to its topography, we find what amounts to a double, counterpointed, chiasmus:

Brewer	England
Jewel merchant	
	Paris
Prince	
Brewer (reappears)	Meudon
	Paris

Prince	Italy
	Paris
Jewel merchant (jewels recognized)	Paris
Jewel merchant (R. recalls putting Amy to bed with him)	England
Brewer (R. hears that he is dead)	Holland

In addition, as in the previous novels, earlier episodes are recapitulated in later ones. And it is here, it seems to me, that the real meaning of the novel is to be found. For just as the incestuous nature of Moll's first marriage governs the very pattern of her later life, so does Roxana's first guilty affair with the landlord-jewel merchant shape her subsequent life.

Roxana's awareness of her sinfulness in yielding to the man is clearly established by Defoe: 'I did what my own Conscience convinc'd me at the very Time I did it, was horribly unlawful, scandalous, and abominable' (39), and her sense of guilt is not alleviated by the plea of necessity:[26] 'But Poverty was my Snare; dreadful Poverty! the Misery I had been in, was great, such as wou'd make the Heart tremble at the Apprehensions of its Return . . .' (ibid.). Amy is her mistress's alter ego here[27] ('the Jade prompted the Crime, which I had but too much Inclination to commit' (40)), even becoming a tempting devil: 'had I consulted Conscience and Virtue, I shou'd have repell'd this *Amy*, however faithful and honest to me in other things, as a Viper, and Engine of the Devil' (38); just as she is when she murders Roxana's daughter (Amy's suggestion provokes Roxana to a rage which is presumably the more intense because she has proposed what Roxana was secretly thinking (pp. 312–13); after the murder is accomplished Roxana 'call'd her a thousand Devils, and Monsters, and hard-hearted Tygers' (324)). And Roxana has already, we recall, degraded the maid to her own level, thereby degrading herself even further, by putting her to bed with her lover and watching them perform together—'as I thought myself a Whore, I cannot say but that it was something design'd in my Thoughts, that my Maid should be a Whore too, and should not reproach me with it' (47)—thereby reminding us again, perhaps, of Moll, who, in like fashion, is driven to involve her own half-brother in her incestuous past and tells him of it; and in marrying him in the first place deepens, and extends, her own guilt.[28]

55

Roxana links the lust of the jeweller and the prince, her next lover, by implication on p. 75: 'I have . . . set down the Particulars of the Caresses I was treated with by the Jeweller, and also by this Prince . . . to draw the just Picture of a Man enslav'd to the Rage of his vicious Appetite.' But the perceptive reader has already noticed an ominous similarity between the two affairs in the manner of their initiation. For the prince takes supper in Roxana's rooms and then declares that he will lodge with her 'for one Night' (63), just as Roxana's first lover, the jeweller, tells Amy (having furnished a room for himself) 'I intend to Lye with you to Morrow-Night; *To Night, if you please Sir,* says *Amy* very innocently, *your Room is quite ready*' (33). And just as the jeweller helps Roxana with food and furnishing before declaring his love for her, so, too, the 'Prince . . . was first a Benefactor, then an Admirer'(64).

Roxana's next lover is the Dutch merchant, and he again is 'my Benefactor; . . . my Deliverer' (135) because of the assistance he gave her in Paris. Now, in Rotterdam, 'he took up his Lodgings in the same House where I lodg'd' (136) and they eventually lie together. And once more, as was the case with the jeweller episode, it is Roxana here, and not the Dutchman, who is guilty of the adultery, because she refuses the marriage that her lover wants even when she becomes pregnant. Ironically, the Dutchman's remarks to Roxana on the 'Mark of Infamy' that the illegitimate child bears from its cradle (156) echo Roxana's own earlier remarks to the prince on their illegitimate son: 'our Affection will ever be his Affliction, and his Mother's Crime be the Son's Reproach; the Blot can never be wip'd out by the most glorious Actions' (81), and thus confirm her guilt. But Roxana's pride and desire for independence force her to incur further guilt: the Dutchman had offered her a way out: 'I had now an Opportunity to have quitted a Life of Crime and Debauchery' (159); they now part, with a warning from him of future ills (160).[29] The Dutchman, a recurring figure in this last half of the novel, replaces the recurring brewer-husband of the first part; and it is his symbolic function to act as a kind of conscience or moral voice, a reminder to Roxana of the security and life of repentance she might have led if she had listened to him when he first proposed marriage to her.[30]

Instead, she relives her adulterous unions with the jeweller and the prince, this time taking the English king as her lover. The echoes are sufficiently apparent: Roxana declares herself 'blinded by my own Vanity' and can think 'of nothing less than of being Mistress to the King himself' (161). In the same paragraph she actually alludes to the prince, to bring that episode once more to our minds, as it were, and the reader should here recall Roxana's remark at the beginning of her first royal affair, 'I was now become the vainest Creature upon Earth' (62). It was the prince who bought Roxana the Turkish slave from whom she 'learnt the *Turkish* Language; their Way of Dressing, and Dancing, and some *Turkish*, or rather *Moorish* Songs' (102)—accomplishments which she will display to the full before the English king at her second ball (180). She lives 'retir'd' 'for three Years and about a Month' (181) as the king's mistress, just as she lived in 'Confinement' as the mistress of the prince (67), when the house was, to all intents and purposes, 'shut up'. Significantly, Roxana has already mentioned the figure of three years in connection with the prince: 'I liv'd in this gay sort of Retirement almost three Years' (75); and, perhaps anticipating her affair with the English king, she has commented: 'I think I may say now, that I liv'd indeed like a Queen' (82).

Roxana's last lover is a lord. She takes a new lodging so that he has access to her whatever time he likes: 'he had a convenient Way to come into the Garden, by a Door that open'd into the Park; a thing very rarely allow'd in those Times' (186). (Compare Roxana's house in Paris, which is convenient for the prince because it has 'a Way out into Three Streets, and [is] not overlook'd by any Neighbours' (66).) It is this lover who is also explicitly associated by Roxana with her first lover, the jewel merchant. Coming in one night 'a little merry', he has to be satisfied that Amy, who is sleeping with Roxana, is a woman. Then follows the passage that I quoted earlier, referring to the time when Roxana put Amy to bed with the jewel merchant: 'Well, he fell foul of poor *Amy*, and indeed, I thought once he wou'd have carry'd the Jest on before my Face, as was once done in a like Case. . . .'

The affair with the lord marks the climax of a 'wicked Scene of Life' which lasts eight years (187); and—perhaps again significantly—her 'prosperous Wickedness' with the prince also lasted eight years (106). All three affairs—prince, king, peer—thus echo each other; and all three also hark back to her first guilt-ridden adultery with the jeweller. Pride has led her to multiply her guilt, and in the last part of the novel she has to try to escape her past, now embodied in the figure of her daughter Susan, offspring of her first and only legitimate marriage. Her 'perfect Retreat' (211) with the Quaker family[31] to escape the consequences of her court reputation is a parody of the earlier retreats which enabled her to be alone with her lovers, and the time is now symbolically ripe for the return of the Dutch merchant. He knows nothing of her past and marries Roxana (243), but only after the reader has been assured of her continuing pride; for at the same time that she hears from Amy of the real death of her first husband (232) she hears also that the prince is looking for her again, news that turns her 'truly craz'd and distracted. . . . I spent most of this Time in the reallizing all the Great Things of *a Life with the Prince*, to my Mind' (234). It is only the prince's repentance after a hunting accident that drives her back to the Dutchman, just as his earlier repentance had led (indirectly, because as a consequence of it she decided to return to England) to her first meeting with the Dutch merchant (111). Once more her life is shaped by the past.

But marriage and a baronetcy are nothing: externals cease to matter to Roxana as she becomes increasingly a prey to mental anguish:

Not all the Affluence of a plentiful Fortune; not a hundred Thousand Pounds Estate; . . . not Honour and Titles, Attendants and Equipages; *in a word*, not all the things we call Pleasure, cou'd give me any relish, or sweeten the Taste of things to me; *at least*, not so much, but I grew sad, heavy, pensive, and melancholly; slept little, and eat little; dream'd continually of the most frightful and terrible things imaginable. . . . (264)

The culmination comes with Susan's murder. And, it should be noted, as Roxana's past presses claustrophobically in on her in this last part of the novel, so is this claustrophobia mimed in the novel's topography, since, after the wide-ranging travels of the first part, her activities now become increasingly localized, centred as they are on London.

Roxana recognizes that there is 'a Supreme Power managing, directing, and governing in both Causes and Events in this World' (121).[32] And although she chooses to ignore it, this 'Supreme Power' is once again attested to in the structure of her narrative, which has the same kind of mysterious inevitability about it that we also find in *Moll Flanders*. As for the ending, I am in full agreement with Robert Hume's praise of its compression as an indication of Defoe's 'growing technical skill' rather than as a sign of any kind of failure.[33] Divine justice demands continuing punishment for the murder of Susan by Roxana's surrogate, Amy. There can be no question of purgation, as there was for Moll's lesser crime; and the near-chiastic structure of the last part of the final sentence surely looks back to the chiastic rhythms of the narrative as a whole, as well as affirming, through its own alliterativelypatterned assurance, that the novel has reached its just conclusion: 'the Blast of Heaven seem'd to follow the Injury done the poor Girl, by us both; and I was brought so low again, that my Repentance seem'd to be only the Consequence of my Misery, as my Misery was of my Crime.'

There is a very real sense, then, in which the structuring of all of Defoe's novels may be regarded as Providential. But in *Moll Flanders* and *Roxana* the iconographical precision of *Robinson Crusoe* has developed into a structural technique at once more fluid and, to the modern reader at least, more suggestive. What the patterning of these two novels finally expresses (that is, over and above their individual psychological insights) is that eminently human search for, and sense of, order in the apparent chaos of unconnected events that is mundane life. Up to the eighteenth century (as attested by *Crusoe* and Fielding's novels except *Amelia*), the search had had the sanction of Christianity: pattern was Providence. With increasing secularism and the consequent abandonment of what came to be regarded as the fiction of Providence, the quest for order remained, but it became merely a personal whim and was less and less (eventually, no longer) related to the divine scheme of things. The old view is expressed by Crusoe in his *Serious Reflections*, in a passage quoted in part in the last chapter, when he cites Exodus 12: 41 in support of his assertions concerning the Providential meaning of the coincidence of dates. As he observes,[34] the pattern applies to private as well as public events: 'I have seen several collections of such things made by private hands, some relating to family circumstances, some to public. . . .' Thomas Dekker had been but one of many to trace a specific instance: he described[35] Elizabeth I's 'life (which was dedicated to Virginitie,) [as] both beginning & closing up a miraculous Mayden circle: for she was borne upon a Lady Eve, and died upon a Lady Eve: her Nativitie & death being memorable by this wonder: the first and last yeares of her Raigne by this, that a *Lee* was Lorde Maior when she came to the Crowne, and a *Lee* Lorde Maior when she departed from it.'

The important thing is that here such coincidences are referred to Providence; they have an emblematic significance. After the eighteenth century, although they were still detected of course, they now possessed only a personal meaning since they could no longer be regarded as divine hieroglyphs. I should like to end by quoting two nineteenth-century examples, one[36] from Browning's life, the other from Mrs Oliphant. Both are instances of that personal obsession with pattern for its own sake that I see Defoe as having anticipated to some extent in *Moll* and *Roxana*; in them, as nearly but not yet in these novels of Defoe's, the Providential paradigm is secularized—that is, emptied of its traditionally affirmative Providential implications:

> 'The cycle is complete,' as Browning said, looking round the room; 'here we came fifteen years ago; here Pen was born; here Ba wrote her poems for Italy. She used to walk up and down this verandah in the summer evenings, when, revived by the southern air, she first again began to enjoy her out-doors life. Every day she used to walk with me or drive with me. . . . Last week when we came to Florence I said: 'We used, you know, to walk on this verandah so often—come and walk up and down once. Just once,' I urged, and she came to the window and took two steps on it. But it fatigued her too much, and she went back and lay down on the sofa—that was our last walk. Only the night she went away for ever she said she thought we must give up Casa Guidi; it was too inconvenient and in case of illness too small. We had decided to go away and take a villa outside the gates. For years she would not give up this house, but at last and, as it were, suddenly, she said she saw it *was* too small for us and too inconvenient. And so it was; so the cycle was completed for us here, and where the beginning was is the end. . . .

For Mrs Oliphant's case it is necessary to know that her husband died in Rome of tuberculosis and that later her daughter died also in Rome; some twenty years after that one of her sons had to be taken to the south of Europe because he had congestion of the lungs. At this point she wrote to Mrs Harry Coghill:[37]

> You know how anxiety of this kind acts upon me. I am in a suppressed fever, and can think of nothing else day and night. I watch every morsel he eats, every varying look and change of colour. How strange it is! All my troubles, and God knows they have been neither few nor small, have been repetitions—always one phase or another coming back, and that makes it all the worse, for I know how far my anguish can go.

NOTES

1 M. E. Novak comments on 'Defoe's growing interest in psychology' in 'Crime and Punishment in Defoe's *Roxana*', *Journal of English and Germanic Philology* (*JEGP*), 65 (1966), 456. Defoe's use of irony is discussed by Dorothy Van Ghent in an influential essay on *Moll* in her *The English Novel: Form and Function* (New York, 1953), and Ian Watt has traced 'The Recent Critical Fortunes of *Moll Flanders*' in *Eighteenth-Century Studies* (*ECS*), 1 (1967–8), 109–26.

2 References are to the modernized text of the first edn (1 vol., 1722) as reprinted in the World's Classics, introd. Bonamy Dobrée (1961). Unfortunately, G. A. Starr's excellent old-spelling text of the novel for OEN (1971) appeared too late for me to use it here, though I am happy to record that he offers justification for my decision to follow the first edn in this chapter: his collation of early edns led to a decision to take the first edn as his copy-text on the grounds that subsequent revisions were unlikely to have been authorial.

3 A. E. Rodway seems to be the only previous critic to have drawn attention to 'the interplay of fraternal relationships' in the novel: '*Moll Flanders* and *Manon Lescaut*', *EC*, 3 (1953), 314–15.

4 E. K. Brown notices such use of repetition only in the nineteenth- and twentieth-century novel, ignoring its earlier history. For its similarity with *Moll* in this respect, though, his discussion of Hardy's *The Well-Beloved* is especially interesting (*Rhythm in the Novel* (Toronto, 1967), pp. 13ff.).

5 Also known as *A Treatise Concerning the Use and Abuse of the Marriage Bed*. I am grateful to Ian Donaldson for first drawing my attention to this work in connection with *Moll Flanders*. Page references are to the facsimile of the first edn, introd. M. E. Novak (Gainesville, Fla., 1967).

6 On Time and Truth, see F. Saxl, 'Veritas Filia Temporis,' in R. Klibansky and H. J. Paton (eds), *Philosophy and History: Essays presented to Ernst Cassirer* (Oxford, 1936), pp. 197–222.

7 A key Biblical text, relevant to the incest idea and cited at the end of *Conjugal Lewdness*, ch. 6, is Genesis 29: 16ff.

8 For example, Orlick, who makes his appearance as Joe's journeyman only after Pip has been bound apprentice (generated by Pip's dissatisfaction with the forge, as it were) and attacks Mrs Joe (as Pip subconsciously wants to) after Pip has acted the part of the apprentice who murders his uncle in *George Barnwell*; and Pip's boy (ch. 27) who, dressed up, becomes an 'avenging phantom' grotesquely parodying Pip himself who, as boy and man, equates gentility with externals (dress, money), etc. G. A. Starr notes that, in persuading Moll to marry Robin, the elder brother is, in a sense at least, a 'projection' of Moll who 'expresses notions which she cannot afford to acknowledge, let alone to advocate, but which she eventually acts upon all the same': '*Moll Flanders*', from *Defoe and Casuistry*, in *Twentieth Century Interpretations of 'Moll Flanders'*, ed. R. C. Elliott (Englewood Cliffs, N.J., 1970), p. 86.

9 A fairly common idea in Defoe's novels: e.g., *Colonel Jack*, p. 244: 'I was next Door to being distempered, and sometimes indeed, I thought my self a little touch'd in my Head', and *Roxana*, ed. Jane Jack (1964), p. 87: 'he started, and turn'd pale as Death.' But I see no reason why this should detract from its thematic relevance here.

10 Moll is prevailed upon by 'a north-country woman' to travel to Lancashire to

61

meet her brother, Jemmy (A); before she does so she meets the bank official (B); she then travels to Lancashire, marries, parts from her husband, returns to London (A), and eventually marries the bank official (B).

11 'Defoe's "Indifferent Monitor": The Complexity of *Moll Flanders*', *ECS*, 3 (1969–70), 361. G. A. Starr discusses Moll's search for the security of the family in his Introd. to *Moll Flanders*, pp. ix–xii.

12 Novak reproduces the table in 'Defoe's "Indifferent Monitor" ', p. 362.

13 Moll herself uses the labyrinth metaphor, but only in Part II ('I was engulfed in labyrinths of trouble' (234)).

14 Jemmy's sudden reappearance just after Moll's marriage to the bank official (213–15) is of the utmost importance. He flits in and out of her life like a reproachful phantom warning her of her false move. Even though he does not waken in Moll any regrets for her marriage to the bank official, she does prevent his arrest, which perhaps indicates some kind of intuitive apprehension of the role he is ultimately to play in her life.

15 Terence Martin, 'The Unity of *Moll Flanders*', *Modern Language Quarterly* (*MLQ*), 22 (1961), 117, suggests that Moll 'steals . . . what might well be wedding rings', but fails to notice their precise echoic function. Martin's article is important in arguing for the structural unity of the novel, without, however, mentioning the incest motif.

16 The pattern is, in fact, broadly chiastic: marriage to brother in Virginia (A); marriage to Jemmy (B); lying-in with governess (C); bank official (D); reappearance of governess (C); reunion with Jemmy (B); return to Virginia (A).

17 On the importance of Newgate for Moll's spiritual regeneration, see Starr, *Defoe and Spiritual Autobiography*, pp. 155ff. As he notes, Moll's repentance and rebirth coincide with the reunion with Jemmy (p. 157). He also comments (pp. 159–60n) on the equation of the New World with moral rebirth.

18 Cf. p. 367, when Moll says of her farewell to the governess as she leaves for Virginia, 'I was never so sorrowful at parting with my own mother as I was at parting with her. . . .'

19 These echoes must, I think, be regarded as deliberate. The formula appears four times in *Moll Flanders* altogether (three times in Part I, once in Part II) and yet only once in Defoe's other novels: 'we were upon *a* Voyage and *no* Voyage, we were bound *some* where and *no* where' (*Captain Singleton*, p. 32).

20 *Colonel Jack*, pp. 266ff. The parallel is commented on by Robert D. Hume, who rightly stresses that the terror which pervades the end of *Roxana* is completely lacking in *Jack* ('The Conclusion of Defoe's *Roxana*: *Fiasco* or Tour de Force?', *ECS*, 3 (1969–70), 485).

21 References are to the OEN reprint of the first edn (1 vol., 1724), ed. Jane Jack (1964).

22 'SUSAN, (for she was my own Name)' (205).

23 It is because she is a projection of her guilt that Roxana talks of Susan 'haunt[ing] me like an Evil Spirit' (310) before her death.

24 John H. Raleigh, 'Style and Structure and Their Import in Defoe's *Roxana*', *University of Kansas City Review*, 20 (1953), 133–4, also sees the passage as 'describing the archetypal movement of the novel', though without really elaborating on the matter. For his comments on the recurrence of characters, see ibid., pp. 132–3.

25 Since this does mark the peak of Roxana's vanity and social climbing ('I . . . was possess'd with so vain an Opinion of my own Beauty, that nothing less than the KING himself was in my Eye' (171–2)), it is significant that she takes the lodgings 'in the *Pall-mall*', which enable her to make the king's acquaintance, at the novel's exact mid-point (p. 165 out of a total of 330). Defoe restores the emphatic central accent.

26 Cf. p. 43: 'I sinn'd with open Eyes, and thereby had a double Guilt upon me.' Novak, 'Crime and Punishment in Defoe's *Roxana*', notes of this episode that Roxana seems intent on affirming her culpability (pp. 448, 450).

27 A point developed by Hume, p. 489.

28 Everett Zimmerman takes a similar view of Amy in his 'Language and Character in Defoe's *Roxana*', *EC*, 21 (1971), 233; and Spiro Peterson discusses the implications of Roxana's whoring of her in 'The Matrimonial Theme of Defoe's *Roxana*', *PMLA*, 70 (1955), 175–6.

29 Roxana sees at this point that there is virtually a predestined pattern to her life: 'he spoke of some particular things which afterwards were to befal me, with such an Assurance, that it frighted me before-hand; and when those things did come to pass, I was perswaded he had some more than humane Knowledge' (160).

30 Peterson, 'The Matrimonial Theme', pp. 184–5, sees the Dutchman as upholding to Roxana 'the orthodox Christian view of marriage'; see also Hume, 'The Conclusion of Defoe's *Roxana*', pp. 478–9.

31 Roxana disguises herself as a Quaker (211), and the Quaker lady she lodges with embodies the ideal that Roxana has failed to live up to in her life; for, like Roxana, she has been abandoned by her husband and left with children to bring up. The analogy is made explicit on p. 252: 'was I, that had tasted so deep of the Sorrows of such a kind of Widowhood, able to look on her, and think of her Circumstances, and not be touch'd in an uncommon Manner?' Homer O. Brown remarks perceptively of the disguise that Roxana 'appears as the self she would like to be (her "spiritual truth") at the same time she is confronted by her past self projected onto the form of her daughter who bears Roxana's true name . . .': 'The Displaced Self in the Novels of Daniel Defoe', *ELH*, 38 (1971), 581.

32 Cf. p. 297: 'What a glorious Testimony it is to the Justice of Providence, and to the Concern Providence has in guiding all the Affairs of Men, (*even the least, as well as the greatest*) that the most secret Crimes are, by the most unforeseen Accidents, brought to light, and discover'd' (cf. p. 44 above).

33 'The Conclusion of Defoe's *Roxana*', pp. 489–90.

34 Ed. Aitken, pp. 189–90.

35 *The Wonderfull Yeare. 1603*, in *The Non-Dramatic Works of Thomas Dekker*, ed A. B. Grosart, Huth Library, 5 vols (1884–6), I. 93. Sir Thomas Browne died on his birthday, and had already commented in his *Letter to a Friend* on the ideal circularity of the coincidence 'that the first day should make the last, that the Tail of the Snake should return into its Mouth precisely at that time, and they should wind up upon the day of their Nativity . . .' (cited in F. L. Huntley, *Sir Thomas Browne: A Biographical and Critical Study* (Ann Arbor, Mich., 1962), p. 4). Cf. Coleridge on the circularity of literary works in the letter quoted as an epigraph above.

36 W. W. Story to Charles Eliot Norton, 15 August 1861, in Henry James, *William Wetmore Story and His Friends* (reprint of 1903 edn, n.d.), II. 65–6.
37 Letter of 19 February 1887, in *The Autobiography and Letters of Mrs M. O. W. Oliphant*, ed. Mrs Harry Coghill (1899), pp. 287–8. Cited by E. K. Brown, *Rhythm in the Novel*, p. 29.

iv Fielding: *Joseph Andrews*

Fielding, as is well known, christened *Joseph Andrews* (1742), in his Preface to that work,[1] 'a comic Epic-Poem in Prose', thereby allying prose fiction as he conceived and executed it with honourable classical antecedents. I have suggested elsewhere that one of the things Fielding draws our attention to by this phrase is an allusive connection between *Joseph Andrews* and the *Odyssey*.[2] I would like to add here that to designate the novel an epic—albeit 'a comic Epic'—would also have had numerological implications. For one thing, the neoclassical preoccupation with the unity of time—in epic as in drama—fostered the habit among readers of counting days in epic actions even as late as the eighteenth century. The following is a typical example:[3]

> The *Epopæa* may take in the Actions of several Years; but
> according to the Criticks, the Time of the main Action, from that
> Part of it where the Poet begins his Narration, must not be
> longer than a Year, as the Time of the *Tragick* Action must never
> be more than a Day. However, *Aristotle* and *Horace* do not lay down
> any such Rule. *Homer* and *Virgil* have observ'd none in this
> Particular. The whole Action of the *Iliad* takes up but fifty Days.
> That of the *Odyssey*, from the Beginning of the Poet's Narration,
> is but about two Months. That of the *Æneid* is a Year.

As I show later, we are meant to count the days occupied by the action of *Joseph Andrews*, as also of *Tom Jones*, where, in the Contents list, Fielding places chronological summaries at the beginning of every book except the first.

But the epic formula would, in addition, have aroused expectations of formal precision in the work as a whole, and not only in the relatively minor matter of chronology. This can be inferred from the practice of Homer, Virgil, Milton, and others,[4] and from the analogy between the relationship of parts in epic narrative and the proportions of the human frame—an analogy that goes back at least to the sixteenth century and survived until the late eighteenth century. The

65

theoretical statements are understandably vague, but their import is clear. Thus, Sir Richard Blackmore, in his Preface to *Prince Arthur* (1695), wrote:[5]

> That which makes the *Unity* of the Action, is the regular
> Succession of one *Part* or *Episode* to another, not only as
> *Antecedents* and *Consequents*, but as it were *Causes* and *Effects*, wherein
> the Reader may discern that the former *Episode* makes the
> following necessary, and the *Connection* between them is such,
> that they *assist* and *support* each other, as the *Members* of the Body
> do, no Episode being out of its place, of a *disproportion'd* size to the
> Rest. . . .

In the first volume of his *Essays upon Several Subjects* (1716) he returned to the proportions of the body, again in connection with the writing of poetry:[6] 'In the Structure of Man, all the Parts are form'd with so much Wisdom, are so exactly proportion'd and dependant on each other in such admirable Order, . . . that all Things appear shap'd and united intirely for Beauty and Majesty. . . .' And as late as 1790 James Ogden, in his 'Introductory Essay on Poetry' prefixed to *The Revolution, An Epic Poem in Twelve Books*, could state[7] that 'none of [the episodes] can be separated from their connection with the main action, without weakening its importance in some respect or other; these under-parts, having the same dependency upon it, and connection with it, as the detached members have with the head in a human body. . . .' Such passages refer, of course, to the traditional notions of bodily proportion which I mentioned in the Introduction and which saw man as embodying, microcosmically, the numerical harmonies of the cosmos.

It was, I suggest, this theoretical background that persuaded Fielding to utilize numerological patterns in his first 'comic Epic', though, as we shall see, Providential considerations also had their part to play in shaping its mathematical symmetries. But Fielding, self-consciously aware that *Joseph Andrews* should, structurally as well as stylistically and morally, be as different as possible from Richardson's *Pamela*, seems to have overcompensated: the novel is perhaps too highly wrought, containing as it does not only an elaborate repetitive structure but, in addition, obscure number symbolisms, some at least of which would clearly have been beyond the grasp of even the most sympathetic reader. There is a close contemporary analogue in this respect in the music of Bach, where numerology—the concern with temporal numbers (the days of the month and the year), and the numerical alphabet, for example—is complemented by less specifically numerically-based structural schemes, such as chiasmus.[8] But Fielding has no real temperamental affinities with Bach's intense mathematical mysticism; so that, even accepting the formal demands of epic and Fielding's desire to affirm in the literary artifact that order which is synonymous with Providence and Divine justice, we must also see in the complexities of *Joseph Andrews* a private game, an almost mannerist piling of difficulty on difficulty[9] to prove to his own satisfaction that the feat can be accomplished. To some extent I suspect that *Joseph Andrews* is, structurally speaking, a virtuoso *jeu d'esprit*.

I

The novel, like *Crusoe*, *Tom Jones*, and Johnson's *Rasselas*,[10] is tripartite, since its four books are so arranged that the first and last, largely static, frame two central books of picaresque movement.[11] The frame effect is reinforced by the echoes of *Pamela*, which are concentrated in Books I and IV;[12] and these two books are further linked by similarity of episode. Thus, I. 5-10, the chapters in which Lady Booby reveals her passion for Joseph, are recapitulated in IV. 1; the discussion between Lady Booby and Slipslop about Joseph in I. 7 is matched by the longer discussion between the two on the same subject in IV. 6; in I. 14 Adams arrives at the Dragon Inn and recognizes Joseph (who is in difficulties with Mrs Tow-wouse), just as, in IV. 15, there is a series of arrivals, all having to do with the 'recognition' of Joseph, concerned this time with the establishing of his true parentage; and in IV. 2 Adams, referring to Joseph and Fanny, tells Lady Booby that 'This Couple were desirous to consummate long ago, and I dissuaded them from it', advice which he originally gave them in I. 11 ('Mr *Adams* had with much ado prevented them from marrying; and persuaded them to wait . . .').

Most important of all is the pairing of part of the Dragon Inn episode in Book I with the final chapter of Book IV. In IV. 16 Joseph and Fanny are married, and go to bed 'to enjoy the private Rewards of their Constancy; Rewards so great and sweet, that I apprehend *Joseph* neither envied the noblest Duke, nor *Fanny* the finest Duchess that Night'. This has been seen—rightly, I think—as an allusion to *Pamela*'s subtitle, 'Virtue Rewarded': here Joseph and Fanny receive their reward.[13] But the full harmony of this union can be fully appreciated only if we

recall its comically-discordant anticipation in I. 17. Mrs Tow-wouse
has just discovered her husband in bed with Betty the chambermaid,
and in the 'most hideous Uproar' that ensues, her voice is heard, 'like
a Bass Viol in a Concert, . . . to articulate the following Sounds.—"O
you damn'd Villain, is this the Return to all the Care I have taken of
your Family? This the Reward of my Virtue? Is this the manner in
which you behave to one who brought you a Fortune, and preferred
you to so many Matches, all your Betters?"'

But though comic, this is full of irony as well. For Mrs Tow-wouse's
emphasis on the monetary side of marriage is a fine dig at the mer-
cenary Pamela, serving to stress the innocent, unmercenary nature of
Joseph's and Fanny's union and 'reward'; while the reader is left with
the impression that Tow-wouse's adultery with the open-hearted
Betty is a more fitting relationship than his marriage to his unchari-
table wife and that it does, in fact, mime, on a lower level, the marriage
of Joseph and Fanny. Another point links the two episodes: Betty
satisfies herself on Tow-wouse only after she has been rejected by
Joseph because he is saving himself for Fanny.

If Books I and IV are paired, so are II and III, and so closely that the
similarities cannot be regarded as fortuitous. A noteworthy feature
here is that parallel episodes appear in the same chapter of their
respective books. Thus, in III. 2 Adams and Joseph, together with
Fanny, encounter what they think are ghosts or murderers (they
turn out to be sheep-stealers), and manage to escape under cover of
darkness. They arrive at a river bank:

> *Adams* here made a full stop, and declared he could swim, but
> doubted how it was possible to get *Fanny* over; to which *Joseph*
> answered, 'if they walked along its Banks they might be certain
> of soon finding a Bridge, especially as by the number of
> Lights they might be assured a Parish was near.' 'Odso, that's
> true indeed,' said *Adams*, 'I did not think of that.'

In terms of Joseph's developing maturity,[14] this episode is important
in itself: his common sense is set over against Adams's blindness to
things practical. The main force of the incident in contrasting the
two, however, derives from the fact that it is an almost exact repetition
of one in II. 2: Adams

> soon came to a large Water, which filling the whole Road, he
> saw no Method of passing unless by wading through, which he

accordingly did up to his Middle; but was no sooner got to the other Side, than he perceived, if he had looked over the Hedge, he would have found a Foot-Path capable of conducting him without wetting his Shoes.

The echo is clear, and is supported by additional ones:[15] in II. 2 Adams 'fell into a Contemplation on a Passage in *Æschylus*', and arrives 'at the Summit of a Hill'; in III. 2 he 'applied himself to Meditation' (after having 'lamented the loss of his dear *Æschylus*') and he and his companions 'found themselves on the Descent of a very steep Hill'.

A similar relationship exists between II. 9 and III. 9. In the former, Adams rescues a woman (who, he discovers later, is Fanny) from rape; in the latter the agents of the 'roasting' squire arrive, and, after a battle, abduct Fanny for their master. She is rescued in III. 12, and this leads to a reunion between her and Joseph at an inn: 'O Reader, conceive if thou canst, the Joy which fired the Breasts of these Lovers on this Meeting'; which recalls chapter 12 of Book II, where Joseph and Fanny are reunited at another inn:

> But, O Reader, when this Nightingale, who was no other than *Joseph Andrews* himself, saw his beloved *Fanny* in the Situation we have described her, can'st thou conceive the Agitations of his Mind? If thou can'st not, wave that Meditation to behold his Happiness, when clasping her in his Arms, he found Life and Blood returning into her Cheeks.

Finally, the last chapter of both books contains a '*Dialogue*' and a disagreement. Perhaps a schematic outline is useful at this point:

BOOK I
Lady Booby and Joseph.
Dialogue: Lady Booby and Slipslop.
Arrival of Adams.
Virtue rewarded.
Joseph and Betty.

> **BOOK II**
> 2 Adams and water, etc.
> 9 Rescue of Fanny (near-rape).
> 12 Reunion.
> Final chapter: Dialogue (Adams and host).

BOOK III
2 Adams and river, etc.
9 Fanny abducted (near-rape).
12 Reunion.
Final chapter: Dialogue (Adams and Pounce).

BOOK IV
Lady Booby and Joseph.
Dialogue: Lady Booby and Slipslop
Various arrivals.
Virtue rewarded.
Joseph and Fanny.

In addition to this, the novel reveals a more pervasive pattern of episode-parallelism which fills out the skeletal frame offered above. For example, soon after his dismissal, Joseph is robbed and stripped (I. 12). The focus now is on theft and charity; but we see how judiciously Fielding has constructed the book: robbery for money is sandwiched between the attempted sexual 'robberies' of Lady Booby and Slipslop in the first half and that of Betty at the Dragon Inn in the second,[16] and he derives a further irony from the fact that it is actually Betty who exemplifies charity by clothing Joseph when he arrives at the Dragon. In II. 3 and II. 5 Joseph is again, as in I. 12, refused entry into a stage-coach, this time because he is a footman.

Book II seems to be relatively free of cross-references after this until chapters 9 and 10, where a parallel with I. 12 is introduced when the gentleman who is accompanying Adams, hearing shrieks from behind some bushes, assumes that a robbery is taking place (both incidents occur at night). But this hint at theft of money is immediately countered by the revelation of the robbery's sexual nature: Adams, 'on coming up to the Place whence the Noise proceeded, found a Woman struggling with a Man, who had thrown her on the Ground, and had almost overpowered her'. II. 9 thus subsumes, in addition to I. 12 (Adams's willingness to come to the rescue contrasts, of course, with the behaviour of the stage-coach passengers), I. 5 and 6, the attempts on Joseph by Lady Booby and Slipslop. Fanny, as yet unnamed, acts here as a surrogate for Joseph in his absence from this part of the novel;[17] and Adams's rescue of her underlines the inseparability of charity and chastity again: the parson, representing the former, rescues Fanny, exemplifying the latter.

The parallel between the attempted seductions of Joseph and Fanny is made explicit when Fanny tells Adams that her would-be ravisher 'desired her to stop, and after some rude Kisses, which she resisted, and some Entreaties, which she rejected, he laid violent hands on her, and was attempting to execute his wicked Will, when, she thanked G—, he timely came up and prevented him'. Compare I. 6: 'so did Mrs. *Slipslop* prepare to lay her violent amorous Hands on the poor *Joseph*, when luckily her Mistress's Bell rung, and delivered the intended Martyr from her Clutches'.[18]

A substantial passage added to the beginning of II. 10 in the second edition starts: 'THE Silence of *Adams*, added to the Darkness of the Night, and Loneliness of the Place, struck dreadful Apprehensions into the poor Woman's Mind: She began to fear as great an Enemy in her Deliverer, as he had delivered her from. . . .' This fulfils a deliberate thematic function by stressing Adams's chastity: he has the opportunity for rape but the thought never enters his head. Hence the irony when, with the arrival of the bird batters in the same chapter, the ravisher, who has by now recovered from Adams's blows, accuses him of being a robber and Fanny of being his whore—a parody of I. 12, with the ravisher now taking Joseph's part of the injured and robbed innocent.

The bird batters' debate over the sharing of the reward money gives the parson, had he been 'a dextrous nimble Thief', a chance to escape: 'but *Adams* trusted rather to his Innocence than his Heels'; which harks back to I. 16, the escape from the 'Dragon' of one of the men who had robbed Joseph. The escape occurred, it is hinted, because the constable guarding him had succumbed to a bribe, as 'not being concerned in the taking the Thief, he could not have been entitled to any part of the Reward, if he had been convicted'. (The bird batters decide to exclude 'the young Fellow, who had been employed only in holding the Nets' from any share in the reward.)

But the parallel extends even further, stressing again, structurally, the intimate relationship between sexual and monetary in the novel. For just as the man who robbed Joseph is caught and then escapes, so is the would-be ravisher caught by Adams, succeeds in 'escaping' by deception (accusing Adams of theft), then escapes properly by slipping away from the justice's house when the identities of Adams and Fanny are revealed (II. 11).

I have already discussed the most obvious instances of repetitive structuring in Book III. But before passing on to Book IV, I should like

71

to examine III. 12 a little more closely, since it serves to unite several thematic strands. In it, Fanny is rescued from the captain who had abducted her on the 'roasting' squire's orders by the arrival of Lady Booby's steward, Peter Pounce. Later in the chapter he offers to take Adams in his chariot, 'finding he had no longer hopes of satisfying his old Appetite with *Fanny*'. This last piece of information is meant to stir the reader's memory: Fanny's rescue by the lustful Pounce (whose desires are never to be satisfied) echoes Joseph's redemption from the 'Dragon' by Slipslop, who, we remember, fails in her attempts to get Joseph into the stage-coach with her, and is again doomed to perpetual frustration.

But if, as I have argued, the reunion of Joseph and Fanny here recalls a similar reunion in II. 12, the rescue of Fanny from rape by the arrival of Pounce in his chariot broadly parallels, in addition, the rescue of the robbed Joseph by the passengers in the stage-coach in I. 12. Once more, sexual counterpoints monetary, attempted rape echoes robbery.

It is this recurring pattern in chapter 12 of each of the first three books, indeed, that is one of the most noticeable features of the novel's structure. In I. 12 Joseph is robbed and rescued; in II. 12 he and Fanny are reunited; in III. 12 Fanny is rescued from rape and reunited with Joseph. The pattern is, in fact, a cumulative one: III. 12 combines the motifs (robbery, reunion) that occur separately in I. 12 and II. 12. And so insistent is it that it almost forces us to predict what Fielding has in store in IV. 12; for if Fielding is to remain true to his scheme there must again be a robbery and a reunion. And so there is. But with a superb twist, since Joseph and Fanny are reunited by becoming brother and sister and are thus apparently prevented for ever from attaining the ultimate union, marriage. Fate, it seems, has stolen Fanny from Joseph this time; so that the scene ironically echoes the robbery-rape motif as well as containing a 'reunion' which is actually the reverse of a reunion.[19]

The final chapter to participate in the system I have been outlining (apart from IV. 16, already considered, and a minor case in IV. 7),[20] is 14, containing the night escapades at Booby Hall. Mark Spilka has made out a convincing case for the climactic force of this episode;[21] but it is a force that derives largely from its heavily recapitulative nature, a point which Spilka failed to note.

Thus, when Adams leaps naked from bed and rescues the soft-skinned Didapper from the amorous clutches of the bearded Slipslop —mistaking the man for the woman and vice-versa—he is unwittingly parodying his rescue of Fanny in II. 9. And when Lady Booby appears on the scene, and, seeing him struggling with Slipslop, immediately accuses him of 'Impudence in chusing her House for the Scene of his Debaucheries, and her own Woman for the Object of his Bestiality', the parody is extended and the comedy heightened; for here is an echo of II. 10, the robber's false accusation of Adams. The echo resounds even louder when the parson, acquitted by the discovery of Didapper's 'Diamond Buttons for the Sleeves', makes his way back to his room. Taking a wrong turning in the dark, he ends up in Fanny's bed and sleeps with her, to her horror in the morning. He is still almost exactly where he was in II. 10; and once again comes the false accusation, this time voiced by Joseph: 'How!... Hath he offered any Rudeness to you?'

II

The above analysis should be sufficient to indicate the kind of care with which Fielding constructed his novel. It is, however, only the first step towards an appreciation of the subtlety and complexity of its structuring. We might begin, for instance, by asking why Fielding should draw attention so deliberately and at such length to the division of his work 'into Books and Chapters' as he does in II. 1, mentioning it (perhaps only half jokingly) as a 'mysterious' and 'secret' business, and actually inviting arithmetical speculation by the explicit reference to addition at the end of the first paragraph: 'These several Places therefore in our Paper, which are filled with our Books and Chapters, are understood as so much Buckram, Stays, and Stay-tape in a Taylor's Bill, serving only to make up the Sum Total, commonly found at the Bottom of our first Page, and of his last.' A page or so later he alludes to numerological speculations which connected the twenty-four books of the Homeric epics with the twenty-four letters of the Greek alphabet: 'These Divisions have the Sanction of great Antiquity. *Homer* . . . divided his great Work into twenty-four Books, (in Compliment perhaps to the twenty-four Letters to which he had very particular Obligations). . . .'[22] It seems to me difficult not to regard these passages as invitations to search for numerical organization in the novel, especially when taken in conjunction with another passage right at the beginning (in I. 3), where Adams refers to the practice of counting the books of the Bible by asking Joseph 'how many Books there were in the New Testament? which were they? how many

Chapters they contained? and such like'.[23] I said earlier that the complexities of *Joseph Andrews* were, to some extent, a private game: it must be admitted, I think, that here at least Fielding confesses publicly what he is up to.

Most obvious, and of primary importance, is the division of the novel into four books. It is too easy to assume that Fielding is here merely glancing at Part I of *Don Quixote*, which is similarly divided, and it might well be that the novel is organized on a four-book plan because 4 was traditionally regarded as symbolizing concord, friendship, and justice. The former meanings derived from the harmonizing of the four elements to create the world-order, expressed as follows by Plato in the *Timaeus*:[24]

what brings solids into unison is never one middle term alone but always two. Thus it was that in the midst between fire and earth God set water and air, and having bestowed upon them so far as possible a like ratio one towards another—air being to water as fire to air, and water being to earth as air to water,—he joined together and constructed a Heaven visible and tangible. For these reasons and out of these materials, such in kind and four in number, the body of the Cosmos was harmonized by proportion and brought into existence. These conditions secured for it Amity, so that being united in identity with itself it became indissoluble by any agent other than Him who had bound it together.

As F. M. Cornford has explained[25] (commenting also on its association with friendship), the significance of 4 as justice is intimately related: Justice . . . completes the tetrad, and assures that the opposite tensions of the contraries shall be held together in harmony. It is easy to see why later authorities also identify the square number with [friendship].'

In narrative terms, concord and harmony are achieved with the marriage of Joseph and Fanny: Andrew Wright has well remarked[26] that 'marriage is the matter of Book IV' since it contains, in addition to the concluding marriage, the arrival of the recently married Pamela and Mr Booby in chapter 4, and the debate between Adams and Joseph on marriage in chapter 8, etc. And justice triumphs explicitly, too, when, in IV. 16, Adams encounters 'the Justice of Peace before whom he and *Fanny* had made their Appearance. The Parson presently saluted him very kindly; and the Justice informed him, that he had found the Fellow who attempted to swear against him and the young Woman the very next day, and had committed him to *Salisbury* Goal, where he was charged with many Robberies'. (At the end of the chapter it is mentioned that the pedlar has been 'made an Excise-man; a Trust which he discharges with such Justice, that he is greatly beloved in his Neighbourhood'.)

Furthermore, as the *Timaeus* passage makes clear, the peculiar stability of 4 arises from the fact that it possesses two means (i.e., water:air::air:fire, etc.), and the interlocking thus achieved was traditionally regarded as having been reproduced in the chiastic dictum attributed to Pythagoras by Iamblichus and Porphyry: friendship is equality, equality is friendship.[27]

Now it will be recalled from the earlier part of this chapter that the four books of *Joseph Andrews* are arranged in just this way; that Books I and IV are linked by echo, repetition, and the *Pamela* parody, as are, even more closely (by the chapter for chapter parallelism noted above), the two central books, II and III, giving us the replicative A B B A pattern.[28]

But the novel's numerology does not function solely to direct us to the 'harmonious' marriage of Joseph and Fanny and ultimate, Providential, justice. It seems to me, indeed, that Fielding's use of this overall replicative scheme brings into focus a basic theme of the novel, that of friendship. The title page is quite explicit in telling us that we are about to read *The History of the Adventures of Joseph Andrews, And of his Friend Mr. Abraham Adams*. And Fielding has emphasized his concern with friendship in several ways. Most noticeable, apart from the title itself, is the interpolated tale in IV. 10, '*The History of two Friends, which may afford an useful Lesson to all those Persons, who happen to take up their Residence in married Families*', which, I have argued elsewhere,[29] is an integral part of the novel because it shows us dissension between the friends Leonard and Paul, and thus affirms by contrast the perfect amity of Joseph and Adams in the chapter immediately following, where Adams comes to Joseph's aid against Didapper despite his wife's and Lady Booby's objections. The notion of friendship appears through literary allusion, too, for both this tale and its counterpart in Book II, '*The History of* Leonora' (chapters 4 and 6), are modelled on 'The Novel of the Curious Impertinent' in *I Don Quixote*, IV. 6–8,[30] the beginning of the first paragraph of which reads:[31] 'Anselmo and Lothario, considerable gentlemen of Florence . . . were so eminent for their friendship, that they were called nothing but the Two Friends.' And so that the reader will not miss the allusion to Cervantes, Fielding drops a broad hint by referring in III. 1 to 'the impertinent Curiosity of *Anselmo*, the Weakness of *Camilla*, the irresolute Friendship of *Lothario*'. The notion of friendship thus permeates the novel explicitly and implicitly.

At this point, then, we can take a more inclusive view of the subject-matter of Book IV than that suggested by Andrew Wright and quoted above. Not only is it about marriage; it also marks the culmination of the related theme of friendship, and, most fittingly (since 4 is the number of concord and union) it is the book of *re*-unions, where Adams is reunited with his young son who is thought to have been drowned (IV. 8), Joseph and Fanny are reunited with their rightful parents, and so on.

But 4 possesses yet another meaning. It signifies virtue because square numbers are particularly virtuous. As Bongo explains,[32] the square consists of four right angles, each of which symbolizes 'right reason, and right reason is the perennial fount of virtue'. Fielding seems to exploit this meaning of 4 as well in the marriage that concludes the novel; for, as we saw above, the marriage of Joseph and Fanny is nothing other than a 'reward' for 'virtue', a re-enactment of the marriage—which itself symbolized 'virtue rewarded'—in Richardson's *Pamela*.[33]

This is underlined in yet another way: the marriage occurs in the sixteenth chapter of Book IV, and 16—as the square of the just and virtuous 4—possesses the meanings of 4, only more so—it is doubly just and virtuous since it is the square of a square.[34] Equally significantly, 16 is specifically connected with love-making and marriage, an association which arose from the biological fact that at the age of sixteen 'incipiant homines veneri indulgere generareque'.[35] And Plato associated the number with marriage when he wrote[36] that 'The limit of the marriage-age shall be from sixteen to twenty years.'

Yet even this is not all. For we might say that the whole movement of the novel is towards 16 and all that it signifies—justice, virtue, and so on—since the total number of chapters is 64, and Book IV is the only book to possess its 'just' (or mean) share of 16 (i.e., $64 \div 4 = 16$).[37] The actual chapter-totals for each book are, in order, 18, 17, 13, and 16, and it will be apparent that the descent towards 16 is made sufficiently clear by the 18–17–16 progression of Books I, II and IV. (Book III is the odd man out here, but Fielding needed it to complete his structural chiasmus—the A B B A scheme outlined above—and also to bring the overall chapter-total to 64.) Thus the very arithmetic of the novel's structure enacts a just sharing of rewards, and it is likely that Fielding would have regarded this as one of the more accessible of his formal schemes, particularly in view of contemporary theories of poetic justice which saw the distribution of rewards and punishments at the end of the play (or novel) as 'an Image of the Divine' and consequently expressive of 'the Being of a God and Providence'.[38] This distribution usually occurred on the level of plot only.[39] But in *Joseph Andrews* and *Tom Jones* Fielding obviously felt the need to affirm his faith in Providence in a more profound way—through number. Samuel Clarke, the divine, had written[40] of the necessity, in an ordered universe, for a 'final vindication of the Honour and Laws of God in the proportionable reward of the best, or punishment of the worst of Men . . . there must at some time or other be such a Revolution and Renovation of Things, such a *future State* of existence of the same Persons, as that by an exact distribution of Rewards or Punishments therein, all the present Disorders and Inequalities may be set right. . . .' It is a vision of this *'future State'* when all will enjoy 'an exact distribution of Rewards or Punishments' that Fielding symbolically offers us as his novel comes to its arithmetically just conclusion.

The reader who has followed my argument this far, incidentally, will not be surprised to learn that 64 itself possesses meanings relevant to the theme of the novel. Like 16 it symbolizes justice (because it can be divided into equal halves until the monad is reached),[41] and it is, in addition, dedicated to Mercury,[42] the god of 'peace and concord',[43] whose zodiacal house is Gemini, the Heavenly Twins (again symbols of concord),[44] and who is the guardian of the fourth day of the planetary week.[45]

III

Up to this point I have discussed *Joseph Andrews* without direct reference to the implications of Fielding's 'epic' formula. In fact, these implications seem to me to be considerable, and I should like to continue by taking up a suggestion of M. C. Battestin's that *Joseph Andrews* is to be related not so much to classical epic as to the Christian epic tradition.[46] This is an important suggestion that has not, so far as I am aware, been developed; and it has a direct bearing on the novel's numerology.

As Battestin has shown,[47] Fielding's heroes, Joseph and Adams, are based (via the writings of Latitudinarian divines) on the figures of the

Biblical Joseph and Abraham, and 'an adaptation of the stories of Joseph and Abraham—already on the Continent the subjects of several epic poems—would be in accord with theories of the biblical epic then prevalent in England.' Moreover, Barbara Lewalski's study of the genre has brought to light points relevant for *Joseph Andrews*. Discussing Milton's *Paradise Regained* as an example of the brief Biblical epic (as opposed to the full-scale epic like *Paradise Lost*), she shows[48] that the Book of Job provided the pattern for the brief epic, having been regarded from patristic times 'as an analogue of the classical epic'; and that the brief Biblical epic was almost invariably divided into three or four books, the former originally in honour of the Trinity, the latter after the four Gospels.[49]

In view of this, it might just possibly have been with specific allusive intent that, in IV. 8, Fielding compared Joseph's patience to that of Job:[50] 'The Patience of *Joseph*, nor perhaps of *Job*, could bear no longer'; and it certainly gives us another reason—if not necessarily the primary one—for the division of *Joseph Andrews* into four books.[51]

But Fielding's novel is an answer to Richardson's *Pamela*; and it is easy to see how *Pamela* might have suggested the Biblical epic to Fielding, prompting him to cast his novel in that form. For example, Pamela's passivity in the face of her adversary might well have reminded Fielding, and Richardson's other readers, of the passive heroes of Biblical epic, Job and Christ.[52] (Characteristically, Adams and Joseph recall that active warrior hero and type of Christ, Hercules, as they brandish crabstick and cudgel.)[53] Then again, as the conflict between Pamela and her master develops, the one becomes an angel and the other a devil, offering her temptation.[54] General echoes become more particular once Pamela is moved to B.'s Lincolnshire estate, however, where she is implicitly identified with Christ. The point has been well made by M. Kinkead-Weekes:[55]

> In the second movement Pamela is imprisoned. This is a period of 'persecutions, oppressions and distress', but it is also a period of spiritual growth. It lasts, pointedly, for forty days and forty nights, and the presence of biblical language in the prayer which opens it, and in the scene by the pond at its heart, should indicate that the new conflict within Pamela herself has a religious dimension.

The identification is reinforced by what appears to be the novel's one instance of typology among an abundance of other Biblical allusions which possess less thematic relevance.[56] This occurs when Pamela has been walking with Mr B. in the garden: 'But I trust, that that God, who has delivered me from the paw of the lion and the bear, that is, his and Mrs. Jewkes's violences, will soon deliver me from this *Philistine*, that I may not *defy the commands of the living God*!' (I. 184). Pamela is misquoting I Samuel 17 (David's encounter with Goliath), verses 26, 'who is this uncircumcised Philistine, that he should defy the armies of the living God?', and 37, 'The Lord that delivered me out of the paw of the lion, and out of the paw of the bear, he will deliver me out of the hand of this Philistine.'[57] The significance of the allusion lies in the traditional interpretation of David's victory over Goliath as a type of Christ's victory over Satan in the wilderness.[58] And Richardson makes the identification, implicit in the allusion, explicit when, on the same page, he has Pamela physically struggling with B. and saying, 'to be sure you are Lucifer himself, in the *shape* of my master, or you could not use me thus' (I. 184).

Pamela, then, might well have prompted Fielding to make his first novel not only a 'comic Epic', but a comic Biblical epic. Moreover, number symbolism flourished to a large extent in the seventeenth-century Biblical epic,[59] and it is worth noting here, I think, that Milton's brief epic, *Paradise Regained*, written—like *Joseph Andrews*—in the almost canonical four books, makes prominent structural use of 64, the number, as we have seen, of the overall chapter-total of Fielding's novel. It appears at the poem's arithmetical centre, and provides the line-total for Christ's speech rejecting Satan's offer of military fame and glory, and his substitution of the *Paradise Regained* ideal of 'the just man', the prime example of which is Job (III. 62ff.). The speech contains, in addition, a condemnation of those who 'all the flourishing works of peace destroy' (III. 80), and his exaltation of the glory achieved 'Without ambition, war, or violence;/By deeds of peace' (III 90–1). In short, Milton seems to be exploiting here two primary meanings of 64 which we encountered earlier on in connection with *Joseph Andrews*: justice and peace.[60] The coincidence is striking; it becomes even more so when we recall that in Book IV of *The Faerie Queene* prominent structural use is again made of 64 (as the stanza total for Canto VIII).

But if *Joseph Andrews* is a comic Biblical epic, and my suggestion that it is organized on numerological lines appears to be confirmed by Richardson's use of number symbolism in *Pamela* (his heroine's forty-day period of imprisonment and trial), the question arises, should not the journey of Joseph and Adams—Fielding's version of Pamela's trial—involve a significant number symbolism? There is, of course, no simple correspondence, as we might have supposed: the journey does not last 40 days; it takes 11.[61] And if we follow Fielding's hints about counting chapter-totals we soon discover that it does not occupy 40 chapters—another possibility—but only 38.[62]

In fact, though, 38 is more relevant to Fielding's purpose than 40 would have been. Like 40, it is specifically associated with the wanderings of the Israelites in the wilderness, as Moses reminds them in Deuteronomy 2: 14, when recapitulating their journey 'in the fortieth year, in the eleventh month, on the first day of the month' (Deuteronomy 1: 3): 'And the space in which we came from Kadesh-barnea, until we were come over the brook Zered, was thirty and eight years.' Moreover, according to Bongo, 38 is not only evil in holy writ; it signifies (to quote his index) 'imperfect and grudging charity' ('*imperfectae, et languidae charitatis significativus*') as well,[63] both of which meanings —but particularly the latter—could not relate more closely to the wretched wanderings of Joseph, Adams, and Fanny, in which, at almost every point, charity is tested and found wanting.[64]

There is a delicate irony in Fielding's use of Biblical numbers here—irony directed at that Puritan habit of mind which could accept the symbolic significance of Pamela's forty days and nights, and of 'Crusoe's twenty-eight years of isolation and suffering'.[65] But Fielding means the numbers seriously, too: they are essential to his conception of the structure of prose fiction.

IV

Further minor instances of numerological decorum may be noted in conclusion. Thus, III. 11 is the scene of Joseph's despair over the abduction of Fanny, or, as the chapter heading has it, '*Containing the Exhortations of Parson* Adams *to his Friend in Affliction*'. The allusion here, surely, is to 11 as the number of grief and mourning.[66] And since 11 is often discussed in connection with 12 (a number of perfection and completion; 11 is imperfect because it falls one short of 12),[67] we might look again at the pattern that I have already traced in the twelfth chapter of each of *Joseph Andrews*'s four books, noting particularly that in the central books the pattern centres round the eleventh *and* twelfth chapters, where suffering yields to joyful reunion. (In II. 11 Fanny and Adams are wrongfully accused before the justice, to be reunited with Joseph in II. 12; in III. 11 Joseph laments Fanny's abduction, and in III. 12 she is rescued and he is reunited with her.) Fielding associates 12 with reunion and rescue, then; perhaps not surprisingly in view of its connection with salvation as well as completion (because it is the number of the disciples, etc.).

The novel also reveals a considerable exploitation of mid-point symbolism. I have postponed discussion of this not because I regard it as less significant than the schemes outlined above, but because, once established, it will enable us to stand back and assess the overall impact of the novel's structure. The reader feels that he has reached the middle of the novel with the opening of Book III (in the original two-volume format, the start of the second volume). Now, the narrative recommences in the second chapter of Book III; and since Joseph, Adams, and Fanny here find themselves on 'a very steep Hill', we can say that the novel literally rises to a peak at its centre. Then, however, it just as rapidly falls: '*Adams*'s Foot slipping, he instantly disappeared, ... rolling down the Hill, ... from top to bottom. ...' The notion of a fall at the centre had already been exploited in Marvell's 'The First Anniversary of the Government under O.C.',[68] and is also to be found in the work of William Hogarth. In view of the friendship between Fielding and Hogarth, it is worth pausing for a moment to consider Hogarth's handling of the iconography of the centre.

The clearest example occurs in the four *Election* plates (1755–8). In Plate 1, 'An Election Entertainment', we note the displacement of the king from his sovereign (central) position: a slashed portrait of William III gazes from the top centre on the scene of corruption below. The 'entertainment' of the title is being given by the Whigs, while the Tories parade outside. As Ronald Paulson suggests,[69] the portrait might have been disfigured by the Whigs themselves, since they were Hanoverian supporters and William was a Stuart by marriage; or, alternatively, the Tories might have been responsible when they gave their earlier entertainment, seeing in William 'the image of usurpation'. In Plate 2, 'Canvassing for Votes', the motif is repeated in a more subtle way: the centre foreground is occupied by a farmer who is being bribed by the hosts of the two inns which we see behind. The nearer of the inns is the 'Royal Oak', representing the Tory interest, the other is the 'Crown', marked out as being Whig in sympathy by the inscription underneath its sign, 'THE EXCISE OFFICE' (an allusion to Walpole's excise bill of 1733). But it is the sign of the 'Royal Oak' that occupies the top centre of the print: complementing the mutilated portrait in Plate 1 is this painting of the oak tree in which Charles Stuart (later Charles II) took refuge after the battle of Worcester. Charles's head is carefully delineated, and symmetrically framed by three crowns, one either side and one above. Ironically, however, the Jacobite Tories have displaced their own emblem of sovereign centrality: over (and partly concealing) the sign they have hung a banner depicting Whig bribes. The upper half of the banner shows the old Treasury, from which money is being poured into sacks which are then conveyed into a waggon; the lower half satirizes the ministry as a Punch and Judy show, with Punch throwing bribery money indiscriminately from his barrow. Moreover, echoing the symbolic displacement of Charles in the centre is the chaotic scene in the background where Tory supporters attack the 'Crown' and one of them begins to saw off the sign itself. Paulson puts it thus:[70] 'The man sawing off the excise sign is unaware that its fall will be his own.'

There is no obvious mid-point symbolism in 'The Polling' (Plate 3). Nevertheless, it should be observed how the waggon and barrow of Plate 2 are now metamorphosed into the coach going over the bridge in the background and, more significantly, into Britannia's coach (on the right in the middle distance): because the coachmen are playing cards rather than controlling their horses, and are unaware that the straps supporting the body of the coach have snapped, it is on the point of overturning. There is perhaps just a hint of the symbolic centre in that the nearer of the two coachmen points with his hand of cards (through a contrived coincidence of perspective) to the keystone of the arch of the bridge behind (presumably the arch of the political constitution which, as the toppling coach implies, is in danger of collapse).

In the final plate the coach becomes a chair—the chair in which, at the centre of the print, the triumphant candidate is borne aloft in a procession but (like Britannia in her coach) is about to fall. Hogarth's meaning is evident enough. And yet the full import of 'Chairing the Members' can be felt only in the light of its iconographical antecedents, that long tradition, particularly rich in the Renaissance, which dictated the central elevation of the triumphator in his chariot and from which Cromwell's fall in a coach accident at the centre of Marvell's 'First Anniversary' derives its symbolic force. Alastair Fowler's *Triumphal Forms* has shown how important the central accent characteristic of the triumph was for literature, architecture, and painting, seeing its influence, for instance, in pyramidal, baroque, façades.[71] And, indeed, the final *Election* plate has long been recognized as an ironic inversion of the traditional triumphal procession and pictorial battle-piece: the goose flying above the candidate in the top centre, for instance, clearly parodies the eagle, symbol of victory, that hovers above the head of Alexander the Great in the top centre of Charles Le Brun's *La Bataille d'Arbelles*.[72]

A quick glance at some of Hogarth's other prints reveals a similar preoccupation with the iconography of the centre. The cosmic centrality of the sun is neatly parodied in the centre of *Strolling Actresses Dressing in a Barn* (1738), where Apollo is just visible behind a declaiming actress dressed as the moon goddess Diana; while the related associations of the centre with judgment (via the *Sol iustitiae*, which I mentioned in connection with *Robinson Crusoe*, and also because the principle of divisibility implied by formal emphasis on the centre traditionally symbolized the notion of just balance) doubtless explain the positioning of the rake in Plate 2 of *A Rake's Progress* (1735) beneath a painting of *The Judgment of Paris* (top centre): compare the dying count in Plate 5 of *Marriage à la Mode* (1745), who occupies the centre of the print in a traditional *Descent from the Cross* pose, with a tapestry of *The Judgment of Solomon* (in which the sword is raised ready to cut the baby in two) behind him.[73] Similarly, in *A Harlot's Progress* (1732), Plate 2, the background is divided equally between two paintings which hang on the wall, one based on Jonah 4: 6–8, depicting the sun of God's justice beating upon Jonah's head, and the other (following II Samuel 6) showing Uzzah 'put[ting] forth his hand to the ark of God': 'And the anger of the Lord was kindled against Uzzah; and God smote him there for his error. . . .' As Paulson explains, these pictures express the rigorous justice which the harlot can expect from her Jewish keeper when he discovers that she has been unfaithful to him[74] and which, I would add, is further expressed in the formal structure of the print, with the Jew in the centre foreground and the two symbolic paintings placed symmetrically behind him.

The disadvantage of a brief survey, though, is that it inevitably oversimplifies. Thus, to return to the *Election*, Plate 2, the iconography of the centre is more complicated than I suggested earlier. As I have said, Charles's 'Royal Oak' is obscured by the banner, a displacement that is echoed in the sawing down of the 'Crown' signboard in the background. But if we look closely at the top right of the banner itself, we see that it depicts the Horse Guards building at Whitehall (completed 1753) and embodies another fall at the centre, this time directed at Hogarth's old enemy, William Kent, the building's architect. Hogarth shows the royal coach going under an arch which, to quote Paulson, being 'based on academic principle rather than utility', is so low that the coachman has been decapitated. Paulson goes on to cite[75] John Ireland's *Hogarth Illustrated* (1791) to the effect that 'the state coach could not pass through until the ground was lowered.'

One of Hogarth's aims was to create his own version of history-painting in the grand manner. In the Preface to *Joseph Andrews* Fielding had called him 'a Comic History-Painter', and stated that 'the Comic Writer and Painter correlate to each other'; so that we find in Hogarth's work, as in Fielding's, the adoption, adaptation, and allusive use of baroque forms not the least of which is the accented centre, though in the case of the *Election* plate just referred to, and not only there, it is tempting to describe the exploitation of multiple centres as having a mannerist feel to it.[76] With Fielding's analogy in mind, however, it is time to turn again to *Joseph Andrews*, to see how far, in their treatment of the centre, 'Writer and Painter' do in fact 'correlate to each other'.

As I have said, the 'steep Hill' of III. 2 gives the novel a firm central accent. Or does it? For closer inspection reveals that this isn't the centre at all: it only *appears* to be if the reader accepts on trust—as, of course, he is inclined to—that the mid-point of the narrative occurs at the beginning of the second volume, with two books read and two to go. In fact, the arithmetical centre (or as near as Fielding can get to an exact centre with an even chapter total) is II. 14 (thirty-second of sixty-four), Adams's visit to Trulliber which, significantly, again begins with a fall when Trulliber 'pushed *Adams* into the Pig-Stye' and one of the pigs 'gave such a sudden spring, that he threw poor *Adams* all along in the Mire'. This confrontation between the two clergymen is the climax of the novel's theme of charity, and its moral as well as physical centre. And, to help his readers grasp this, Fielding supplied a pointer in the preceding chapter (II. 13) by ending it with an inn bill, written out in full and including the 'Balance' when Adams's sixpence-half-penny has been deducted from the total of seven shillings. For from the sixteenth century on the inclusion of the word 'balance' at or near the mid-point had been regarded as a substantive clue to the symbolism of the centre.[77]

A similar decorum is present in the individual books. Book I (eighteen chapters) is divided into two by the balance at the end of chapter 9 ('the Balance of Opinion'; the simile is remarkably extended, occupying as it does a whole paragraph) and by Joseph's departure from Lady Booby's establishment in the next chapter; the central action of Book II—Adams's encounter with the coward (7 to 9)—takes place on 'the Summit of a Hill' (II. 7) and is complemented by the middle of Book III (chapter 7 out of a total of thirteen) where Adams is entertained by the 'roasting' squire: this episode concludes with the erection of a 'Throne' (Fielding's word: we recall the traditional association of the centre with sovereignty)[78]—in fact a blanket over a tub of water—on either side of which sit 'the King and Queen, namely, the Master of the House, and the Captain'. The climax comes when the parson 'was led up to his Place, and seated between their Majesties. They immediately rose up, when the Blanket wanting its Supports at either end, gave way, and soused *Adams* over Head and Ears in the Water.' Finally, in the centre of Book IV we have the near-drowning of Adams's son Dick (ch. 8), and the deflation of Adams's philosophy of submission to the demands of Providence which this entails.

With its double and subsidiary centres, then, particularly when they are viewed in the light of the numerical schemes already outlined, *Joseph Andrews* is distinctly mannerist. And yet, just as the symbolic centres in Hogarth's second *Election* print are all thematically related, so are the centres in *Joseph Andrews*: apart from that in Book I, they all involve Adams in some way, so that their ultimate effect is to unify rather than diversify: to make Adams structurally the novel's centre of interest (on other grounds, of course, readers have always felt him to be that anyway).[79] And if we bear this in mind as we think back on the novel's chiastic, A B B A, form, we see that for all its complexities it has a structure that is fundamentally baroque: Hogarth's fondness for the pyramid as a compositional framework (clear enough in the *Election*, Plate 2),[80] Fielding's use of the chiasmus with its central accent in *Joseph Andrews*, Defoe's tripartite *Robinson Crusoe* with its mid-point—all manifest that symmetry about the centre that is the *sine qua non* of baroque art.[81] The same is true of *Tom Jones*, which I discuss in the next chapter.

NOTES

1 Quotations are from the 'Wesleyan' *Joseph Andrews*, ed. M. C. Battestin (Oxford, 1967).

2 See my 'Abraham Adams and Parson Trulliber: The Meaning of *Joseph Andrews*, Book II, Chapter 14', *Modern Language Review* (*MLR*), 63 (1968), 794–801, and my Introd. to the OEN '*Joseph Andrews*' and '*Shamela*' (1970).

3 'A Discourse upon Epick Poetry', in *The Adventures of Telemachus*, tr. J. Ozell, 2 vols (1735), I, p. xxviii. Alastair Fowler, *Triumphal Forms*, p. 129 and n, cites examples from Pope, Addison, and Zachary Grey's edn of *Hudibras*.

4 On recessed symmetry (A B C C B A) in Homer, see Cedric H. Whitman, *Homer and the Heroic Tradition* (Cambridge, Mass., 1958), chaps 11 and 12. Virgil is discussed in Brooks Otis's *Virgil: A Study in Civilized Poetry* (Oxford, 1964), and structural analyses of *Paradise Lost* appear in Gunnar Qvarnström's *The Enchanted Palace: Some Structural Aspects of 'Paradise Lost'* (Stockholm, 1967), and Alastair Fowler's Introd. to *Paradise Lost* (*The Poems of John Milton*, ed. Carey and Fowler, pp. 440ff.). Qvarnström's *Poetry and Numbers* (Lund, 1966) analyses Edward Benlowes's *Theophila* (1652) in detail.

5 Cit. H. T. Swedenberg, *The Theory of the Epic in England 1650–1800* (Berkeley and Los Angeles, Calif., 1944), pp. 220–1. On p. 11 Swedenberg traces the idea back to the sixteenth-century theorist Geraldi Cinthio.

6 Cit. ibid., p. 145.

7 Cit. ibid., p. 239.

8 On numerology in Bach generally, see Karl and Irene Geiringer, *The Bach Family: Seven Generations of Creative Genius* (1954), p. 203; the same authors' *Johann Sebastian Bach: The Culmination of an Era* (1967), pp. 134–5; and Friedrich Blume, *Renaissance and Baroque Music: A Comprehensive Survey*, tr. M. D. Herter Norton (1968), p. 117. Wilfrid Mellers's article on numerology in music ('Tuning in to the Natural Law', *The Times Literary Supplement* (*TLS*), 1 October 1971, pp. 1179–80) has interesting things to say about Bach, while Paul H. Lang refers to temporal numbers in one of the New Year Cantatas in 'The Enlightenment and Music', *ECS*, 1 (1967–8), 96.

9 I follow John Shearman's definition in his excellent *Mannerism* (Harmondsworth, 1967), p. 21. Shearman stresses the importance of the notion of difficulty overcome, the appearance of effortless mastery over technical problems, which encouraged the proliferation of complexities for the challenge they provided.

10 See Emrys Jones, 'The Artistic Form of *Rasselas*', *RES*, n.s. 18 (1967), 387–401, where *Rasselas*'s forty-nine chapters are analysed as falling into three groups of 16 + 1.

11 Andrew Wright, *Henry Fielding: Mask and Feast* (1965), p. 60, states that in Book I 'of a total of eighteen chapters, nine (2–10) are devoted to Joseph in London, and nine (11–18) to Joseph on the road'. But Joseph does not arrive in London until ch. 4, and from chaps 12 to 18 he is at the Dragon Inn; so that Book I's main matter is contained in two static seven-chapter units. On the similarities between Books I and IV, see also Robert Alter, *Fielding and the Nature of the Novel* (Cambridge, Mass., 1968), pp. 134ff.

12 See, for example, Robert Donovan, *The Shaping Vision: Imagination in the English Novel from Defoe to Dickens* (Ithaca, N.Y., 1966), ch. 4; and my 'Richardson's *Pamela* and Fielding's *Joseph Andrews*', *EC*, 17 (1967), 158–68.

13 Maurice Johnson, *Fielding's Art of Fiction* (Philadelphia, Pa., 1961), p. 56.

14 Dick Taylor, Jr, 'Joseph as Hero in *Joseph Andrews*', *Tulane Studies in English*, 7 (1957), 91–109, has made out a case for Joseph's growth in the novel.

15 The similarity between the openings of the two books is also noticed by Alter, op. cit., pp. 134–5.

16 Thus dramatically illustrating the intimate relationship in the novel between charity and chastity and their obverse, on which see M. C. Battestin, *The Moral Basis of Fielding's Art* (Middletown, Conn., 1959), ch. 3.

17 Her function in this respect is brought out by the physical similarities between her and Joseph. The two are, in fact, identical: compare their descriptions in I. 8 and II. 12.

18 Not too much importance can be attached to the 'violent hands' phrase in itself, however, since it was a particular favourite of Fielding's: e.g., *Tom Jones*, IV. 12; VI. 2; IX. 7; XII. 1, 3, and 7.

19 An analogous pattern appears in what is generally agreed to be the earlier *Jonathan Wild* (though it was not published until 1743), where similar events occur in a similar position in all four books. Thus, in I. 9 Wild makes an attempt on Laetitia Snap's chastity and is repulsed; in II. 9 we are presented with his plans for seducing Mrs Heartfree; and in IV. 10 Mrs Heartfree is nearly raped by Count La Ruse. In I.10 Laetitia, having rejected Wild, yields to Tom Smirk the apprentice; in II. 10 Mrs Heartfree withstands, and is rescued from, Wild; in III. 10 there is a reference to Wild in the boat in which he was cast away at the end of II. 10, and also to Laetitia's infidelity with Fireblood; finally, in IV. 11 Wild catches '*Fireblood in the Arms of his lovely Laetitia*'. I follow the text of the first edn, as reprinted in the World's Classics (1932).

20 In IV. 7 Joseph rescues Fanny from one of Didapper's servants, and the fight recalls that of Adams in II. 9. Interestingly, although there is no identification of chapter-numbers at this point, the two fights occur in the same position in their respective volumes in the early editions of the novel: in the first edn the fight in II. 9 covers vol. I. 224–7, and that in IV. 7, vol. II. 225–7 (second edn, I. 224–6; II. 225–6).

21 'Comic Resolution in Fielding's *Joseph Andrews*', reprinted from *College English* in *Fielding. A Collection of Critical Essays*, Twentieth Century Views, ed. Ronald Paulson (Englewood Cliffs, N.J., 1962), pp. 59–68.

22 On Homer and the twenty-four letters of the alphabet see, e.g., 'An Essay on the Life, Writings, and Learning of Homer', in Pope's *Iliad* (1715), I. 38, and *Spectator* 632 (13 December 1714). For 24 as an alphabetical number in Biblical exegesis, see Fowler, *Triumphal Forms*, pp. 7–8.

23 The total number of books in the Old and New Testaments (Authorized Version) is sixty-six. Alastair Fowler drew my attention to the importance of Adams's questions. For the kind of answer he was expecting see the table from Ostervald's Bible reproduced in the Appendix.

24 *Timaeus*, 32 B–C, tr. R. G. Bury, Loeb edn (1929), pp. 59–61.

25 'Mysticism and Science in the Pythagorean Tradition', *Classical Quarterly*, 17 (1923), 4.

26 *Henry Fielding: Mask and Feast*, p. 68. The idea of marriage as concord and harmony is, of course, a commonplace. See, e.g., Sir John Davies, *Orchestra*, sts 110–11, and Jonson's masque *Hymenaei*: 'the *rite* was to ioyne the marryed payre with bandes of silke, in signe of future *concord*' (*Ben Jonson*, ed. Herford and Simpson, VII (Oxford, 1941), 210).

27 Cornford, 'Mysticism and Science', p. 4, n. 6.

28 A pattern that is also reminiscent of the contemporary da capo form in music: divided into two main parts, the first 'set out in the tonic and ended

emphatically on the dominant, the second departure began in the dominant with the same idea, reversed the modulation and ended in the tonic'; Manfred Bukofzer, *Music in the Baroque Era*, p. 361.

29 'The Interpolated Tales in *Joseph Andrews* Again', *Modern Philology* (*MP*), 65 (1968), 208–13.

30 See Homer Goldberg, 'The Interpolated Stories in *Joseph Andrews* or "The History of the World in General" Satirically Revised', *MP*, 63 (1966), 295–310, and also my 'Interpolated Tales'.

31 Tr. P. Motteux, Everyman edn, 2 vols (1943), I. 262.

32 Pietro Bongo, *Numerorum mysteria* (Bergamo, 1599), p. 195, where 4 as justice is also mentioned. For further documentation, see below, p. 119, n. 40.

33 This is made abundantly clear in that novel immediately after the wedding when Mr Williams tells Pamela: 'I will say, that to see so much innocence and virtue so eminently rewarded, is one of the greatest pleasures I have ever known'; Everyman edn, ed. M. Kinkead-Weekes, 2 vols (1962), I. 309–10.

34 Bongo, p. 415.

35 Bongo, p. 411. Did Fielding notice that Pamela is sixteen when she marries (e.g., I. 357, 369)? On p. 176 she states: 'I have lived about sixteen years in virtue and reputation.'

36 *Laws*, VI, 785 B; tr. R. G. Bury, Loeb edn (1926), I. 501.

37 I am indebted to Alastair Fowler for pointing this out to me.

38 John Dennis, *The Usefulness of the Stage* (1698), cit. Richard H. Tyre, 'Versions of Poetic Justice in the Early Eighteenth Century', *Studies in Philology* (*SP*), 54 (1957), 35.

39 Hence, understandably, modern criticism seeking a Providential pattern in the works of Fielding and other writers tends to concentrate solely on plot. See, for example, M. C. Battestin, '*Tom Jones*: The Argument of Design', in *The Augustan Milieu: Essays Presented to Louis A. Landa*, ed. H. K. Miller, E. Rothstein, G. S. Rousseau (Oxford, 1970), 289–319, and the two articles by Aubrey Williams cited above, p. 17, n. 30.

40 *A Discourse Concerning the Unchangeable Obligations of Natural Religion*, in *Works* (1738), II. 597–8, cit. Battestin, '*Tom Jones*: The Argument of Design', p. 317.

41 Bongo, p. 413, discusses 4, 16, and 64 together. He mentions the principle of equal division on p. 486.

42 In the well-known tradition of planetary squares. Bongo, p. 345, makes passing mention of the fact. For a more expansive treatment, see Cornelius Agrippa, *Three Books of Occult Philosophy*, II. 22 (p. 241). In this tradition 16, attributed to Jupiter, still retains associations similar to those already outlined above for that number: 'love, peace, and concord'; ibid., p. 240.

43 Agrippa's words, II. 43 (p. 302).

44 The Twins could be male, or male and female, and even bride and bridegroom: see Alastair Fowler, *Spenser and the Numbers of Time* (1964), p. 167, nn. 1 and 2.

45 The notion of reconciliation and concord at the end of the novel appears in a more subtle way still. For there is, in effect, a double marriage, since the wedding of Joseph and Fanny is an exact re-enactment of that between Richardson's heroine and Mr B., who are present at the *Joseph Andrews* wedding: see my 'Richardson's *Pamela* and Fielding's *Joseph Andrews*', p. 159. Fielding is in this way symbolically reconciling his novel with Richardson's.

46 Battestin makes the connection in *The Moral Basis of Fielding's Art*, p. 41.

47 Introd. to *'Joseph Andrews' and 'Shamela'* (1965), p. xxx; and see *The Moral Basis*, ch. 3. One may note, as an obvious allusive instance of Fielding's attention to numerical detail, that Joseph is seventeen when he becomes Lady Booby's footboy (I. 2), the age of the Biblical Joseph when he was sold to Potiphar (Genesis 37:2 and 36).

48 *Milton's Brief Epic: The Genre, Meaning, and Art of 'Paradise Regained'* (Providence, R.I., 1966), p. 11. On pp. 32ff. will be found references to seventeenth-century Biblical epics which used Job as a structural model.

49 Ibid., p. 67. Four-book epics are mentioned on, e.g., pp. 43, 82, 85, 89, 91, and 102.

50 This follows two other references to patience under affliction, in III. 11 and earlier in IV. 8.

51 It is difficult to determine priorities in a case like this. But it seems obvious— from *The Faerie Queene* and *Paradise Lost*, for instance—that adherence to a canonical number by no means hindered far more elaborate number symbolisms. It was merely fortunate for Fielding that 4 was so rich in meanings.

52 See Lewalski, p. 36, for Richard Blackmore's comments on, and defence of, the heroic nature of Job's passivity, in contrast to the 'very active' heroes of Homer and Virgil. The Introd. to the second edn of *Pamela* (February 1741) referred to 'the poor passive PAMELA' (*Samuel Richardson's Introduction to 'Pamela'*, ed. Sheridan W. Baker, Jr, Augustan Reprint Society Pub. No. 48 (Los Angeles, Calif., 1954), p. xxvi).

53 Their versions of the club of Hercules. See my Introd. to the OEN *'Joseph Andrews' and 'Shamela'*, pp. xii–xiii.

54 E.g., Everyman edn, I. 24, 43, 47, 72, 89 (angel and devil); I. 15, 51, 58 (temptation).

55 Introd. to *Pamela*, I, p. ix. In fact, Pamela's 'worst trial' (I. 174), when the disguised B. climbs into bed with her, occurs on Sunday, the thirty-eighth day of her imprisonment, though it is true that she recounts it on Tuesday, the fortieth, which is also the day of her interview with B. when the movement towards reconciliation begins. For an interesting expansion and explanation of religious patterns in *Pamela*, see M. D. Bell, 'Pamela's Wedding and the Marriage of the Lamb', *PQ*, 49 (1970), 100–12.

56 As Lewalski points out (e.g., p. 86), typological symbolism was a feature of Biblical epic, though it was also, as we have seen, fundamental to the Puritan world-view (Hunter, *The Reluctant Pilgrim*, pp. 99ff.). The Biblical allusion in *Pamela*, I. 217, incidentally, reinforces the suggestion of the number 40. It is to Numbers 11: 5 and is related contextually to the Israelites' forty-year sojourn in the wilderness.

57 Pamela also mentions the lion and bear (among other animals) on p. 146; but it is unlikely that she has this passage in mind.

58 Lewalski, p. 279 (and p. 230 on the analogy with Hercules's victory over Antaeus). Goliath oppressed the Israelites for forty days (I Samuel 17:16). Are B.'s articles—which offer Pamela clothes, money, servants, etc.—a parallel to Satan's offering Christ 'all the kingdoms of the world' (Luke 4:5, Matthew 4:8)?

59 For references, see above, p. 86, n. 4.

60 This is the only sixty-four-line speech in the poem. Gunnar Qvarnström, *The Enchanted Palace*, pp. 114 and 157, has already noted another case of this type of numerology in *Paradise Regained*, involving the number 33.

61 F. Homes Dudden, *Henry Fielding: His Life, Works, and Times*, 2 vols (Oxford, 1952), I. 344–50. As Dudden remarks, 'the time-scheme has been carefully worked out.' I have pointed out above how used the eighteenth-century reader should have been to counting days in epic works.

62 Joseph's journey begins in I. 11 after his dismissal by Lady Booby (he has 'just set out on his Travels'), and he and Adams return home at the very beginning of IV. 1. To the chapter-totals for Books II and III (seventeen and thirteen respectively), therefore, must be added the final eight chapters of Book I (I include the two prolegomenous chapters, II. 1 and III. 1 in my count). The allusion may well be to the precise period of Pamela's trials; though as I have already indicated, Richardson seems to have had 40 in mind as the significant figure.

63 Pp. 499–500, and Appendix, pp. 48–9, citing among other texts John 5:5, 1 Kings 16:29, and II Kings 15:8.

64 Does Fielding intend the individual totals for Books II and III to be meaningful? 17 is evil and unfortunate in Pythagorean, Roman, and Jewish thought (Bongo, pp. 416–17, 420), and 13 signifies transgression of divine law, and impiety and irreverence (pp. 400–1). It might also be worth noting that 18, the total for Book I, was regarded by divines as 'unhappy' (Agrippa, *Three Books*, II. 15 (p. 222)) because 'the children of Israel served Eglon the king of Moab eighteen years' (Judges 3:14).

65 Hunter, *The Reluctant Pilgrim*, p. 204.

66 Bongo, p. 383 (classified in the index as *luctui sacer*; Lewis and Short define *luctus* as '*sorrow, mourning, grief, affliction, distress, lamentation*, esp. over the loss of something dear to one'). The symbolism appears to have been fairly common and accounts for the eleven stanzas of Milton's 'On the Death of a Fair Infant' and of *Lycidas*. Note, in addition, that the journey in *Joseph Andrews* takes eleven days: if read symbolically it accords well with the interpretations I have offered of the other journey numbers, 38, 17 and 13. It is interesting that Deuteronomy 1:2 (the chapter immediately preceding that containing the reference to 38) reads: 'There are eleven days' journey from Horeb by the way of mount Seir unto Kadesh-barnea.' Similarly, if we pursue the chronological clues provided in the Contents pages and the heading to each book of *Tom Jones*, we discover that the action of the novel from the time of Tom's expulsion by Allworthy when '*The World*, as *Milton* phrases it, [lies] *all before him*' at the beginning of Book VII to his marriage with Sophia in Book XVIII is forty-two days, the number of the 'pilgrimage of this life' (Bongo, p. 513).

67 Agrippa, II. 13 (p. 216).

68 The central line describes 'Cromwell falling' as a result of his coach accident of 29 September 1654. For a full discussion, see Fowler, *Triumphal Forms*, pp. 81–4.

69 Ronald Paulson, *Hogarth's Graphic Works*, 2 vols (New Haven, Conn., and London, 1965), I. 229.

70 Ibid., I. 231.

71 Pp. 31–2.

90

72 See *Graphic Works*, I. 235, and Paulson's *Hogarth: His Life, Art, and Times*, 2 vols (New Haven and London, 1971), II. 201. (Hereafter cited as *Hogarth*.) Hogarth refers to 'Alexander's battles painted by Le Brun' in *The Analysis of Beauty* (1753); ed. Joseph Burke (Oxford, 1955), p. 11. As M. C. Battestin notes, Fielding invokes one of Le Brun's Alexander paintings in *Tom Jones*, V. 12: 'Fielding's Definition of Wisdom: Some Functions of Ambiguity and Emblem in *Tom Jones*', *ELH*, 35 (1968), 212.

73 Analysed in detail by Paulson, *Hogarth*, I. 486–8.

74 *Graphic Works*, I. 145.

75 Ibid., I. 232.

76 On Hogarth and history-painting, see Paulson, *Hogarth*, I. 259ff. and 470–1. In calling this complication of the centre 'mannerist', I follow Fowler, *Triumphal Forms*, pp. 99ff.

77 *Triumphal Forms*, p. 71, n. 1.

78 See above, Introd., p. 13, and *Triumphal Forms*, ch. 4.

79 Adams's falls can be interpreted in two ways: they express the rejection of his Christian values by a hostile world and, simultaneously, symbolize Adams's limitations, reminding us that to some extent he rides through life on inadequate theories and assumptions from which he has, literally, to be toppled. The best discussion of these limitations (Adams's belief in appearances, for example, which he 'elevates . . . , in the form of physiognomics, into an elaborate and total philosophic system') is by Leo Braudy, *Narrative Form in History and Fiction: Hume, Fielding, and Gibbon* (Princeton, N.J., 1970), pp. 103ff.

80 Hogarth praises the pyramid as a 'beautiful form' in *The Analysis*, ed. cit., p. 35 (cf. p. 39), and Paulson discusses Hogarth's use of pyramidal forms in *Hogarth*, I. 218, 224, 332, and 397.

81 On the centre in baroque architecture see, e.g., Emil Kaufmann, *Architecture in the Age of Reason* (New York, 1968), pp. 4, 11–12, and 14. Karl and Irene Geiringer analyse Bach's use of chiastic schemes and the accented centre in *Johann Sebastian Bach: The Culmination of an Era*, pp. 148, 176, 180–2, 196, 209–20, 227–8, 241, 243, and 336–9. See also Friedrich Blume, *Renaissance and Baroque Music*, pp. 136–7.

v   Fielding: *Tom Jones* and *Amelia*

Wilbur L. Cross, Fielding's biographer, detected the ideas of Shaftesbury in *Tom Jones*, seeing Fielding as playing here with notions put forward in the *Inquiry concerning Virtue*:[1]

> This essay, like others in the 'Characteristicks,' had profoundly influenced Fielding; in a sober mood he would have accepted as completely as did Square the moral doctrines of 'the great Lord Shaftesbury.' He never burlesques or parodies Shaftesbury, never quite uses his phrases; he rather puts to a sort of humorous test his lordship's ethical system by bringing it into conjunction with real life. From the moment we first see Tom, he has all of Shaftesbury's 'social virtues'. . . .

If Cross was right, and there is little doubt that he was, then we might suspect that the neo-Platonic philosophy of the Third Earl—his view that virtue was harmony, that the poet was an architect with an eye for 'interior numbers' whose works should exemplify 'that exterior proportion and symmetry of composition which constitutes a legitimate piece',[2] is evident in something more than the character of Fielding's hero. We might suspect, indeed, that Shaftesbury's many references in the *Characteristics* to number, harmony, and proportion played their part, too, in dictating the elaborate symmetries of *Tom Jones* and also of *Joseph Andrews*.[3] The question of background and influence in such matters is, of course, large and complex. All one can hope to do is merely to suggest its extent: the average eighteenth-century man was far more aware of numerological modes of thought than we are even yet prepared to concede.

92

I

Some of the points I want to make about the novel have already been anticipated in the perceptive work of Frederick W. Hilles and Robert Alter.[4] Nevertheless, if a convincing case is to be made for the full complexity of its structure it will be necessary to repeat, or at least allude to, their findings here.

In my discussion of *Joseph Andrews* I indicated that certain symmetries were apparent only if one read the novel in its original two-volume format.[5] The inference seems to be that volume divisions themselves could contribute in a significant way to the structural harmonies of an eighteenth-century novel, and this is borne out by several of Smollett's works, by Richardson's *Clarissa*, and at least one of Fanny Burney's novels.[6] It is also borne out by *Tom Jones*, which was originally published in six volumes, three books per volume. The scheme was maintained for the second edition but abandoned for the revised third edition, which appeared in four volumes. The six-volume format was somewhat extravagant for a novel which was, after all, nowhere near as long as *Clarissa*,[7] and I would suggest that one reason at least for this generous disposition of the novel's eighteen books was to assist its first readers by emphasizing the work's fundamental structural pattern. It is, Fielding implies, to be understood (initially) in terms of six groups of three books. Moreover, the reader is expected to notice that the chapter-totals yield the following information, which I reproduce in tabular form overleaf.

It will be seen that the first and last volumes answer each other exactly, the 13–9–10 pattern of the opening (vol. I) being reversed as the novel draws to its close (vol. VI), thus indicating that a large-scale chiasmus will, in all likelihood, be operating, as indeed it does in *Joseph Andrews*.

Another feature to emerge is the pairing of volumes II and V, since through their chapter-totals they share a similar formal scheme (ABA) even though the totals involved are different: 14–12–14; 12–10–12. The implication must be that there will be a thematic relationship between the framing books in each triad (those having the same number of chapters), and also between these two similarly organized triads as a whole: that is, we would expect volume V to echo volume II.

Finally, the table hints at a bipartite arrangement which will complement, yet run counter to, the novel's chiastic scheme; for the chapter-totals for Books X to XIII correspond exactly and in sequence to those for Books II to V: 9, 10, 14, 12. It is now necessary to see how far these putative schemes are substantiated by the narrative.

Volume	Book	Chapter-total	
I	I	13	
	II	9	
	III	10	
II	IV		14
	V		12
	VI		14
III	VII		15
	VIII		15
	IX		7
IV	X		9
	XI		10
	XII		14
V	XIII		12
	XIV		10
	XV		12
VI	XVI	10	
	XVII	9	
	XVIII	13	

Books I and XVIII both possess thirteen chapters: the one initiates the mystery of Tom's birth, the other resolves it. The affinities are, however, far more exact than this. For example: in XVIII. 3, when Nightingale and Mrs Miller are talking to Allworthy about Tom, Allworthy comments:[8] 'I still remember the innocent, the helpless Situation in which I found him. I feel the tender Pressure of his little Hands at this Moment.' If we check back, we discover that this echoes the third chapter of Book I, in which Mr Allworthy 'had now got one of his Fingers into the Infant's Hand. . . .' In XVIII. 6 Jenny Waters is seen by Allworthy for the first time since Book I (though she has been reintroduced to Tom in XVII. 9), and in chapter 7 she reveals Tom's parentage, prefacing her account with the words: 'You may be pleased to remember, Sir, I formerly told you, you should one Day know.' Again, we must actually refer to Book I if the precision of the symmetry is to be fully apparent. Jenny had, in fact, first appeared in the novel in I. 6, when she was brought before Allworthy under suspicion of being Tom's mother; and in I. 7 she has admitted the charge while refusing 'to declare the Father of [her] Infant.' She continues: 'I promise you faithfully, you shall one Day know.'

The correspondences between Books II and XVII are less marked, and it may well be that here Fielding was relying in part on the identical chapter-totals themselves to imply a relationship which, however formally desirable, the demands of the narrative prevented him from fulfilling as completely as he would have liked. Even so, certain parallels emerge: in XVII. 2, Blifil does his best to make Tom fall lower in Allworthy's estimation by telling him about the duel with Fitzpatrick. He is thus the true son of Captain Blifil, who, in II. 2, does his best to prevent Allworthy adopting Tom because, as Fielding tells us, he is jealous of Allworthy's fondness for the child. Next, Partridge's fight with his wife over Jenny (II. 4) seems, in retrospect, to be a comic, anticipatory, parody of Tom's duel with Fitzpatrick (XVI. 10): found guilty of 'incontinency', Partridge is forced—like Jenny—to leave the neighbourhood (II. 6); as a consequence of the duel Tom languishes in prison throughout Book XVII. Tom is accused (wrongly) of having struck the first blow, and Blifil bribes witnesses to confirm the accusation. It is thought at one point that Fitzpatrick is dead, but in XVII. 5 Partridge brings news that he 'was still alive', and Tom comments that 'he should always lament the having shed the Blood of one of his fellow Creatures, as one of the highest Misfortunes which could have befallen him.' Compare Mrs Partridge's false accusation of Partridge in II. 4, 'which the Reader will, I believe, bear Witness for him, had greatly exceeded the Truth; for indeed he had not struck her once . . . but when his Wife appealed to the Blood on her Face, as an Evidence of his Barbarity, he could not help laying claim to his own Blood, for so it really was; as he thought it very unnatural, that this should rise up (as we are taught that of a murdered Person often doth) in Vengeance against him.' The heading to II. 6 tells us that Partridge is to stand trial '*for Incontinency*': he has confessed his guilt, even though he is innocent, because his wife has 'vowed, that as she was sure of his Guilt, she would never leave tormenting him till he had owned it.' The corresponding event at the other end of the novel occurs in XVII. 6; it is, surely, Tom's confession to Sophia by letter of his guilt and unworthiness over the proposal of marriage to Lady Bellaston. One supposed infidelity balances another, and Tom's confession is in a sense as unjustified as Partridge's; for, as the reader knows and as Sophia is to discover, the proposal was a stratagem of Nightingale's to remove Tom from Lady Bellaston's clutches.[9]

As far as Books III and XVI are concerned, the reintroduction of Blifil (Book XVI), which continues his attempts on Sophia and hence also his enmity to Tom, answers his introduction in Book III and the initiation of the enmity between the two in that same book. Similarly, III. 2 introduces us to Black George, who is reintroduced in person in XVI. 3. But the novel's bipartite structure dictates that Book XVI should have a more significant relationship with Book VII, and I want now to turn to the two complementary triads, Books IV, V, and VI and XIII, XIV, and XV.

I have already mentioned the clearly-defined ABA structure. And what is stated numerically is confirmed by symmetries within the narrative itself. There is, for example, a close similarity between Books IV and VI in that the former establishes Tom's commitment to Moll Seagrim and the latter the unwelcome courtship of Sophia by Blifil: both are paired off with false lovers just as, in the corresponding books in the second half of the novel, Tom associates with Lady Bellaston (XIII) and Sophia has the attentions of Lord Fellamar forced upon her (XV). These are, however, only general parallels which can be supported in more detail.

The opening chapters of Book IV affirm Sophia's affection for Tom and hatred of Blifil (in IV. 5 she declares: 'I hate the Name of Master *Blifil*'), while the opening chapters of Book VI, as I have said, establish Sophia's courtship by Blifil and confirm her love for Tom (VI. 5 mentions the 'strong . . . Disinclination' she has to Blifil). In IV. 8 there is the battle in the churchyard in which Tom comes to the rescue of the bloody Moll; in VI. 8 Tom discovers Sophia 'just risen from the Ground where her Father had left her, with the Tears trickling from her Eyes, and the Blood running from her Lips'. IV. 9 ('*Containing Matters of no very peaceable Colour*': in it Mrs Seagrim rails at her daughter for being pregnant but is 'mollified' when she sees the gold Tom has given the girl) is echoed in VI. 9: '*tempestuous*', according to the chapter heading, it contains a confrontation between Western and Jones over Sophia, Western's objection to Tom being his lack of fortune. There are, too, echoic relationships between IV. 10 and VI. 10 (in the one Supple tells Sophia about the battle in the churchyard and Moll's pregnancy; in the other Blifil reveals to Allworthy the love-making between Tom and Moll and also the battle between Tom, Thwackum, and Blifil, which began in V. 10), and between IV. 11 and VI. 11 (in the former, Tom's appeal to Allworthy prevents Moll being sent away to Bridewell, and the chapter ends by remarking that Allworthy's mind had received its 'first bad Impression concerning *Jones*'; in the latter, Tom is dismissed by him). Finally, there is a simple and obvious parallel between the last chapter of each of the two books. The heading to IV. 14 reads, in part, '*a long Dialogue between* Sophia *and her Maid*'; that to VI. 14 reads: '*A short Chapter, containing a short Dialogue between Squire* Western *and his Sister*'.[10]

As we would expect, the pattern observed above is echoed in Books XIII to XV. In Book XIII Tom's affair with Lady Bellaston begins; in Book XV it is broken off. And other correspondences include the eighth chapter of both books (Mrs Miller's account of her cousin's 'Love-Match' with the impoverished Anderson in XIII. 8; the marriage of Nightingale and Nancy in XV. 8) and the ninth, XIII. 9 containing letters from Lady Bellaston, XV. 9 also containing letters from her. In addition, Nightingale's reference to 'the Queen of the Fairies' in this same chapter (XV. 9) takes us back to Tom's invitation to the masquerade received in Book XIII (ch. 6).[11]

But as well as possessing these internal symmetries the two triads answer each other substantively. Thus, Tom is expelled at the end of Book VI and is forced to leave Sophia: in Book XIII he arrives in London and there meets Sophia for the first time since Book VI, at which reunion he hands her the lost pocket-book (XIII. 11): Tom, it will be recalled, had lost his own pocket-book in VI. 12. Furthermore, in XIII. 6 Tom quotes Allworthy's exact words when he expelled him: 'I am resolved from this Day forward, on no Account, to converse with you any more' (compare VI. 11). When Mrs Honour visits Jones in XIV. 2, Lady Bellaston, who is already with him, conceals herself behind the bed: the link with V. 5, when Square had hidden himself 'behind the Arras' in Moll's room, is sufficiently obvious, as is that between XIV. 3, where Tom feigns sickness to avoid paying a visit to Lady Bellaston because he is attempting to re-establish his relationship with Sophia, and V. 2, where he is genuinely sick with a broken arm after saving Sophia when she has been thrown by her horse. Finally, Nancy Miller's pregnancy is revealed in XIV. 6, and it is in V. 6 that the identity of the father of Moll's child is discovered.

This discussion of the affinities between the contents of vols II and V has of necessity touched on the parallels between Books IV and XV, which need not, therefore, be considered separately.[12] We are now in a position to confirm that the first and last sections of the novel, divided into two sets of three books each, answer each other in recessed-symmetrical (or chiastic) fashion.

II

F. W. Hilles's diagram of the middle section of *Tom Jones* (Books VII to XII)[13] cannot, it seems to me, be bettered. In it, Hilles indicates the centrality of the Upton episode (Books IX and X) and shows how—continuing the chiastic scheme I have outlined above—Book XI (in which Mrs Fitzpatrick tells her story) corresponds to Book VIII (the Man of the Hill's narrative), and Book XII (Tom's pursuit of Sophia) answers Book VII (Sophia's escape from confinement and journey in search of Tom). I have no wish to modify this analysis in any way, but merely to expand on it.

It is important to note, for instance, that throughout this section Fielding is thinking in terms of three sets of two books rather than two sets of three, a symmetry which the original volume divisions somewhat obscured. The principle of pairing is established firmly, however, by the identical chapter-totals of Books VII and VIII: both possess fifteen chapters, and the numerical relationship again hints at a substantive relationship.[14] In somewhat similar fashion, the same period of time is allotted by Fielding to Books IX and X (twelve hours each) and to Books XI and XII (the heading to Book XII reads: '*Containing the same individual Time with the former*').

The thematic and narrative importance of the Upton episode is apparent enough. For the moment I should like merely to draw attention to the way in which Fielding announces his chiastic intentions both before and after it by having Tom arrive at Upton in the third chapter of Book IX, and having him leave it in X. 7, the third chapter from the end of Book X. The heading to the next chapter (X. 8) reads: '*In which the History goes backward*', and what Fielding does here is to recapitulate the events leading to the arrivals of Sophia and her father at Upton. But it should also be understood as a self-referring directive: having passed its mid-point the novel as a whole is now going to move 'backward'.[15] This is the penultimate chapter of Book X. It corresponds, therefore, to the second chapter of Book IX (in fact, the central chapter of the whole novel, 104th out of a total of 208), in which we see Tom standing on the top of Mazard Hill[16] indulging in what can (on one level) again be interpreted as actions aimed at making explicit the structural movement of the novel. For while on the hill Tom first looks 'towards the South', that is, back over the novel so far, as he makes quite clear: 'I was endeavouring to trace out my own Journey hither.' Then he turns in the almost diametrically opposite direction, looking forward over what is to come, as it were ('They now walked to that Part of the Hill which looks to the North-West'), and immediately hears the screams of Jenny Waters—whom we first met in Book I, and who, in the final book, will reveal Tom's parentage. Significantly, Fielding begins this chapter with a hint as to the mystery (a structural one, I suggest) that it contains:

> *Aurora* now first opened her Casement, *Anglicè*, the Day began to break, when *Jones* walked forth in Company with the Stranger, and mounted *Mazard* Hill; of which they had no sooner gained the Summit, than one of the most noble Prospects in the World presented itself to their View, and which we would likewise present to the Reader; but for two Reasons. *First*, We despair of making those who have seen this Prospect, admire our Description. *Secondly*, We very much doubt whether those, who have not seen it, would understand it.

It should also be noted how carefully, having established the symmetrical framework to the Upton episode, Fielding has bound Books IX and X together by fairly obtrusive cross-references: Jenny Waters's cries of 'Murder! Robbery! and more frequently Rape!' when Fitzpatrick bursts into her room (X. 2) hark back to IX. 2, in which Tom rescues her from Northerton after hearing her 'violent Screams'; Sophia's arrival with Honour in X. 3 parallels the arrival of 'a young Lady and her Maid' (Harriet Fitzpatrick) in IX. 3; the events in X. 4 take place round the kitchen fire, and IX. 4 ends with everyone 'rang[ing] themselves round the Kitchen Fire'; Jenny starts to ogle Tom in IX. 5, with inevitable results, and in X. 5 Honour tells Sophia that Tom is 'in Bed with a Wench'.

The chiastic correspondences between the remaining books— VIII and XI, VII and XII—cut across the pattern of pairing mentioned above: in Book XI Sophia meets up with her cousin, Harriet Fitzpatrick, just as, in Book VIII, Tom meets up with his travelling companion, Partridge. And, as has been noted, Mrs Fitzpatrick's story (which is relevant to Sophia's situation in the novel: she has married imprudently and is fleeing her husband; Sophia refuses to marry imprudently and is fleeing her father in consequence) complements the Man of the

Hill's autobiography, which is applicable in some ways to Tom himself.[17] Moreover, there are specific links between the two stories: when Tom and Partridge arrive at the Old Man's cottage, his housekeeper, whom Partridge takes for a witch, opens the door. Fielding comments: 'nor can the Reader conceive a Figure more adapted to inspire this Idea. . . . She answered exactly to that Picture drawn by *Otway* in his Orphan' (VIII. 10). And when Harriet has been taken to Fitzpatrick's Irish estate, she tells us that 'An old Woman, who seemed coeval with the Building, and greatly resembled her whom *Chamont* mentions in the *Orphan*, received us at the Gate' (XI. 5). In addition, just as the Old Man's narrative is interrupted by Partridge with his ghost story (VIII. 11), so is Mrs Fitzpatrick's narrative interrupted, this time by the Jacobite landlord who mistakes Sophia for Jenny Cameron and tells her that the Pretender 'hath given the Duke the Slip; and is marching as fast as he can to *London*, and ten thousand *French* are landed to join him on the Road' (XI. 6).

The structural device of the interruption—the one to deflate the Old Man's narrative, the other to recall in the middle of Mrs Fitzpatrick's melodramatic tale a more fundamental, political, reality—itself invites the reader to relate the two stories.[18] But the landlord's error fulfils another function by reminding us that, in VIII. 9, Partridge has made a similar error about Tom in thinking that he is a staunch Jacobite, thereby reaffirming the parallel between the historical events narrated by the Old Man and those of 1745—a parallel that Tom himself makes explicit in VIII. 14.

At the beginning of Book XII (ch. 3) we once more follow Tom as he sets off from Upton. Not sure which road to take, he decides to abandon the pursuit of Sophia and join the army. Just before this, Partridge has begged him to return home and not 'travel thus about the Country like a Vagabond'. The link with Book VII is unmistakable; for it is here that Tom first decided to join the army, and here, too, he (or rather his guide) lost his way (ch. 10).[19] We recall as well that at the beginning of the book (ch. 2) Tom indulged in similar histrionics to those in XII. 3, crying out—again over his separation from Sophia— 'Shall I lurk about this Country like a Thief. . . ?'; and that in XII. 6 there is a reference to 'the Inn where the Accident of the broken Head had happened' (i.e., Northerton's throwing of the bottle at Tom in VII. 12). But perhaps the most noticeable link between the books is provided by the subsidiary interpolated actions they contain, namely, Tom's encounter, in VII. 10, with the Quaker who buttonholes him with a retrospective tale (the Quaker's attitude to his daughter's marriage echoes that of Western's to Sophia too closely for Tom's comfort), and the puppet show of 'the fine and serious Part of the *Provoked Husband*' in XII. 5. As the chambermaid (who has just been caught 'in Company with the *Merry Andrew*, and in a Situation not very proper to be described') indignantly points out, 'What was the fine Lady in the Puppet-show just now [but a whore]? I suppose she did not lie all Night out from her Husband for nothing' (XII. 6). The show is thus prospective, preparing us as it does for the sexual corruption of Lady Bellaston in the next book;[20] so that the four interpolations are themselves arranged in chiastic fashion:

VII	VIII	XI	XII
Quaker	Man of Hill	Mrs Fitzpatrick	Puppet show
(retrospective)			(prospective)

III

I said at the beginning of this chapter that there appear to be two main structural schemes operating in *Tom Jones*—a large-scale chiasmus, in which each of the books in the first half of the novel is answered in reverse order by the books of the second half (ABCDDCBA), and also a bipartite scheme, in which the second half is a direct echo of the first (ABCD; ABCD). This kind of complexity again seems characteristically mannerist; but it is significant, I think, that the bipartite scheme is not carried through with the thoroughness which distinguishes the chiasmus: virtuosity (and the author's interest in formal patterning) has its limits, especially in a period when such things are becoming less and less admired.

Our first and most important lead to the bipartite arrangement is given, as we have seen, by the chapter-totals: those for Books X to XIII echo the totals for Books II to V (9, 10, 14, and 12 respectively). Why Book X fails to correspond to Book I (as we would expect it to) will become clear, I hope, later on. For the moment I want to try to determine how far the numerical parallels just outlined are substantiated in narrative terms. The brief answer is that they aren't; or at least, that the parallels available for even the most scrupulously attentive reader are few and unremarkable. When, for example, Sophia is missed in X. 8, Squire Western gives 'Orders for the Bell to be rung in the Garden', presumably recalling the ringing of 'the Bell . . .

without the Doors' in II. 9 for Captain Blifil, who has died while out for a walk. The captain's death releases Bridget from a man whom she loathes; Sophia's escape is from Blifil's hated son. Book XI introduces Mrs Fitzpatrick, who was brought up with Sophia as a child: their contrasting dispositions earned them the nicknames 'Miss *Graveairs*, and Miss *Giddy*' (XI. 4), and the antithetical pair of girls seems to look back to the antithetical pair of boys, Tom and Blifil, introduced in Book III.

Here the narrative pointers cease: Book XII should correspond to Book IV, since both have fourteen chapters, but I detect no parallels. And when the pairing of halves is resumed, as it is in Book XIII, the system of correspondence that I have been tracing so far is abandoned, to be replaced by one that is at once simple and more direct. That is to say, whereas Book XIII should have answered Book V, XIV should have answered VI, etc., what now happens is that XIII answers IV, XIV answers V, in a straightforward sequential scheme which pairs the fourth book of the second half with the fourth book of the first, the fifth with the fifth, and so on until the end, as Robert Alter has noticed.[21] In Book XIII the introduction of Lady Bellaston and reintroduction of Sophia look back to the introduction of Sophia and Moll in Book IV; Tom's liaison with Lady Bellaston is confirmed in Book XIV, as is his love for Sophia and sense of obligation to Moll in Book V; Fellamar's unwelcome attentions to Sophia in XV correspond to those of Blifil in Book VI; Sophia is confined by her father in Books XV and XVI as she is in the sixth and seventh books of the first part, until released by Aunt Western in both instances. Finally, Books VII and XVI both end in fights (Tom and Northerton, Tom and Fitzpatrick), and XVIII. 2 contains an explicit directive to the reader to turn back to Book IX for certain information: 'If the Reader will please to refresh his Memory, by turning to the Scene at *Upton* in the Ninth Book, he will be apt to admire the many strange Accidents which unfortunately prevented any Interview between *Partridge* and Mrs. *Waters*, when she spent a whole Day there with Mr. *Jones*.' As Alter says, at this point the 'mechanism of the plot and the significant symmetries of structure' become one.[22]

IV

Among other things, the foregoing analysis has demonstrated the close affinity between the opening and closing triads of books, namely,

Books I to III and XVI to XVIII. As I have shown, clear narrative links, particularly between Books I and XVIII, reinforce the obvious and unique numerical echo in the chapter-totals (13, 9, 10; 10, 9, 13). Moreover, the novel's chiastic structure inevitably throws emphasis onto the central block of two books, Books IX and X, which I have again shown to be a closely integrated unit. This accenting of beginning, middle, and end has, it seems to me, ineluctable numerical implications: the observant and responsible reader is to be concerned, as in *Joseph Andrews*, with overall chapter-totals; and elementary addition reveals the following symmetry:

I	II	III		IX	X		XVI	XVII	XVIII
13	9	10		7	9		10	9	13
	32			16			32		

Significantly, Fielding utilizes the same number—16—that had also provided the key to the earlier novel:[23] just as *Joseph Andrews* demonstrated the ultimate triumph of virtue and justice, so does the structure of *Tom Jones* affirm (to quote Ralph Cudworth[24] on the analogy between the plot of 'a dramatick poem' and God's creation) 'that a thread of exact justice did run through all, and that rewards and punishments are measured out in geometrical proportion'. Once more we are confronted with the formal realization of a mathematically conceived poetic justice.

As for the virtue to which Tom aspires throughout the novel, it is expressed in the person of Sophia (Wisdom): Battestin has remarked[25] how his pursuit of her 'after the crisis at Upton will symbolize his gradual and painful attainment of *prudentia*, of self-knowledge and clarity of moral vision'. Battestin is absolutely right in singling out the thematic importance of Upton here; for it is this episode that embodies the novel's central moral dilemma, as we shall see.

Tom Jones has a clearly defined mid-point: in IX. 2, the 104th chapter out of 208, Tom is elevated on Mazard Hill, looking back then forward.[26] When he hears the screams of Jenny Waters he symbolically rejects the Old Man (apparent wisdom)[27] by 'slid[ing] down the Hill' to rescue her. (The abrupt descent is in itself sufficient confirmation of Tom's continuing rashness or imprudence.) But the central accent is far more developed in *Tom Jones* than in *Joseph Andrews*. The even chapter-total ideally demands two chapters with a central emphasis, the 104th and 105th. Such a detail had not bothered Fielding before. But he carefully observes the decorum now in his more profound and morally searching second novel; for IX. 3 contains an elaborate balance-image which must be regarded, in context, as an explicit numerological pointer.[28] It appears towards the end of 'the Battle of *Upton*', which is raging between two sides of equal strength:

> Now the Dogs of War being let loose, began to lick their bloody Lips; now Victory with Golden Wings hung hovering in the Air. Now Fortune taking her Scales from her Shelf, began to weigh the Fates of *Tom Jones*, his female Companion, and *Partridge*, against the Landlord, his Wife, and Maid; all which hung in exact Ballance before her. . . .

The balance is more than a mere structural directive, however. Implications of moral equilibrium[29] emerge a short time later in the complementary amorous battle between Tom and Jenny (IX. 5): 'To confess the Truth, I am afraid Mr. *Jones* maintained a Kind of *Dutch* Defence, and treacherously delivered up the Garrison, without duly weighing his Allegiance to the fair *Sophia*'; and since Tom's 'masculine Person and Mein' [*sic*] have been compared to those of Hercules earlier in the chapter, it is perhaps not fanciful to see in Tom's dilemma a re-enactment of that paradigm especially dear to the eighteenth century, the 'Choice of Hercules' or 'Hercules at the Crossroads', in which the young Hercules was faced with the choice between Pleasure and Virtue, symbolized in the figures of two women.[30]

The 'just' division of the novel into two equal halves by Mazard Hill and the balance-image itself mimes that virtue—Prudence— which Tom is striving to acquire. To be prudent, according to the traditional classical and Christian definition of the virtue, is to exercise memory, intelligence (or judgment) and foresight in a threefold act devoted to weighing the consequences of all activities and events: this is why Tom looks back then forward (south then north) on the top of Mazard Hill;[31] and this is why the balance is concretized for us in the following, equally central, chapter. For, as the tripartite division of the prudential act (and of the novel itself?) in part implies, we are also concerned here with the traditional concept of virtue as balance, as a mean between extremes. Indeed, Battestin draws attention to John Denham's poem 'Of Prudence',[32] in which imprudence (adherence to the will and its 'low Pleasures') is castigated and Prudence herself explicitly associated with 'the Golden Mean'.

All this is mimed in addition in the chapter-totals of the two central books—seven and nine respectively. The interpretation of these numbers had always been a relatively easy matter; and there is no reason to suspect that they would have presented any difficulty even in the mid-eighteenth century. For Fielding's friend John Upton,[33] writing in the 1750s, the association of 7 with the body and the mutable part of man and 9 with his intellectual, incorporeal nature was simple enough, and supported by references to the basic authority, Macrobius (he is glossing *The Faerie Queene*, II. 9. 22):[34]

> This stanza is not to be understood (I believe) without knowing the very passage our poet had in view; namely Cicero's *Somnium Scipionis*, which Macrobius has preserved and commented upon: *Proportioned equally*, agrees with *them both*, viz. mind and body; which receive their harmonic proportion, relation, and temperaments from the *seven* planetary orbs, and from the *ninth* orb, infolding and containing all the rest. What influence the *seven* planets have upon man, you may learn from Manilius, and the astrologers: but the *ninth* orb,
> ——*The circle sett in heavens place,*
> *Summus ipse Deus, arcens & continens caeteros,*—What theist doubts this influence? This is the source, the sea, the sun, of all beauty, truth and MIND.

The 7 and 9 in *Tom Jones* seem to possess the same significance as they do in Spenser and Dryden: as Tom demonstrates his imprudence by rejecting Sophia and succumbing to the fleshly lures of Jenny Waters, so does the structure of this part of the novel counterpoint his action by recalling, symbolically, man's true moral nature in which the passions are tempered by the reason, corporeal 7 is moderated by 9, the number of the mind.

Moreover, 7 and 9 are explicitly mentioned in the text. Prepared as we have been by the nicely-calculated ambiguity and irony of the statement that 'Poetry . . . demands Numbers, or something like Numbers; whereas to the Composition of Novels and Romances, nothing is necessary but Paper, Pens and Ink, with the manual Capacity of using them' (IX. 1), the first allusion, in X. 1, should come as no surprise. Fielding is talking about the 'main Design' of his work. Invoking the commonplace of the artifact as heterocosm, he writes:

> This Work may, indeed, be considered as a great Creation of our own; and for a little Reptile of a Critic to presume to find Fault with any of its Parts, without knowing the Manner in which the

Whole is connected, and before he comes to the final Catastrophe,
is a most presumptuous Absurdity. . . .

Another Caution we would give thee, my good Reptile, is, that
thou dost not find out too near a Resemblance between certain
Characters here introduced; as for Instance, between the
Landlady who appears in the Seventh Book, and her in the
Ninth.

The second allusion occurs in X. 8, the chapter '*In which the History goes
backward*' 'in order to account for the extraordinary Appearance of
Sophia and her Father at the Inn at *Upton*'; for it contains the following
reminder: 'The Reader may be pleased to remember, that in the
Ninth Chapter of the Seventh Book of our History, we left *Sophia*, after
a long Debate between Love and Duty, deciding the Cause, as it
usually, I believe, happens, in Favour of the Former.' Although there
is no need to see these passages as directing attention to the symbolic
antithesis of 7 and 9 in the novel, I would suggest that the evidence
tends in that direction, especially in view of the other self-referring
pointers already noticed here and in *Joseph Andrews*.

VII. 9, which is mentioned in X. 8, ends, as we have just seen, in a
moral dilemma familiar to the period: love against duty. The problem
of judgment, of weighing the consequences, is again posed. It is also
posed in X. 1, the other chapter to allude to 7 and 9. For in this chapter,
too, Fielding talks about judgment, the judgment of character:
'Every Person . . . can distinguish between Sir *Epicure Mammon*, and Sir
Fopling Flutter; but to note the Difference between Sir *Fopling Flutter* and
Sir *Courtly Nice*, requires a more exquisite Judgment' (the kind of
judgment, one is tempted to add, possessed only by the truly prudent
man). Fielding then outlines his theory of characterization: *Tom Jones*
contains no 'Models of Perfection' because its author has 'not, in the
course of [his] Conversation, ever happened to meet with any such
Person'. He continues:

Nor do I, indeed, conceive the good Purposes served by inserting
Characters of such angelic Perfection, or such diabolical
Depravity, in any Work of Invention: Since from contemplating
either, the Mind of Man is more likely to be overwhelmed with
Sorrow and Shame, than to draw any good Uses from such
Patterns; for in the former Instance he may be both concerned
and ashamed to see a Pattern of Excellence, in his Nature, which
he may reasonably despair of ever arriving at; and in contem-

plating the latter, he may be no less affected with those uneasy
Sensations, at seeing the Nature, of which he is a Partaker,
degraded into so odious and detestable a Creature.

Fielding here offers two extreme alternatives, 'angelic Perfection' and
'diabolical Depravity'. He rejects both and chooses to present the
mean: a 'mixed' character who will function as an instructive exem-
plar to the reader.[35]
It was a commonplace, deriving from Aristotle, that this middle
way was to be understood quite literally as an arithmetic mean.[36]
We are surely meant to notice, then, that X. 1, embodying a theory of
the mean, itself occupies the mean position between the seven chapters
of Book IX and the nine chapters of Book X, since it is the eighth
chapter from the beginning of this central block. Moreover, as I have
pointed out, we also find a reference to 7 and 9 and to the problem of
moral choice in the *eighth* chapter of Book X. Fielding clearly alludes
to the harmonious, integrative, octave: Spenser's 'goodly diapase',
which Upton associated with the 'Diapason closing full in Man' of the
first stanza of Dryden's *Song for St. Cecilia's Day*.[37] Even more important,
the symbolism of the large-scale symmetry by which the virtuous 16
of Books IX and X is framed by the 'just' 32 of Books I to III and XVI
to XVIII now becomes intelligible: it appears that Fielding is thinking
in *proportional* terms, so that 32:16:32 becomes 2:1:2; and 1:2 is the
octave proportion which, in Pythagorean thought, symbolized the
relation between the rational soul and the concupiscible faculty.[38]
Tom's search for, and acquisition of, this aspect at least of the cardinal
virtue, Prudence, is thus expressed with a simple yet beautiful clarity
by the novel's numerological structure.
I suspect, too, that we are now in a position to understand the
bipartite arrangement which is to be inferred from the identical
chapter-totals for Books II to V and X to XIII. A diagram will perhaps
prove a useful reminder:

I	II	III	IV	V	VI	VII	VIII	IX	
13	9	10	14	12	14	15	15	7	
	9	10	14	12	10	12	10	9	13
	X	XI	XII	XIII	XIV	XV	XVI	XVII	XVIII

The novel's eighteen books emerge as having been conceived of in the
following fashion: 1+16 (or 8+8)+1, with emphasis again firmly on
the virtuous 16 (we recall that the number of chapters in the novel is

208, i.e. 16×13)[39] and on the median and justly divisive 8. Notice, in addition, the juxtaposed totals of Books IX and XVII: 7 and 9.

V

The structure of *Tom Jones* is in accord with Augustan aesthetic and theological proportional theory (the latter is exemplified in the quotation from Ralph Cudworth cited above, affirming that in a Providential universe 'rewards and punishments are measured out in geometrical proportion'). And yet one must ask the question, What about Square the deist, to whom we are introduced in III. 3 and who is clearly an object of Fielding's satire? He is described, it will be remembered, as being 'deeply read in the Antients, and a profest Master of all the Works of *Plato* and *Aristotle*. Upon which great Models he had principally form'd himself, sometimes according with the Opinion of the one, and sometimes with that of the other. In Morals he was a profest *Platonist*, and in Religion he inclined to be an *Aristotelian*.' His 'favourite Phrase . . . was *the natural Beauty of Virtue*', and he 'measured all Actions by the *unalterable Rule of Right*, and the *eternal Fitness of Things*.' In IV. 11 he declares: 'I am resolved, . . . never to give Way to the Weakness of human Nature more, nor to think any Thing Virtue which doth not exactly quadrate with the unerring Rule of Right', thereby rendering explicit the significance of his name: he is Aristotle's *homo quadratus*, the 'faultless cube', emblem of rectitude and 'right reason'.[40] Square is the embodiment of deist commonplaces as voiced by Shaftesbury, Samuel Clarke, and many others.[41] The inadequacies of those who claimed to 'govern . . . themselves only by the infallible Guide of Human Reason' had been attacked in *Joseph Andrews*, III. 3. Fielding continues the offensive in *Tom Jones* with Square, who, significantly, sees the error of his ways at the end of the novel and dies a good Christian: 'The Pride of Philosophy had intoxicated my Reason, and the sublimest of all Wisdom appeared to me, as it did to the *Greeks* of old, to be Foolishness. God hath however been so gracious to shew me my Error in Time, and to bring me into the Way of Truth, before I sunk into utter Darkness for ever' (XVIII. 4).

From one point of view, of course, the appearance of the Aristotelian-Platonic Square confirms my numerological reading of the novel. He is its ultimate symbol, since the key to its structure is 16 (4×4). But Fielding is satirizing him: does this mean that the novel's symbolism becomes only an elaborate joke? I think the answer to this question

108

must be 'no'. For Fielding obviously shared certain basic assumptions with Clarke and the deists: for example, he admired Shaftesbury, as we saw at the beginning of this chapter, even though that admiration was qualified in certain respects. Ruthven comes to similar conclusions:[42] namely, that while Fielding satirized Clarke for his ineptitude (linguistic and intellectual), he himself retained his belief in 'the eternal fitness of things', a belief that Ruthven sees as being mimed in the manipulation of the novel's plot 'toward a "just" conclusion'. I would only add that, as in *Joseph Andrews*, the formal realization of 'eternal fitness' is not restricted to plot but is expressed through the symbolic numbers embodied in *Tom Jones*'s structure.

Nevertheless, the satire at Square's expense clearly functions as a warning—a warning not only against proclaiming the self-sufficiency of reason but also against taking the numerology as an end in itself. In other words, it is merely a symbol, and of value only in so far as it directs us to the ultimately ineffable mystery of God's Providence.

VI

In *Tom Jones* we have one of the finest expressions of the humanist assumption that the well-made artifact symbolizes the self-knowledge, the moral virtue, of its creator.[43] It is also the most elaborate attempt, in the Augustan period at least, to realize the ancient ideal, *ut architectura poesis*.[44] The general background relating to this concept has been outlined in the Introduction, and its relevance for Fielding's novel has been too well explored by Martin Battestin for me to need to go into it again here.[45] We may note, however, that *Tom Jones* has the structural massiveness that *Joseph Andrews* lacks, so that it strikes us more immediately as having affinities with baroque architecture (or, more precisely, with what Emil Kaufmann calls 'Palladian Baroque'),[46] and our suspicions are confirmed by the strongly accented centre which manifests none of the mannerist ambiguity present in the earlier novel, where, we recall, we have to choose between two possible centres, II. 14 and the beginning of Book III. Also Palladian baroque is the clarity of the tripartite arrangement of *Tom Jones*'s eighteen books; while the chiastic pattern, whatever its literary pedigree, has its analogue in Palladian architectural theory:[47] 'The Anti-Chambers and Chambers ought to be so divided and disposed, that they may fall on each side of the Entry and of the Hall, taking care that those on the right hand may exactly answer to those on the left'—just as the books correspond to each other in reverse order on either side of the novel's centre.

Even 'Orbilius', one of Fielding's more wrongheaded critics, saw that the architectural analogy was important, though he—perhaps wilfully—misapplied it. Noting that Allworthy's house is described in I. 4 as having been executed after 'the *Gothick* Stile of Building', he remarks:[48] 'A *Gothic Building* indeed is an ill Presage of want of Symmetry in the Pile, which our Author has raised to eternize his and *Allworthy's* Memory, in the present Work.' Now Fielding liked 'the *Gothick* Stile', probably having heard about it from Sanderson Miller, as Cross suggests.[49] But there is, of course, nothing '*Gothick*' about *Tom Jones's* structure, a more explicit and elaborate architectural comment on which is to be found in XI. 9 where Fielding mentions Esher, Stowe, Wilton, Eastbury, and Prior Park in connection with the economical writing of a novel, and invites his reader to use his 'Sagacity to apply all this to the *Bœotian* Writers, and to those Authors who are their Opposites.'

Esher (1711) had been designed by Vanbrugh for himself. He also designed Stowe and Eastbury.[50] There are no hints of Palladian baroque here, then, though Inigo Jones had had a considerable hand in the seventeenth-century alterations to Wilton (Jones is praised by Pope in the *Epistle to Burlington*, l. 43, as possessing that 'Good Sense, which only is the gift of Heav'n'—that is, in context, an intuitive feeling for harmony and proportion), and Ralph Allen's Prior Park, designed by John Wood the elder and begun *c.* 1735, has typical Palladian baroque characteristics.[51] But it seems clear that Fielding is alluding to the grounds rather than the houses themselves, the importance of this being that, with the exception of Eastbury (designed by Charles Bridgeman on the older, formal geometrical principles),[52] these parks embody the new ideal of cultivated irregularity, epitomized by Pope in the *Epistle to Burlington* (ll. 55–6): 'He gains all points, who pleasingly confounds, / Surprizes, varies, and conceals the Bounds.' And this ideal was intimately bound up with the Palladian revival. Its chief theorist had been Shaftesbury, and its arch-practitioner was William Kent, protégé of 'that truly English Vitruvius, Richard Earl of Burlington'.[53] In fact, Kent designed the grounds at Esher,[54] and completely remodelled Bridgeman's work at Stowe;[55] Wilton possesses the celebrated Palladian bridge (1736; later copied at Prior Park among other places),[56] and Pope—involved in the theory and practice of neo-Palladianism and the new style of gardening[57]—took a very personal interest in the progress of the landscaping of Ralph Allen's new estate.[58]

This passage, therefore, with its invitation to the reader to employ his 'Sagacity' in approaching *Tom Jones* as he would (for example) the house and grounds at Prior Park, confirms by implication the Palladian baroque structure of the novel and the symmetries I have detected in it. There is little evidence of mannerism in *Tom Jones*; and I would conclude that its formal clarity may justifiably be seen as an expression of Fielding's increasing desire for moral (and hence artistic) explicitness.

VII *Postscript: Amelia*

It would be surprising if, in his last novel, Fielding had abandoned entirely the structural procedures of *Joseph Andrews* and *Tom Jones*. And indeed, although there is no number symbolism, the narrative symmetries in *Amelia* echo those of the earlier novels, with the volume divisions again fulfilling an elucidatory function. Published in four volumes, *Amelia*'s twelve books fall into four blocks of three with the following chapter-totals: vol. I (Books I, II, III), ten, nine, twelve chapters; vol. II (Books IV, V, VI), nine, ten, nine chapters;[59] vol. III (Books VII, VIII, IX), ten chapters each; and vol. IV (Books X, XI, XII), nine chapters each. The first volume is an obviously independent unit, containing as it does the past histories of Miss Matthews and Booth; vol. II sees the beginning of the narrative proper by introducing Amelia in person, as well as Mrs Ellison and Mrs Bennet, and by initiating the noble lord business, and it ends with the anonymous warning against going to the masquerade; in vol. III the masquerade ceases to be the main concern: instead, Booth is imprisoned at the bailiff's, and Colonel James begins to pursue Amelia; while the fourth volume returns to the masquerade and takes us to the novel's conclusion.

Book VII may be regarded as marking the inception of the second half of the novel since eight of its ten chapters are devoted to the history of Mrs Bennet, parts of which recall the histories of Booth and Miss Matthews as narrated in the first half.[60] Just as the first half begins with a long narrative, therefore, so does the second; and just as Booth is in prison throughout Books I to III, so is he imprisoned at the end of Book VII, to remain in confinement throughout Book VIII.

111

Moreover, *Amelia* may be said to pivot round its two central books, VI and VII. There is a balance-image in VI. 3 which, as we would expect, has clear moral implications (the character of Booth is being weighed, and, by Mrs Ellison at least, found wanting): ' "O my dear Mrs. *Ellison*, what Fortune can be put in the Balance with such a Husband as mine?" "I am afraid, dear Madam," answered Mrs. *Ellison*, "you would not hold the Scale fairly." ' This is complemented by a similar passage in VII. 10, in which Mrs Bennet says to Amelia: 'Let us compare your Serjeant now, with the Lord who hath been the Subject of Conversation; on which Side would an impartial Judge decide the Balance to incline?'

It seems that the balances here have a structural as well as an ethical significance, especially when we notice that VI. 8, one of the central chapters in the first edition,[61] also contains a balance: Mrs Ellison 'continued to give only dark Hints to Mrs. *Bennet's* Disadvantage; and, if ever she let drop something a little too harsh, she failed not immediately to contradict herself, by throwing some gentle Commendations into the other Scale. . . .'[62]

A key—if commonplace—image in *Amelia* sees the loss of virtue in terms of a physical fall. Amelia tells Mrs Bennet[63] in VII. 7: 'I look upon you, and always shall look upon you, as my Preserver from the Brink of a Precipice; from which I was falling into the same Ruin, which you have so generously, so kindly, and so nobly disclosed for my Sake.' The actual preservation occurs in VI. 9 with the note warning Amelia not to go to the masquerade, which Amelia recognizes as being in Mrs Bennet's hand. Are we not to understand this symbolically? The mid-point of *Amelia* is, in its quieter, less obtrusive way, as emphatic as that in *Tom Jones*: in this, the second of the novel's central chapters, the heroine is explicitly saved from a moral fall, as Mrs Bennet affirms, symmetrically, in the ninth chapter of Book VII, by again mentioning her note and saying: 'I am convinced, by what I have lately seen, that you are the destined Sacrifice to this wicked Lord; and that Mrs. *Ellison*, whom I no longer doubt to have been the Instrument of my Ruin, intended to betray you in the same Manner.'[64]

Other links between the two central books are provided by Booth's arrest on the orders of Harrison (VII. 10) (who by searching the Booths' apartment in VI. 4 had found evidence which eventually persuaded him to take out a writ against Booth; VI. 8 hints that the arrest is imminent), and by the letter of Mrs Bennet's shown to Amelia by Mrs Ellison in VI. 3, which introduces a piece of her life story and thus anticipates Book VII, where, as we have seen, her story is narrated in full.

The pairing of Books VI and VII after the manner of *Tom Jones*, IX and X, promises an overall chiastic arrangement of the novel's twelve books, though the promise is only partly fulfilled: Books IV and IX, II and XI, and I and XII correspond, but (apart from VI and VII) no others. To consider them in order: IX. 1 reminds us that 'We have already partly seen in what Light *Booth* had been represented to the Doctor abroad'—a reference, in fact, to Harrison's letter in IV. 3; in IX. 2 Booth is reunited with Amelia after being released from the bailiff's, as he is after being released from prison in IV. 2; and IX. 7 recalls 'the Dislike [Amelia] had taken to Mrs. *James* at her first seeing her in Town' (i.e., in IV. 6). The third chapter of Book XI (containing another interpolated narrative, this time '*The History of Mr.* Trent') narrates how '*Trent* burst from the Closet into which he had convey'd himself' as the noble lord was beginning to make love to his wife. Similarly, in II. 3, Booth describes to Miss Matthews how 'Mrs. *Harris* burst from the Closet, where she had hid herself, and surprised her Daughter, reclining on my Bosom. . . . 'In XI. 6 Atkinson is convinced that he is dying; and it is in II. 7 that he is first introduced to us.

The parallels between the first and last books are slightly more elaborate. An obvious symmetry emerges when Booth reveals to his wife 'the whole that had pass'd between him and Miss *Matthews*, from their first Meeting in the Prison' (XII. 2)—the meeting which had, of course, occurred in Book I. And at the beginning of Book XII Booth is again imprisoned (at the bailiff's), having been arrested, fittingly enough for the novel's symmetry, on his way to Miss Matthews. Robinson is also at the bailiff's, and, because he thinks he is dying, confesses the part he had in the suppression of Mrs Harris's will. In XII. 7 Booth meets Robinson face to face and is reminded by him of where they encountered each other before: 'do you not remember, a few Weeks ago, that you had the Misfortune to be in a certain Prison in this Town. . . ?'—an explicit reference, in the third chapter from the end of the novel's final book, to I. 3, the chapter in which Booth had first made Robinson's acquaintance.

It is important to notice that these symmetries are not indulged in for their own sake. Indeed, the correspondences between Books I and XII and the completion of the circle implied by them render explicit Fielding's moral purpose and the symbolism of *Amelia*'s structure, which is, again, to affirm and mime that benevolent Providence whose order is always to be discovered by the wise and virtuous man (or woman)[65] under the myriad apparent incoherences of human life. For it is in I. 3 that Booth's and Robinson's philosophies are described as 'very nearly coincid[ing]'. Booth, says Fielding, 'was in the wavering Condition so finely described by *Claudian*' in his *In Rufinum* (I. 14–19). He believes that Fortune holds sway, not design and art:

> In short, poor *Booth* imagined, that a larger Share of Misfortunes had fallen to his Lot than he had merited; and this led him, who (tho' a good classical Scholar) was not deeply learned in religious Matters, into a disadvantageous Opinion of Providence. A dangerous Way of reasoning, in which our Conclusions are not only too hasty, from an imperfect View of Things; but we are likewise liable to much Error from Partiality to ourselves; viewing our Virtues and Vices as through a Perspective, in which we turn the Glass always to our own Advantage, so as to diminish the one, and as greatly to magnify the other.

And it is at the end of the novel that Booth's and Robinson's doubts are resolved: Booth's in XII. 5, and Robinson's in the following chapter: 'an Accident happened to me Yesterday, by which, as Things have fallen out since, I think I plainly discern the Hand of Providence.'

As in *Tom Jones*, moreover, the novel's large-scale symmetries are supported by local cross-references. Book XI, for instance, begins with '*a very polite Scene*', and concludes with '*A very tragic Scene*'. The '*polite Scene*' involves Colonel and Mrs James, and is thus echoed in the '*polite History*' which opens Book XII and in which the Colonel and his wife again appear. In VII. 10 Atkinson comes 'running into the Room, all pale and breathless' to tell Amelia that Booth has been arrested at the suit of Dr Harrison; in VIII. 10 the sergeant once more comes 'running, out of Breath, into the Room'. This time it is the room in the bailiff's house in which Booth is imprisoned, and he is followed by Harrison and others who have come to bail Booth out. Among many other instances which could be cited, I shall mention only the splendid irony of the juxtaposition of V. 8 (7 in the revised version) and VI. 7: in the former Atkinson tells Booth that he has 'had an Offer of Marriage' (from Mrs Bennet, though this is not revealed until later), and in the latter we see Mrs Bennet railing learnedly against second marriages.

The symmetries in *Amelia*, then, are designed to support Fielding's affirmation in I. 1 which champions Providence over against Fortune and continues: 'Life may as properly be called an Art as any other; and the great Incidents in it are no more to be considered as mere Accidents, than the several Members of a fine Statue, or a noble Poem.' But the complex patterns of the earlier novels are lacking. And significantly, as I said earlier, there is no number symbolism. It is perhaps no coincidence that a parallel can be drawn with Hogarth. *Amelia's* simplicity of structure, and the appearance here of an authorial voice that utilizes few of the teasing and demanding ironic strategies so characteristic of *Joseph Andrews* and *Tom Jones*, are reminiscent of the greater simplicity of Hogarth's work from the 1740s on: as Hogarth moved away from the complexity (both structural and allusive) of his comic histories—the *Harlot*, the *Rake*—to the 'simplified forms' of a series like *Industry and Idleness* (1747),[66] so did Fielding move from the world of his comic epics to the starker and more explicitly heroic[67] world of *Amelia*, though the transition in Fielding's case is more abrupt.

But although, as I said in the last chapter, I detect mannerist elements in Hogarth's handling of the mid-point as late as the *Election* series, there are no such elements in *Amelia*. It is Fielding now—unconsciously following in Defoe's earlier footsteps—who feels more than Hogarth that complexity of structure no longer reliably conveys meaning. Hogarth, in the *Election* and *The Cockpit* (1759), was still requiring his reader to observe and analyse the allusive function of baroque forms and traditions.[68] Admittedly, in *Amelia* Fielding utilized the *Aeneid* and the symmetrical patterns I have outlined above, but—and this is important—with less conviction than is demonstrated in Hogarth's use of allusion.[69] (Thus the saving of Amelia from a fall in the centre has none of the dark exuberance of Hogarth's inversion of the sovereign and triumphal mid-point in the *Election*, for example.)

What we have in *Amelia*, I think, is a moving testament to Fielding's confrontation and reluctant acceptance of the limitations of his earlier clear-cut faith in 'the eternal fitness of things'. At bottom a personal matter, it also coincided with the official contemporary rejection of the belief in the metaphysical significance of number and proportion in such works as Hogarth's own *Analysis of Beauty* (1753) and Burke's *Philosophical Enquiry* (1757), itself merely one manifestation of the mid-century reaction against the neoclassical and objective and the increasing preoccupation with the psychology of the individual and the subjective.[70]

The inevitable result of this reaction was the advocation of the relativity of aesthetic judgment. Hence, it seems to me, the formal tensions in *Amelia*, where Fortune appears to be stronger than Providence and the happy ending strikes one as being so contrived, and where the structure only barely sustains its paradigmatic function. The novel's imagery, too, evidences a new, almost Richardsonian, sensibility:[71]

> [Amelia] past a miserable and sleepless Night, her gentle Mind torn and distracted with various and contending Passions, distressed with Doubts, and wandring in a kind of Twilight, which presented her only Objects of different Degrees of Horrour, and where black Despair closed at a small Distance the gloomy Prospect. (XI. 9)

And notice the way in which the celebration of a sane and ordered 'Art of Life' (I. 1) is immediately subverted by the narrative itself, which begins 'On the first of *April*' (All Fools day), and by the following description of the imperfections of the English legal system:

> It will probably be objected, that the small Imperfections which I am about to produce, do not lie in the Laws themselves, but in the ill Execution of them; but, with Submission, this appears to me to be no less an Absurdity, than to say of any Machine that it is excellently made, tho' incapable of performing its Functions. Good Laws should execute themselves in a well regulated State; at least, if the same Legislature which provides the Laws, doth not provide for the Execution of them, they act as *Graham* would do, if he should form all the Parts of a Clock in the most exquisite Manner, yet put them so together that the Clock could not go. In this Case, surely we might say that there was a small Defect in the Constitution of the Clock. (I. 2)

While in the next paragraph the reader is literally presented with a 'world upside-down' (to borrow a phrase that has been given new currency by Ian Donaldson):[72] 'Butler in the Coach-box, . . . Steward behind [the] Coach'.

There is a sense in which Fielding's pessimism is still characteristically Augustan, as the second chapter of Book XI—on '*Matters political*', with its analogy between Rome and contemporary England—attests. But it is also something more. It is, to repeat, the product of the transitional period—transitional philosophically, artistically, politically—in which *Amelia* was written.[73] Little wonder, then, that the novel should show signs of unease.

NOTES

1 *The History of Henry Fielding*, 3 vols (New Haven, Conn., 1918), II. 212.
2 *Advice to an Author*, III. 3, in *Characteristics*, ed. Robertson, I. 216. Fielding owned a copy of the 1737 edn of the *Characteristics* (item 499 in the sale catalogue of his library, reprinted in the Appendix to Ethel M. Thornbury's *Henry Fielding's Theory of the Comic Prose Epic*, University of Wisconsin Studies in Language and Literature, 30 (Madison, Wisconsin, 1931)).
3 Compare *Advice to an Author*, III. 3 (ed. Robertson, I. 227–8): 'harmony is harmony by nature. . . . So is symmetry and proportion founded still in nature, let men's fancy prove ever so barbarous, or their fashions ever so Gothic in their architecture, sculpture, or whatever other designing art. . . . Virtue has the same fixed standard. The same numbers, harmony, and proportion will have place in morals, and are discoverable in the characters and affections of mankind. . .'; *An Inquiry Concerning Virtue or Merit*, I. 3. 3 (Robertson, I. 279): 'the admiration and love of order, harmony, and proportion, in whatever kind, is naturally improving to the temper. . .'; and *The Moralists, A Philosophical Rhapsody*, II. 4 (Robertson, II. 63): 'Nothing surely is more strongly imprinted on our minds, or more closely interwoven with our souls, than the idea or sense of order and proportion. Hence all the force of numbers, and those powerful arts founded on their management and use.' This list is representative rather than exhaustive.
4 F. W. Hilles, 'Art and Artifice in *Tom Jones*', in Maynard Mack and Ian Gregor (eds), *Imagined Worlds: Essays on Some English Novels and Novelists in Honour of John Butt* (1968), pp. 91–110, and Robert Alter, *Fielding and the Nature of the Novel*, pp. 136–8.
5 E.g., the balancing of the fight in IV. 7 against that in II. 9 (see above, p. 87, n. 20).
6 Smollett is discussed in chaps 6 and 7 below; *Clarissa* is analysed by F. W. Hilles, 'The Plan of *Clarissa*', *PQ*, 45 (1966), 236–48; and the Fanny Burney instance is touched on by Edwine Montague and Louis L. Martz in 'Fanny Burney's *Evelina*', in F. W. Hilles (ed.), *The Age of Johnson: Essays Presented to Chauncey Brewster Tinker* (New Haven, Conn., and London, 1964), pp. 174–5.
7 The first and second edns of Richardson's novel appeared in seven vols, the third and later edns in eight.
8 Quotations are from the third edn, 4 vols, 1749.
9 The duel with Fitzpatrick also parallels the duel with Northerton in Book VII, as Irvin Ehrenpreis has noted in *Fielding: Tom Jones* (1964), p. 47.
10 To unify the triad even further, Fielding links V. 6 and VI. 6: Tom, Sophia, and the canal feature in both.
11 In XV. 6 Fielding refers to 'the third Chapter . . . of the preceding Book' in order to explain 'by what Method the Squire discovered where his Daughter was'. But he means XIII. 3, not XIV. 3. Does this imply that he wrote Books XIII and XV in sequence, or merely that he flipped through his manuscript too hurriedly to check the reference, and misread it?
12 One may note in addition, however, the way in which Sophia's concern for Tom (when he falls into the canal, when he is reported dead in a duel) connects IV. 3 and XV. 3, and the parallel with a difference between IV. 5 (in which Tom 'snatched [Sophia's] Hand, and eagerly kissed it') and XV. 5 (Fellamar's attempted rape, the prelude to which is 'laying hold of her Hand').
13 Reproduced in 'Art and Artifice in *Tom Jones*', p. 95.

14 For example: Honour's resolution to travel with Sophia in VII. 7, and Partridge's resolution to travel with Tom in VIII. 6–7; Tom's meeting with the Quaker and the Quaker's tale in VII. 10, and his meeting with the Man of the Hill in VIII. 10, who subsequently narrates his autobiography; Tom as 'ghost' in VII. 14, and Partridge's ghost story at the end of VIII. 11, etc.

15 An idea familiar in modern musical constructivism: see Misha Donat on the slow movement of Berg's *Chamber Concerto*, which moves backward as soon as the mid-point is reached ('Mathematical Mysticism', *The Listener*, 2 April 1970).

16 The name itself reminds us that we have arrived at a peak, since 'mazard' means 'head' (*OED*, s.v., 2a) as well as being a dialect word for a small black cherry.

17 The tales are discussed by Irvin Ehrenpreis in *Fielding: Tom Jones*, pp. 45–6, and Alter, *Fielding and the Nature of the Novel*, pp. 110–12.

18 Just as an interruption is one way in which the tale of Leonora and '*The History of two Friends*' are connected in *Joseph Andrews*. See my 'The Interpolated Tales in *Joseph Andrews* Again', *MP*, 65 (1968), 208–13.

19 Tom, Partridge, and their guide also lose their way in XII. 11.

20 On the relevance of *The Provoked Husband* and the Quaker, see Ehrenpreis, op. cit., pp. 41, 44.

21 Op. cit., pp. 137–8.

22 Ibid., p. 138.

23 Note that the total number of chapters—208—can be factorized as 16×13. 32 was also—like 16—a Pythagorean number of justice (Bongo, *Numerorum mysteria*, p. 486).

24 *The True Intellectual System of the Universe* (1678), cit. Battestin, '*Tom Jones*: The Argument of Design', in *The Augustan Milieu*, p. 295. Fielding owned the 1678 edn (library catalogue, item 463).

25 'Fielding's Definition of Wisdom: Some Functions of Ambiguity and Emblem in *Tom Jones*', *ELH*, 35 (1968), 206.

26 The hill at the centre balances that at the beginning: 'Reader, take Care, I have unadvisedly led thee to the Top of as high a Hill as Mr. *Allworthy*'s, and how to get thee down without breaking thy Neck, I do not well know' (I. 4). A moral contrast is thus implied between Allworthy and the Old Man of the Hill.

27 Or, more specifically, apparent 'Good Counsel', allegorized in Ripa's *Iconologia* as an old man (Erwin Panofsky, *Meaning in the Visual Arts*, p. 163 and Fig. 41).

28 See above, p. 84. It is, therefore, touchingly fitting that Christopher Smart's 'Epitaph on Henry Fielding, Esq.' (1763) should have as its central lines: 'Hence pow'r consign'd the laws to his command, / And put the scales of Justice in his hand' (reprinted in Ronald Paulson and Thomas Lockwood (eds), *Henry Fielding: The Critical Heritage* (1969), p. 436).

29 For the ethical significance of the balance in the period, see Paul Fussell, *The Rhetorical World of Augustan Humanism* (1969), pp. 182–3. Cf. Shaftesbury, *The Moralists*, II. 4: 'few have heard of the balance of their passions, or thought of holding these scales even' (*Characteristics*, II. 69), and Fielding's periodical *The Champion*: 'as a just Ballance of Power can only support any Degree of Liberty in a Political Constitution, so must the exact Ballance of the Passions preserve Order and Regularity in the Mind' (2 vols, 1741 edn, I. 233).

30 Xenophon, *Memorabilia*, II. 1. 21–33. I discuss the importance of the fable for

Joseph Andrews in my Introd. to the OEN edn of that novel; and see Ronald Paulson, *Hogarth*, I. 271–6 and 417–20 for Hogarth's use of it. Note that, framing the central block of *Tom Jones*, there are two references to Tom's being lost at crossroads: in VII. 10 and XII. 5 (cf. XII. 11).

31 The three faculties (memory, intelligence, foresight) were, to use Panofsky's word, 'co-ordinated' with the three modes of time (past, present, future): Tom thus looks to the past, then to the future. Battestin's excellent account of prudence in the novel in 'Fielding's Definition of Wisdom' cites classical and later sources, and draws in part on Panofsky's *Meaning in the Visual Arts*, ch. 4, which is devoted to the iconography of Titian's *Allegory of Prudence*.

32 Ibid., p. 192.

33 Battestin, in his annotations to the forthcoming 'Wesleyan' edn of *Tom Jones*, VIII. 11, shows that Fielding was friendly with the Uptons (John and his father).

34 *Spenser's 'Faerie Queene'. A New Edition with a Glossary, and Notes Explanatory and Critical* (1758), II. 481. Spenser's stanza describes Alma's castle as having a 'frame' that 'seemd partly circulare, / And part triangulare'; it continues: 'And twixt them both a quadrate was the base / Proportioned equally by seven and nine; / Nine was the circle set in heavens place, / All which compacted made a goodly diapase.' The stanza is discussed exhaustively by Alastair Fowler in *Spenser and the Numbers of Time*, pp. 260–88. For Dryden's use of 7 and 9, see Fowler and Brooks, 'The Structure of Dryden's *A Song for St. Cecilia's Day, 1687*', in *Silent Poetry*, pp. 185–200.

35 Notice that the next chapter, X. 2, announces that 'it was now Midnight': another directive to the middle way?

36 *Nicomachean Ethics*, II. 6. 4–17 (1106 A–B).

37 Upton, *Spenser's 'Faerie Queene'*, II. 480.

38 Pico della Mirandola, *Conclusiones secundum mathematicam Pythagorae*, nos. 8–10; in *Opera omnia* (Basel, 1601), I. 53; and Agrippa, *Three Books*, II. 28 (quoted above, Introd., p. 6). The symbolism had been used by, among others, Milton (Fowler's Introd. to *Paradise Lost* in *The Poems of John Milton*, pp. 445–6) and Dryden ('The Structure of Dryden's *A Song*', pp. 191–2 and 195–6). See also Fowler, *Triumphal Forms*, pp. 99–100, and 159–60.

39 The number 13 is uniformly unfortunate in meaning (Plutarch, *Moralia*, tr. Philemon Holland (1657), p. 848; Bongo, *Numerorum mysteria*, pp. 399–401), and it is significant that I. 13 embodies, as no other chapter in the novel, the evil represented by the Blifils (here, Captain Blifil's 'strange, cruel, and almost unaccountable Ingratitude' to his brother; in atonement for his own wrongs young Blifil has to ask 'Pardon of his Brother' (Tom) before being dismissed in XVIII. 11); so that the novel's insistence on 13 and 16 re-enacts symbolically what is effected by the vanquishing of Blifil in the narrative: i.e., as the 208th chapter is reached, 13 is multiplied by (and elevated to) the 16 of justice and virtue.

40 *Nicomachean Ethics*, I. 10. 11 (1100 B). For the square as 'right reason', see Bongo, p. 195. Cf. Henry More's definition of 'quadrate': 'A figure with foure equall sides, and foure right angles. The rightnesse of the angles, is a plain embleme of erectnesse or uprightnesse of mind' (*Philosophicall Poems* (Cambridge, 1647), p. 432). K. K. Ruthven discusses the symbolism of the name in 'Fielding, Square, and the Fitness of Things', *ECS*, 5 (1971–2), 248–9.

41 Miriam Allott, 'A Note on Fielding's Mr Square', *MLR*, 56 (1961), 69–72. Not that Clarke was himself a deist, since, unlike the deists, he believed in revelation. However, as Ruthven puts it, he 'seems to have given the impression of being of the deists' party without knowing it; and Fielding's Square is Clarke assessed from this point of view' (art. cit., p. 246).

42 Ibid., p. 255.

43 Cf. Shaftesbury, *Advice to an Author*, I. 3 (ed. Robertson, I. 136–7): 'As for poets in particular (says the learned and wise Strabo), Can we possibly imagine that the genius, power, and excellence of a real poet consists in aught else than the just imitation of life in formed discourse and numbers? But how should he be that just imitator of life whilst he himself knows not its measures, nor how to guide himself by judgment and understanding?'

44 Fussell, *The Rhetorical World*, pp. 189ff., discusses the ideal.

45 See his '*Tom Jones*: The Argument of Design', passim.

46 *Architecture in the Age of Reason*, p. 14. Kaufmann here discusses the retention of the baroque emphasized centre by the early eighteenth-century English neo-Palladians, with particular reference to Colen Campbell's *Vitruvius Britannicus* (1715ff.). Sir John Summerson, *Architecture in Britain: 1530–1830* (Pelican History of Art (Harmondsworth, 1970)), chaps 20 and 22, provides an excellent survey of the Palladian movement which, in fact, had a threefold allegiance—to Vitruvius's *De architectura*, to Palladio, and to Inigo Jones. Historically, and also on the evidence of *Tom Jones*, XI. 9 (discussed below), it is this tradition which is most likely to have influenced Fielding.

47 *The Architecture of A. Palladio; In Four Books*, tr. Giacomo Leoni (1742), I. 21 (p. 26).

48 'Orbilius', *An Examen of the History of Tom Jones, a Foundling* (1749), in Paulson and Lockwood (eds), *Henry Fielding: The Critical Heritage*, p. 194.

49 *The History of Henry Fielding*, II. 112–13, 164.

50 On Esher, see Summerson, op. cit., p. 277; and on Stowe and Eastbury, H. Avray Tipping and Christopher Hussey, *English Homes*, Period IV, vol. ii: *The Work of Sir John Vanbrugh and his School, 1699–1736* (1928), chaps 6 and 8. On Eastbury, see also Emil Kaufmann, *Architecture in the Age of Reason*, p. 18.

51 John Summerson discusses Wilton, op. cit., pp. 142–4; for Jones and 'the metaphysical belief in the universal efficacy and beauty of numbers', see Rudolf Wittkower, *Architectural Principles in the Age of Humanism*, pp. 143–4. An illustration, plan, and discussion of Prior Park appear in Summerson, pp. 323ff.

52 Summerson, op. cit., p. 346, and Edward Malins, *English Landscaping and Literature 1660–1840* (1966), p. 61.

53 Quoted from Drake's *Eboracum* (1736) by H. Avray Tipping in *English Homes*, Period V, vol. i (1921), p. xxiii. On Shaftesbury, Burlington, Kent, and the new gardening, see James Lees-Milne, *Earls of Creation: Five Great Patrons of Eighteenth-Century Art* (1962), p. 16, and Margaret Jourdain, *The Work of William Kent* (1948).

54 Cf. Pope's *Epilogue to the Satires*, Dialogue ii, 66–7, which refers to 'Esher's peaceful Grove / (Where Kent and Nature vye for PELHAM's Love)'.

55 Cf. the *Epistle to Burlington*, ll. 70ff., and Bateson's note (*Epistles to Several Persons*, ed. F. W. Bateson; Twickenham edn, vol. III. ii (1961), 141).

56 See Lees-Milne, op. cit., pp. 96–7, and Summerson, op. cit., pp. 360–1.

57 See Maynard Mack's *The Garden and The City: Retirement and Politics in the Later Poetry*

of Pope 1731–1743 (Toronto, Buffalo, and London, 1969), chaps 1 and 2, esp. pp. 32ff. and 53ff.

58 Malins, op. cit., pp. 42–5, and Plate vi (facing p. 51), and Pope's letter to Allen of 15 May 1740 (*The Correspondence of Alexander Pope*, ed. George Sherburn, 5 vols (Oxford, 1956), IV. 238–9).

59 The original second chapter of Book V—'*Containing a Brace of Doctors, and much physical Matter*'—was omitted on Fielding's authority in Murphy's edn of the novel in *The Works of Henry Fielding, Esq.* (1762) and subsequent edns. The usual chapter-total for Book V is therefore nine. All quotations are from the first edn (4 vols, 1752).

60 For example, Mrs Bennet announces herself as 'an Adulteress and a Murderer' (VII. 1), and Miss Matthews is imprisoned for murder (I. 6); 'Mrs. *Harris* burst from the Closet' to interrupt an interview between Booth and Amelia (II. 3), and Mrs Bennet's aunt 'burst in upon' her and Mr Bennet as they were talking 'in a very thick Arbour in the Garden' (VII. 5), etc.

61 Depending on whether we allow nine or ten chapters to Book V, the total for the novel is either 115 or 116. With the 116 total, VI. 8 and 9 are both central (fifty-eighth and fifty-ninth); with the revised total, VI. 9 is exactly central (fifty-eighth).

62 Other allusions to balances—in X. 1 and XII. 6—are much more perfunctory, and thus serve to highlight the cluster of important references at the novel's centre.

63 Cf. I. 8 ('every Woman . . . walks on a Precipice, and the bottomless Pit is to receive her, if she slips'); IV. 2 ('so slippery is the Descent of Vice'); VIII. 9 ('Innocence . . . tumbles into the Pit, which [guilt] foresees and avoids'); X. 2 (Amelia is described in Harrison's letter against adultery as 'a Precipice which it is impossible [James] should ever ascend'); and X. 8 (Mrs Atkinson on the antiquity of the notion of the 'slippery Descent' of 'all the Ways of Vice').

64 For the fall at the centre, which Fielding had exploited in *Joseph Andrews,* see above, pp. 81–5.

65 At the beginning of VIII. 4 Amelia refers to 'that Divine Will and Pleasure, without whose Permission at least, no Human Accident can happen. . . .' On Fortune and Providence in the novel, see D. S. Thomas, 'Fortune and the Passions in Fielding's *Amelia*', *MLR*, 60 (1965), 176–87.

66 Ronald Paulson, *Hogarth*, II. 71. Paulson sees in *Industry and Idleness* 'a kind of heroic opposition' that recalls the opposition of gods and devils in 'sublime history painting' (ibid.).

67 'Heroic' in its closeness to the *Aeneid*, particularly at the beginning of the novel. Hence, too, *Amelia*'s twelve books. Fielding's use of Virgil's epic in this novel has been sensitively analysed by George Sherburn, 'Fielding's *Amelia*: An Interpretation', *ELH*, 3 (1936), 1–14, and in more (but less convincing) detail by L. H. Powers, 'The Influence of the *Aeneid* on Fielding's *Amelia*', *Modern Language Notes (MLN)*, 71 (1956), 330–6. Fielding writes of Virgil as his 'noble model' in connection with *Amelia* in *The Covent-Garden Journal*, 28 January 1752.

68 Paulson, *Hogarth*, II. 357–8.

69 C. J. Rawson, 'Nature's Dance of Death. Part II: Fielding's *Amelia*', *ECS*, 3 (1969–70), 520, remarks that the *Aeneid* parallels operate for the most part in a non-satiric, non-Augustan, way; and Robert Alter sees Fielding's use of the

Aeneid as a means of helping him establish a meaningful relationship between public and private in so domestic a novel (*Fielding and the Nature of the Novel*, pp. 141–7). Alter's chapter on *Amelia*, incidentally, seems to me to be the best critical account of the novel to date.

70 Another symptom was the cult of sensibility. Robert Alter, op. cit., pp. 166–71, describes its adverse effects on *Amelia*, particularly on character and language.

71 Compare Atkinson's nightmare in IX. 6. Also new in Fielding's work is the use of the novel's topography—London, the verge of the court, prison—to reinforce the numerous references to darkness in order to create the impression of a world that is oppressive and claustrophobic (cf. the end of *Roxana*).

72 See his suggestive *The World Upside-Down: Comedy from Jonson to Fielding* (Oxford, 1970).

73 See Paulson, *Hogarth*, II. 402–6, for a parallel with the late Hogarth, and particularly the 'premonition of impending change' which culminates in 'Tailpiece, or The Bathos' of 1764, where Time himself is shown expiring.

vi Smollett: *Roderick Random, Peregrine Pickle, Ferdinand Count Fathom*

I *Roderick Random*

Form mattered to Fielding. Even in *Amelia*, as we have seen, its iconographical implications can still be detected, if only faintly. In Smollett's first novel, published in 1748, on the other hand, the overriding impression is one of disorder and fragmentation, in subject-matter and in structure. Robert Alter has justly remarked on the way it reflects the phrenetic and neurotic quality of life in the period;[1] and it does so with a fidelity and awareness of the grotesque and the chaotic that has, once again, its visual counterpart in the middle and late works of Hogarth. But to concentrate on this aspect of *Roderick Random* is to do Smollett an injustice by ignoring his attempts to impose arithmetical schemes on his material, attempts which make his novels structurally very different from their picaresque antecedents.[2] I use the word 'impose' advisedly, however: the young Smollett was too much a man of the transitional mid-century to achieve, or even want to achieve, at this stage of his development, the kind of formal complexity manifested in, say, *Joseph Andrews*. Nevertheless, before writing *Roderick Random* he had obviously studied Fielding's novel with some care, as the several echoes of it in his own work attest,[3] and doubtless one of his reasons for reading *Joseph Andrews* was to seek guidance on the structuring of a long prose fiction.

Like *Joseph Andrews*, *Roderick Random* was published in two volumes. This format obviously assisted Smollett in working out his narrative symmetries, as it assists the reader in grasping them. It should be recorded here, then, that vol. I contains thirty-six chapters, and vol. II, thirty-three chapters. The chapter numbering is continuous (i.e., running from 1 to 69), though in later eighteenth-century editions there seems to have been a tendency to number each volume separately.[4]

The novel's fundamental circularity is announced in chapter 1 with the sage's interpretation of Roderick's mother's dream as meaning that he 'would be a great traveller, that he would undergo many dangers and difficulties, and at last return to his native land, where he would flourish with great reputation and happiness'. It is also in this first chapter that Roderick's father mysteriously disappears, 'and notwithstanding all imaginable inquiry, could not be heard of, which confirmed most people in the opinion of his having made away with himself in a fit of despair'. Both Roderick and his father return to Scotland and regain the family estate in the final chapter.

Such a balancing of beginning and end is elementary enough. More interesting is the way Smollett prepares us for the rediscovery of Roderick's father. Don Rodrigo is, it will be recalled, encountered in chapter 66, living in Buenos Aires. No sooner have he and his son been reunited than they sail from the Rio de la Plata to Jamaica where they meet Roderick's former shipmate Thomson (ch. 67). Leaving Thomson they set off for England and almost immediately lose a man overboard:

> About two hours after this melancholy accident happened . . . I heard a voice rising, as it were, out of the sea, and calling, 'Ho, the ship, ahoy!' Upon which one of the men upon the forecastle cried, 'I'll be d—n'd, if that an't Jack Marlinspike, who went over-board!' Not a little surprized at this event, I jumped into the little boat that lay along-side, with the second mate and four men, and rowing towards the place, from whence the voice (which repeated the hail) seemed to proceed, we perceived some-thing floating upon the water; when we had rowed a little farther, we discerned it to be a man riding upon a hen-coop. . . .

The man turns out to be from another ship; but this apparent resurrection of the drowned sailor is a clever retrospective analogue to the unexpected discovery of Roderick's father, thought to be dead long since. The incident makes full structural sense, however, only if we remember what happened to Thomson earlier on in the novel. Because of Mackshane's brutality (Thomson mentions Mackshane at the beginning of chapter 67) he had thrown himself overboard from the ship in which he and Roderick were serving together (ch. 29). Nothing more is heard of him (and he is presumed dead) until chapter

36, when Roderick goes ashore at Morant and notices a horseman who turns out to be 'the very person of my lamented friend'. Thomson then explains how he comes to be alive: once in the water he had 'hailed a large vessel' but her crew had not wanted 'to lose time, by bringing to; however, they threw an old chest over-board, for his convenience, and told him that some of the ships a-stern would certainly save him. . . .'

The parallel could scarcely be closer. And this episode itself has been prepared for by Roderick, who, in chapter 34, after nearly dying of a fever, pretends to be dead and suddenly to come to life in order to startle Morgan. We might say, then, that *Roderick Random*'s basic structure is planned round the disappearance and rediscovery of Don Rodrigo, and that the 'resurrections' noted here, but especially that of Thomson at the very end of the first volume, have a deliberate anticipatory function—a function that is made the more explicit by Thomson's reappearance in chapter 67 immediately after Roderick's reunion with his father, and by the echo of his original plight by the sailor on the hen-coop.

If the end of the first volume looks forward, the first chapter of the second (37) looks back and also marks a new beginning for Roderick. Returning to England with wealth and clothing and seeing himself 'as a gentleman of some consequence' (ch. 36), it is suddenly apparent that his quest for gentility[5] has reached only a contrived, not a genuine, conclusion. For in chapter 37 there is a storm, and Roderick, who tells us 'I cloathed myself in my best apparel', fights with his enemy Crampley and is left destitute on a Sussex beach, where 'I cursed the hour of my birth, the parents that gave me being', and so on.[6] This curse is important; for it is clearly intended to take us back to chapter 1. And as a further reminder that the novel is, in a sense, beginning again, Roderick finds himself a surrogate mother in Mrs Sagely (chapter 38; his own mother had died in chapter 1): the old woman 'drew a happy presage of my future life from my past sufferings' (recalling the sage's prediction in chapter 1)[7] and Roderick 'contract[s] a filial respect for her', but only after he has heard her life history: she had married beneath her and without her parents' consent, and they had disinherited her. The story echoes that of Roderick's own father, who had married 'a poor relation' without parental consent and had again been disinherited. Mrs Sagely then leaves the novel until near the end (chaps 65 and 67);[8] and in chapter 67 she alludes to her words in chapter 38: 'she thanked heaven that I had not belied the presages she had made, on her first acquaintance with me. . . .' Beginning, middle, and end of the novel are thus closely bound together as they are also by the disappearance of Roderick's father, the disappearance and reappearance of Thomson, and the reappearance of Don Rodrigo.

Miss Williams provides another link between the two halves of the novel. Roderick, already in his eyes 'a gentleman in reality' (ch. 20), had first encountered her when he pursued her as a supposed heiress, and had met her again as an abandoned prostitute in the following chapter. This hints at a theme that is developed in more detail in vol. II with the courtesan picked up by the deluded Roderick in chapter 45 and Melinda (chaps 47ff.). Miss Williams's function is therefore proleptic: she acts as a warning of the sexual and social temptations that will confront him on his return to London, though the relevance of her 'history' (chaps 22, 23) becomes apparent only after Roderick has met his beloved Narcissa in the second volume. As a girl Miss Williams had been attacked by a drunken squire in a wood and rescued by a young man who 'was the exact resemblance of' Roderick. He had seduced her and then 'left [her] without remorse'. The parallel (with a difference) with the main narrative emerges in chapter 41, when Roderick rescues Narcissa from an indecent attack by Sir Timothy Thicket. Moreover, the link thus forged between the two women is strengthened when Miss Williams appears as Narcissa's maid in chapter 55 (acting as a warning to him once more: he had pursued her unsuccessfully as an heiress in Part I and had nearly married her; now she brings Roderick and Narcissa together when he is again on a false trail by chasing another heiress, Miss Snapper). Roderick first met Miss Williams in chapter 20; chapter 55 is the nineteenth chapter of vol. II.

Miss Williams's story is interrupted at the beginning of chapter 23 by her wrongful arrest. She is driven off to the Marshalsea, but is released when the mistake is realized. The interruption is as much a structural matter as anything else; for Roderick hears the second interpolated story, that of Melopoyn, in chapters 62 and 63, when he has been arrested for debt and is himself imprisoned in the Marshalsea. Both narratives last for two chapters, and although the Marshalsea provides the only substantive link between them, and their relative positions in their respective volumes by no means correspond, we have here yet another indication, I think, of Smollett's anxiety to give his first novel all the trappings of formal unity even if, in his treatment of the interpolated narrative, he was unable to live up to the examples of Fielding and Fielding's own model, Cervantes.

The symmetries created by the appearances of Bowling are also worth comment. We last hear from him in the first volume in chapter 6; Roderick then encounters him in France in chapter 41, and he departs in chapter 42 (i.e., the sixth chapter of vol. II), to reappear to rescue his nephew from the Marshalsea in chapter 64 (the sixth chapter from the end of the novel). Strap, too, is involved in analogous symmetries: he and Roderick meet and decide to travel together in chapter 8, and they meet up again in France in chapter 44, the eighth chapter of vol. II.

If we now turn from large-scale patterns to the internal organization of the individual volumes, an interesting contrast is apparent. There is an undeniable arithmetical patterning in vol. I, since its thirty-six chapters are clearly divided into three sets of twelve by Roderick's arrival in London (ch. 13) and his being press-ganged into the navy (after the beginning of chapter 24, which is therefore transitional). Smollett was obviously working to the following scheme:

1–12	13–24	25–36
Scotland; Journey	London	Navy

While in addition, the following subdivisions may be detected: chapters 1 to 6, Scotland, and 7 to 12, journey (i.e., the first block falls into two sets of six chapters); chapters 13 to 15, various London matters; 16 to 18, the navy office; 19 to 21, Lavement; 22 to beginning of 24, Miss Williams (four sets of three). The third block is similarly divided: nearly four chapters (24 to 27) are devoted to Roderick's initial experiences on board ship; three chapters (28 to 30) recount events on the voyage to Carthagena, and Carthagena itself takes up three chapters (31 to 33); finally, the last three chapters of the volume (34 to 36) form a single unit centring round Captain Whiffle and Crampley.

But the second volume lacks such a precise individual arithmetical structure, though it does contain the few symmetries already noted. Of *Roderick Random* as a whole, it can be said that Smollett here reveals no firm sense of structural direction, and that the patterns I have described lack any real iconographical import despite the lip service paid to the power of Providence in the novel.[9] I suspect, in fact, that they are little more than mere scaffolding.

II *Peregrine Pickle*

The symmetries in Smollett's much longer second novel, however, possess more symbolic significance. Indeed, we might anticipate a little here, and say that from the structural point of view at least Smollett's development is the exact opposite to that of Defoe and of Fielding, in that it manifests an increasing concern with architectonics and such numerological details as mid-point symbolism. As we shall see, this concern coincides with a move towards greater thematic and moral clarity.

The question of structural schemes in *Peregrine Pickle* (1751) is complicated by the considerable revisions made for the second edition (1758). For the time being, therefore, I shall consider the first edition, and since the volume divisions once again have an important part to play, I supply the following table:[10]

Volume	Chapters	Total
I	1–38	38
II	39–78	40
III	79–93	15
IV	94–114	21

Only with this information before us can we appreciate, for example, how carefully Trunnion's death at the garrison at the beginning of the third volume (ch. 79), together with his warning to Peregrine not to abuse Emilia, is balanced by the death of Peregrine's aunt at the beginning of vol. IV (ch. 94), which again brings Peregrine to the garrison. And chapter 94 can also serve as a useful introduction to the kind of less symmetrical repetitive structuring that we encounter in *Peregrine Pickle*. For Peregrine here meets Emilia, whom, despite his uncle, he has abused, and with whom he is on bad terms. He asks Sophy to be his advocate with her, and in so doing he draws the parallel with her previous identical role in vol. I (ch. 26) by remembering 'that fond, that happy day, on which the fair, the good, the tender-hearted Sophy became my advocate, though I was a stranger to her acquaintance, and effected a transporting reconciliation between me and that same inchanting beauty, that is now so implacably incensed'. The parallel here has both a moral and a structural function. The first incident, caused by the letter fabricated by Pipes, had been a comic misunderstanding. But the second involves a much more serious alienation

128

between the two, brought about by Peregrine's pride and his failure to recognize and live up to the virtue embodied in Emilia. And just as Pipes, because of the letter, had had a major part in chapter 26, so he does in chapter 94, trying to help Peregrine's case by pretending that his master has 'hanged himself for love'. Again, Peregrine draws the parallel: 'this is the second time I have suffered in the opinion of that lady by your ignorance and presumption; if ever you intermeddle in my affairs for the future, without express order and direction, by all that's sacred! I will put you to death without mercy.'

The parallel deaths of Peregrine's uncle and aunt are not the only way in which Smollett has linked the last two volumes: the third volume, beginning as it does with Trunnion's death, sees Peregrine in possession of his uncle's estate and his initiation into the fashionable world; at the end of vol. IV (ch. 111) Peregrine's father, Gamaliel, dies. Having squandered his first inheritance, Peregrine can handle with temperance the 'more ample' fortune he now receives. The point is made explicitly: Peregrine has 'a stock of experience that [will] steer him clear of all those quicksands among which he had been formerly wrecked' (ch. 112).

Further instances of such patterning abound. For example, the series of misunderstandings and reconciliations between Peregrine and Godfrey near the end of the first, second, and fourth volumes: in chapter 30 (ninth from the end), chapter 73 (sixth from the end) and chapter 109 (also sixth from the end); or the satirical adventures of the two at the end of the first volume (chaps 34ff.) and of the second volume (chaps 73ff., where they have a more moral aim and are not mere practical jokes as they were earlier). It is here (ch. 76) that Peregrine becomes acquainted with Crabtree, and near the end of vol. III (chaps 89ff.) occur several satirical *exposés* in which Peregrine and Crabtree engage together (including Peregrine's unmasking of 'a couple of sharpers' in chapter 92—compare the '*Scheme*' in chapter 74 '*by which a whole Company of Sharpers is ruined*').

Similarly, towards the end of vol. I, in chapter 35, Peregrine's sister Julia is alienated from her family because of her affection for her brother. In a corresponding position in vol. II (ch. 72) she is married to a Mr Clover who, at the end of the fourth volume, is instrumental in seeing that Peregrine gets his rightful inheritance (ch. 111); while a couple of chapters from the end of vol. III Peregrine claims to have seen an apparition of 'the commodore . . . , in the very cloaths he wore at [Julia's] wedding' (ch. 92). Finally, there is the repetitive

129

pattern created by Godfrey's military promotions: in chapter 33 Trunnion discovers that he knew Godfrey's father, and he and Peregrine give Godfrey money which enables him to purchase an ensigncy; in chapter 73 Peregrine, again unknown to Godfrey, helps him to a lieutenancy, and in chapter 92 he gets him 'a captain's commission'. The sequence is completed when, in the fourth volume, Godfrey is again seeking promotion and discovers who his benefactor has been (ch. 109). At this point Pipes refers Godfrey to the first event in the sequence: 'That same money you received from the commodore, as an old debt, was all a sham, contrived by Pickle for your service. . . .' (In the first, second, and last instances the relevant event occurs in the sixth chapter from the end of the volume.)

I suggested that *Roderick Random* begins again, as it were, with the opening of the second volume. We have already seen Defoe (in *Robinson Crusoe*) and Fielding (in *Tom Jones* and *Amelia*) using the centres of their novels in a similar way, and, as I said earlier, I regard this pre-occupation with the centre as deriving (in part at least) from the rich tradition of mid-point symbolism in seventeenth-century poetry. Interestingly, though, in *Peregrine Pickle* Smollett's concern for the thematic possibilities of the centre is much more evident than in his first novel: it is here that we sense him, however tentatively, beginning to explore the iconographical implications of pattern. In fact, he places Trunnion's death exactly in the middle, that is, in the first chapter of vol. III (in Clifford's edition, on p. 394 out of a total of 781). The volume divisions are essential in directing us to the symmetry; for we are prepared to take on trust that, as we open the third volume, we have reached the half-way stage in a four-volume work. (Though in terms of chapter-totals, of course, chapter 79 is considerably beyond the mid-point; this is because of the imbalance created by Lady Vane's 'Memoirs', which occupy the greater part of vol. III.) The counting of pages, therefore, merely confirms what the external (i.e., volume) divisions have already made explicit. The death of Trunnion is, of course, crucial to Peregrine's career and moral development. Significantly, then, Smollett underlines the event and its centrality with the traditional image of elevation which is here invoked to affirm Peregrine's pride: 'The possession of such a fortune, of which he was absolute master, did not at all contribute to the humiliation of his spirit, but inspired him with new ideas of grandeur and magnificence, and elevated his hope to the highest pinnacle of expectation.'[11]

Moreover, vols I, II, and IV themselves possess symbolic centres. Of the first volume's thirty-eight chapters, the first nineteen narrate (among other matters) Peregrine's schoolboy pranks and practical jokes. His Winchester rebellion fails in chapter 20, and at this point 'he plunged into a profound reverie that lasted several weeks, during which he shook off his boyish connections, and fixed his view upon objects which he thought more worthy of his attention.' He is, Smollett tells us, 'in the utmost hazard of turning out a most egregious coxcomb', and there are hints of unstable equilibrium and potential fall: 'While his character thus wavered between the ridicule of some, and the regard of others, an accident happened, which, by contracting his view to one object, detached him from those vain pursuits that would in time have plunged him into an abyss of folly and contempt.' This 'accident' is his meeting with Emilia; so that the second half of vol. I is concerned with Peregrine and Emilia, the transition coming in the centre with Peregrine's character change and the appearance of Emilia. An element of chiastic patterning reinforces the symmetry:

17   Trunnion (sends Peregrine away from garrison to Winchester)
   18
      19   Insurrection (leaves school)
         20   Failure of insurrection; Emilia
      21   Elopes from school (because of Emilia)
   22
23   Trunnion (summons Peregrine to garrison)

Like Sophia in *Tom Jones*, Emilia represents that virtue to which Peregrine is aspiring as he journeys through the novel. He is especially forgetful of her (and hence of her symbolic significance) during his travels in vol. II, and returns from France prepared to violate her. His attempt to do so, which occurs in chapters 80 to 84, is Smollett's profoundest comment on his hero's moral decadence; and, it is essential to note, the episode has been carefully prepared for by the pattern of sexual encounters in the second volume. First of all frustrated in his attempts on Mrs Hornbeck (chaps 40ff.), Peregrine meets up with her again and finally enjoys her 'without restraint' (ch. 64). But this successful amatory adventure frames an unsuccessful one with an unknown girl whom Peregrine dubs his 'Amanda'. The Amanda episode resolves itself into a series of frustrations at the very moment of consummation, the last frustration being the most important for the comment it elicits from Amanda: 'she hoped last night's adventure would be a salutary warning to both their souls; for she was persuaded, that her virtue was protected by the intervention of heaven; that whatever impression it might have made upon him, she was enabled by it to adhere to that duty from which her passion had begun to swerve . . .' (ch. 62).

In other words, 'the intervention' is to be read as a Providential warning to Peregrine, which he fails to heed.[12] And its function in this respect is reinforced structurally in a way that should by now come as no surprise: for Amanda occupies the centre of the second volume and is thus implicitly contrasted with Emilia, who, as we have seen, is introduced in the centre of vol. I (the central chapters of vol. II are 58 and 59, twentieth and twenty-first out of a total of forty). The whole episode is, in addition, symmetrical in itself: Peregrine meets Amanda in a coach (ch. 56) and parts from her in a coach (62); in the central chapter of the group and of the volume Peregrine arranges a coach accident so that he might seduce her at an inn:

```
56    A and P meet in coach
   57    A and P interrupted by Jolter and Jew
      58    A and P interrupted by Pallet
         59    Coach accident
      60    A and P interrupted by Pallet
   61    A and P interrupted by Jolter and Pallet
62    A and P part in coach
```

Two other symmetries in this volume are worth noting. First, in the seventh chapter (45) Peregrine receives a letter from Godfrey and fails 'to honour the correspondence which he himself had sollicited' and also begins 'to conceive hopes of [Emilia] altogether unworthy of his own character and her deserts'; in chapter 71 (eighth from the end) Peregrine, now in England, 'remembred, with shame, that he had neglected the correspondence with her brother, which he himself had sollicited', and we are told that 'Tho' he was deeply enamoured of miss Gauntlet, he was far from proposing her heart as the ultimate aim of his gallantry. . . .' Second, Peregrine dismisses Pipes in chapter 56 (just before the Amanda affair begins); and in chapter 64—shortly after its conclusion—Pipes reappears.

As I have said, the Amanda episode, far from being a warning to Peregrine, seems rather to act as an incitement. He returns to England intent on seducing Emilia, and, significantly, his attempt on her contains several echoes of the earlier attempts on Amanda. Thus, the failure of his attempted seductions leads to a fit of rage and madness ('he raved like a Bedlamite, and acted a thousand extravagancies' (ch. 82)) which recalls the 'distraction', 'delirious expressions', 'agitation', and 'extasy of madness' that are the result of Amanda's refusal to see him any more (ch. 62); he chases unsuccessfully after Emilia (ch. 84) as he does after Amanda (ch. 66); and, as if to confirm the parallel, Emilia has already been referred to as 'his Amanda' at the beginning of chapter 84. It takes 'a dangerous fever'—the consequence of his passion—to bring 'him to a serious consideration of his conduct' (chaps 84, 85). But again, Smollett's attention to structural detail ensures that the point is made more subtly. For in chapter 85 Peregrine returns to the garrison—always associated with integrity and right thinking in the novel—not only to assist in Hatchway's courtship of Mrs Trunnion but also 'to give orders for erecting a plain marble monument to the memory of his uncle' (the chapter begins with Peregrine writing a letter to Mrs Gauntlet expressing his sense of shame at having abused Emilia). Now immediately before Peregrine's attempt on Emilia, the dying Trunnion had warned his nephew, 'if you run her on board in an unlawful way, I leave my curse upon you . . .' (ch. 79); and since the actual seduction attempt on Emilia occurs in the central chapter (82) of the group of five devoted to Peregrine's scheme against her (80 to 84), we get the following symmetry: garrison / two chapters // attempt on Emilia // two chapters / garrison. Peregrine's involvement in the erection of the commodore's tombstone thus functions as a tacit, symbolic, reminder of his abuse of Emilia and of his uncle's trust, his abandonment of Trunnion's values.

The mid-point of vol. IV has even more obviously iconographical implications than those in the first two volumes. Here, in chapter 104 (eleventh out of twenty-one), we see Peregrine disappointed in his expectations of preferment from Sir Steady Steerwell, and his resultant despair. Just as, at the mid-point of the novel as a whole, Peregrine was 'elevated' in pride and fortune, so now, with that fortune squandered, he has reached his nadir: he has undergone a 'reverse of fortune' and 'such a gush of affliction would sometimes rush upon his thought, as overwhelmed all the ideas of his hope, and sunk him to the very bottom of despondence' (ch. 104)—the inversion of the traditional central image of elevation again. And at the end of the chapter the 'lady of quality' calls upon him to redirect his attentions to Emilia ('it is now high time for you to contract that unbounded spirit of gallantry, which you have indulged so long, into a sincere attachment for the fair Emilia . . .'), who thus occupies the centre of this last volume as of the first. Moreover, chapter 104 is framed in such a way as to affirm unequivocally its median position. The preceding chapter concludes with a squabble between the fly-fancier and mathematician whom Peregrine has encountered at the virtuoso's public breakfast—a squabble that is announced with a comic balance-image: 'the engineer proceeded to the illustration of his mechanicks, tilting up his hand like a ballance, thrusting it forward by way of lever, embracing the naturalist's nose like a wedge betwixt two of his fingers. . . .' The function of this as a numerological pointer is reinforced by a complementary passage in chapter 105, where Peregrine is imprisoned in the Fleet and 'in this microcosm' discovers a concern with justice that puts the greater world to shame: 'Justice is here impartially administered, by a court of equity, consisting of a select number of the most respectable inhabitants, who punish all offenders with equal judgment and resolution, after they have been fairly convicted of the crimes laid to their charge.'

And in between we have the blatant injustice of the minister Sir Steady Steerwell, whose name, which graces the heading of the 104th chapter, parodies that ideal of just government which it so manifestly expresses.[13] Deflated on the one side by the *Dunciad* world of the college of authors (itself a transparent comment on hierarchy and preferment in the political sphere) and of the virtuosi, Sir Steady is shamed on the other by the just world of the Fleet and—the irony is a manifestly numerological one—by the 'just' division of the volume itself into two equal halves with Sir Steady maintaining the mean.[14]

There can be no doubt, it seems to me, that these patterns are deliberate on Smollett's part. And their effectiveness is both a symptom and a result of *Peregrine Pickle*'s moral and thematic clarity. In *Roderick Random* Narcissa had been introduced too late to act convincingly as a moral cynosure; but, as Rufus Putney showed long ago,[15] in Smollett's second novel the Emilia-Peregrine relationship is crucial: we measure Peregrine's growth in terms of his attitudes to Emilia, who is thus given the central positions of sovereignty. *Peregrine Pickle* quite literally revolves round her.

In addition to these exact symmetries, as I have already suggested, *Peregrine Pickle* reveals the less significant repetitions and episode-parallelisms that we are familiar with from the novels discussed in earlier chapters, and there is no need to cite further examples. But before going on to consider how the revisions for the second edition affected the symmetries outlined above, a word or two should be said about the long interpolated narratives, 'The Memoirs of a Lady of Quality' (ch. 88), and the history of MacKercher and the Annesley case (ch. 106). It is evident from the facts that, although it is possible to detect links between the 'Memoirs' and the story of Peregrine, they were included in the novel for extra-literary reasons. It would be a mistake, therefore, to attempt to isolate every possible parallel; and the Annesley case has only slightly more relevance: together with Peregrine's tale at the end of chapter 106 of a child deprived of an estate which is subsequently restored to him, it obviously anticipates the restoration to Peregrine of his family estate at the end of the novel.[16] Clearly, Smollett's concern for a tighter, symbolic, structure in his second novel did not extend to the interpolated tale, which he had handled with more sensitivity in *Roderick Random*.

The revisions for the 1758 text have been analysed in detail by Howard S. Buck.[17] In effect, they amount to the omission of various personal attacks (against Fielding and Garrick, etc.) and of episodes regarded by Smollett in retrospect as being in bad taste—the homosexual episode in chapter 49 and Pallet's urinating at the masquerade, the business between Peregrine and the nun in chapter 66, and so on. These changes considerably reduced the length of the novel and entailed the renumbering of chapters, the total now being 106 instead of 114. Inevitably, some of the symmetries that I have noticed in connection with the first edition disappear: looked at from one point of view, they had been the novel's scaffolding which could now be dismantled without incurring structural collapse. Thus, Peregrine's Winchester rebellion is omitted, and with it the chiasmus at the centre of vol. I; but Smollett ensures that Emilia still occupies the volume's mid-point (she is introduced in the seventeenth chapter of a total of thirty-four). And although certain alterations to vol. II mean that the Amanda episode is no longer exactly central in that volume (it is narrated in chapters 52 to 58; chapters 53 and 54 mark the middle of the revised total of thirty-eight), its slight shift in position is a trifling matter and in no way affects its central 'feel'. Moreover, the position of Trunnion's death is unaffected at the beginning of vol. III; and since the chapter-total for the final volume stays at twenty-one, its symmetries, too, remain intact.

III *Ferdinand Count Fathom*

Ferdinand Count Fathom (1753) manifests a stark simplicity of structure which is a fitting complement to the novel's moral schematism as announced in the Dedication.[18] Smollett here exploits the tradition of mid-point symbolism in which, as we have seen, he had shown increasing interest, with full awareness of its iconographical implications (its association with sovereignty, the midday sun, elevation, and the triumph), and once again utilizes the volume-divisions to direct attention to the novel's symmetries. In addition, the Dedication contains an explicit authorial statement to the effect that this novel—and presumably the others—was conceived of in visual and spatial terms by defining 'A Novel [as] a large diffused picture, comprehending the characters of life, disposed in different groupes, and exhibited in various attitudes, for the purposes of an uniform plan, and general occurrence, to which every individual figure is subservient. . . .'

The novel, like poetry, is *ut pictura*. And as we read *Ferdinand Count Fathom*, taking note of the symbolism of the centre, it is worth recalling Hogarth's preoccupation with the mid-point in the *Election* (1755–58), which I have discussed above (ch. iv): a glance at the allusive structures which Hogarth incorporated in even his popular prints leaves one in little doubt as to the contemporary reader's ability to detect and interpret spatial schemes of considerable complexity. In the mid-eighteenth century literature and painting were still very much sister arts.

Fathom appeared in two volumes, vol. I containing the first thirty-five chapters and vol. II containing chapters 36 to 67 (i.e., thirty-two chapters). The first volume traces Fathom's rise in fortune and reputation, and the climax occurs in chapter 35 with the heading's explicit allusions to sovereignty and elevation: '*He repairs to Bristol spring, where he reigns Paramount during the whole season.*' The opening paragraph of this chapter, by again hinting at centrality ('Fathom, as usual, formed the nucleus or kernel of the beau monde'), confirms that he has built on the success that was his in chapter 32 where, we are told (presumably as an early directive to the iconography of the centre), 'he . . . shone in the zenith of admiration.'

Fathom arrives at Bristol claiming knowledge of medicine, and this is the beginning of his downfall.[19] For as vol. II opens (ch. 36) he becomes involved with one of his patients, Mrs Trapwell, 'the young wife of an old citizen of London'. He is betrayed by her, prosecuted, and imprisoned: 'Thus, he saw himself, in the course of a few hours, deprived of his reputation, rank, liberty and friends; and his fortune reduced from two thousand pounds, to something less than two hundred, fifty of which he had carried to goal in his pocket.' And the second half of the novel abounds in references to Fathom's decline, speaking of it specifically in terms of 'eclipse': the heading to chapter 54 announces '*His eclipse, and gradual declination*', and in chapter 63 Madame Clement has 'traced him in all the course of his fortune, from his first appearance in the medical sphere to his total eclipse'.

There is, incidentally, an important ironic comment on this imagery in chapter 40, where the just imprisonment of Fathom is contrasted by Smollett with the unjust treatment of the historical figure of Theodore, King of Corsica, whom Fathom meets in gaol. The heading reads: '*He contemplates majesty and its satellites in eclipse*'; so that for once in the novel the solar imagery is used seriously with the full significance that it had long enjoyed in the iconography of kingship.[20] And Smollett's belief in Theodore's rightful sovereignty emerges clearly from the following passage: he 'actually possessed the throne of sovereignty by the best of all titles, namely, the unanimous election of the people over whom he reigned. . . .' Theodore plays a minimal part in the plot. Nevertheless, this piece of political propaganda functions thematically to illustrate by contrast the villainy of Fathom, who is Theodore's antithesis, and who, as we have seen, '*reigns Paramount*' over the beau monde at the structural centre. The contrast is expressed emblematically at the beginning of chapter 40 when Theodore greets Fathom 'with a most princely demeanour' and 'seat[s] him on his right hand, in token of particular regard'.

There can be no doubt, then, that Smollett exploited the numerological device of mid-point symbolism in *Fathom* to illustrate the rise and fall of the count's fortunes, since the break—from good to bad fortune—comes unequivocally in the centre as marked by the volume divisions. Moreover, the individual volumes are themselves divided exactly into two. In vol. I a change of scene and subject-matter is announced in the heading to chapter 18 (central out of a total of thirty-five): '*Our hero departs from Vienna, and quits the domain of Venus for the rough field of Mars*'; and the central chapters of the second volume, 51 and 52 (sixteenth and seventeenth out of a total of thirty-two), echo his moment of triumph at the middle of the novel as a whole. For he is again a physician, and '*Triumphs over a medical rival*' (heading to chapter 51); but in chapter 52 he moves to London, becomes well known and (ch. 53) seduces one of his patients, a clergyman's wife, and is prosecuted by her husband (as he was prosecuted by Trapwell at the beginning of the volume). Chapter 50 has already reminded us that his second appearance as a physician, this time not as a nobleman who knows about medicine but as a man who 'professed himself one of the faculty', is an indication of 'the decline of his fortune'. And it is now, once the mid-point of the second volume, with its echoes of his earlier triumph, is past, that the images of decline and overthrow increase apace. Chapter 54—as we have seen—proclaims '*His eclipse, and gradual declination*' and tells us that 'our hero was exactly in the situation of a horseman, who, in riding at full speed for the plate, is thrown from the saddle in the middle of the race. . . .' He has a coach accident ('Then was his chariot overturned with a hideous crash . . .'), and it is finally revealed that he has, all the time, been enlisted under the banner of capricious Fortune: 'Fathom, finding himself descending the hill of fortune, with an acquired gravitation, strove to catch at every twig, in order to stop or retard his descent.'[21] It is impossible to read these substantive references to physical falls and to being 'thrown . . . in the middle of the race' without relating them to the novel's physical structure—its observance of mid-point symbolism—especially when we notice that the sentence immediately succeeding the one just quoted ('the hill of fortune', etc.) reminds us of Fathom's former glory in terms that should by now be familiar: 'He now regretted the opportunities he had neglected, of marrying one of several women of moderate fortune, who had made advances to him, in the zenith of his reputation. . . .'

In chapter 56 he suffers a further 'torrent of misfortunes' which induces him for the first time to recognize his guilt and to invoke Providence: 'Shall the author of these crimes pass with impunity? Shall he hope to prosper in the midst of such enormous guilt? It were an imputation upon providence to suppose it—Ah, no! I begin to feel myself overtaken by the eternal justice of heaven! I totter on the edge of wretchedness and woe, without one friendly hand to save me from the terrible abyss.' And Fathom's fall is complemented, as we might expect, by an increasing number of allusions to Providence, especially in connection with the reappearance of Monimia: 'Mysterious powers of providence! this is no phantome!', etc. (ch. 63).[22] However, before we can see how the concepts of Fortune and Providence (the former relating to Fathom, the latter to Renaldo and Monimia) are inter-related in the novel, it is necessary to look at its structure even more closely.

In the foregoing analysis I have regarded the division between volumes I and II as marking the novel's mid-point which, to all intents and purposes, it does. But in fact the arithmetically central chapter is the thirty-fourth (out of a total of sixty-seven), and this, significantly, contains yet another instance of Fathom's iniquity, his seduction of Celinda, whom he leaves an alcoholic. This means, then, that Fathom is only *apparently* elevated at the centre, because his triumph at Bristol occurs at the centre as marked by the division between the two volumes; and that the exact—arithmetical—centre is dedicated to stripping away appearances and conveying, to quote the chapter heading, '*a true idea of his gratitude and honour*'. And with this structural subtlety established, further symmetries are revealed. The Celinda episode harks immediately back to Fathom's treatment of Elinor, whom he has left deranged in the madhouse in chapter 31; and it also has affinities with Don Diego's narrative in chapter 26: just as Fathom destroys Celinda and Elinor, so does Diego think he has killed his wife and daughter. Furthermore, it functions proleptically by anticipating Fathom's most heinous piece of villainy, the alienation of Monimia from Renaldo and his attempted seduction of her, which leads to her illness and apparent death.

If *Fathom*'s symmetries are now reassessed by taking the arithmetical centre (ch. 34) as the starting point, it emerges that they are designed to bring Renaldo and Monimia, the novel's symbols of virtue, into prominence, and, simultaneously, to accentuate the count's vices. For Don Diego's story of his daughter Serafina and her lover Orlando is narrated to Fathom in chapter 26. In chapter 42 Renaldo arrives at the gaol where Fathom is imprisoned, arranges his release, and tells him that

> he was captivated by the irresistible charms of a young lady on whose heart he had the good fortune to make a tender impression: that their mutual love had subjected both to many dangers and difficulties, during which they suffered a cruel separation; after the torments of which, he had happily found her in England, where she now lived entirely cut off from her native country and connexions, and destitute of every other resource but his honour, love, and protection. . . .

She is introduced in the next chapter with a clear hint that her real identity will be announced later: 'It was not without reason he had expatiated upon the personal attractions of this young lady, whom (for the present) we shall call Monimia. . . .' And in chapter 64 we discover, if we haven't guessed already, that Monimia is Serafina; so that Diego's story in chapter 26 and Renaldo's brief *résumé* in chapter

42 are about the same person. I reproduce in diagrammatic form the pattern thus created:

1–25	26	27–33	34	35–41	42	43–67
25 chapters	Don Diego, Serafina	7 chapters	Celinda	7 chapters	Renaldo, Monimia	25 chapters

There are, finally, additional symmetries which link the beginning and end of the novel. Chapter 57 is recapitulatory, narrating Renaldo's journey to Vienna and his preparations there for regaining his rightful inheritance from his stepfather, Count Trebasi. Renaldo travels to Vienna in company with a Major Farrel, who had served under the old Count Melvile and who 'owed his promotion' to him. Farrel is a symbol of gratitude as Fathom, who again owes everything to the old count, is an arch-symbol of ingratitude. This journey to Vienna—in chapter 57—occurs in the eleventh chapter from the end of the novel; and it was in chapter 10 that Renaldo had made his first journey to that city, accompanied by Fathom. In chapter 59 Renaldo's sister, Mlle de Melvile, is released from the Viennese convent in which she had been confined by Trebasi, and reveals Fathom's treachery, including his alliance with Teresa, which had been dedicated to systematic theft. Smollett writes: 'She then explained their combination in all the particulars, as we have already recounted them in their proper place. . . .' If we turn to the beginning of the novel, we find that the thefts occurred in chapters 9 and 10; and chapter 59 is the ninth from the end. It will be recalled that Fathom had devised the plan for stealing from Renaldo's sister because he had been unsuccessful in his attempts to possess her fortune by marrying her (chaps 6 to 8). Once again there is a structural relationship with, and moral contrast to, Major Farrel, who explains openly to Renaldo in chapter 60 that he has contracted some debts, that he is attracted to Mlle de Melvile, and that he would like to marry her, in part for her fortune. Renaldo agrees and the marriage takes place. The major's frankness contrasts with Fathom's deception; and just as Fathom's last attempt on Mlle de Melvile had occurred in chapter 8, so is chapter 60 the eighth chapter from the end of the novel.

Fathom, then, possesses an elaborate symmetrical structure, which clearly fulfils a symbolic function by exalting the forces of good (Renaldo, Monimia, Farrel, etc.) over Fathom, the embodiment of evil. We do Smollett and the 'uniform plan' of his work a gross injustice if we fail to detect the patterns outlined above and to note how Fathom's rise and fall, with its apparent observance of the mid-point as marked out by the volume divisions, is undercut by the numerically exact symmetries revolving round the story of Celinda in chapter 34. Fathom's story, as Smollett indicates, is that of a child of Fortune; but Monimia's and Renaldo's is just as explicitly Providential. The asymmetry of the one is overridden by the precise balance of the other to create, for the first time in Smollett's fiction, a compelling Providential paradigm.

NOTES

1 *Rogue's Progress: Studies in the Picaresque Novel* (Cambridge, Mass., 1964), pp. 62–3.

2 Smollett does, of course, mention his indebtedness to *Don Quixote* and *Gil Blas* in the Preface to *Roderick Random*, though, so far as I can see, the debt is not in any significant sense a formal one. Paul-Gabriel Boucé gives a detailed discussion of the influence of these works on Smollett's novels in *Les Romans de Smollett: Étude Critique* (Publications de la Sorbonne; Littératures, I (Paris, 1971)), Pt. II, ch. 1.

3 E.g., the bedroom mix-ups in ch. 11; the business over Roderick's diary (which is written in Greek characters) in ch. 30; and the hospitality given to the destitute Roderick by Mrs Sagely in ch. 38. Compare *Joseph Andrews*, IV. 14; II. 11 (where Adams's Æschylus is mistaken for 'a Book written . . . in Ciphers'; a passage added in the second edn), and I. 12 respectively. Tuvia Bloch, 'Smollett's Quest for Form', *MP*, 65 (1967–8), 103–13, incidentally, argues for Fielding's formal influence on Smollett. She concentrates mainly on *Ferdinand Count Fathom* and *Launcelot Greaves*, however, and her discussion is limited largely to plot patterns and Smollett's attempts to imitate Fielding's detached, ironic, narrator. Her concept of form does not include the kind of structural parallelisms that I am concerned with.

4 This is the case with the text printed in *The Novelist's Magazine*, II (1780). In quoting from the novel I have used the first edn, since Smollett's subsequent revisions had no effect on its structure as outlined in this section. For a collation of textual variants, see O. M. Brack, Jr, and James B. Davis, 'Smollett's Revisions of *Roderick Random*', *Papers of the Bibliographical Society of America*, 64 (1970), 295–311.

5 An important theme here as in *Colonel Jack*, though not so consistently sustained. As early as ch. 20 Roderick has rejected Strap as an unworthy companion and has told us 'I now began to look upon myself as a gentleman in reality.'

6 M. A. Goldberg, *Smollett and the Scottish School* (Albuquerque, New Mexico, 1959), pp. 39–42, detects five main catastrophes or reversals in *Roderick Random* of which this is the central one, though he fails to note the significance of its position at the novel's approximate structural centre. Also worth mentioning is P.-G. Boucé's analysis of the novel in terms of a capital 'W', with the three top points representing Roderick's birth, encounter with Narcissa at Bath, and marriage, and the two bottom points his shipwreck and fight with Crampley, and his

imprisonment in the Marshalsea: see his *Les Romans de Smollett*, pp. 169 and 193–4. Boucé makes no comment on its arithmetical structure, however.

7 Boucé also notices the parallel, ibid., p. 159.

8 Where her maternal relationship with Roderick is again insisted on: in ch. 65 Roderick calls her 'Dear mother' and she 'received me with a truly maternal affection'; in ch. 67 her 'maternal affection' is divided between Roderick and Narcissa.

9 In ch. 41 (where Mrs Sagely and Bowling mention Providence); ch. 43 ('I could not comprehend the justice of that providence, which after having exposed me to so much wretchedness and danger, left me a prey to famine at last in a foreign country. . .'); ch. 44 ('providence or destiny acted miracles in their behalf'); ch. 66 (Roderick's father cries out 'Mysterious Providence!', and refers to 'this amazing stroke of providence'); and ch. 67 (Narcissa 'observed that this great and unexpected stroke of fate seemed to have been brought about by the immediate direction of providence').

10 This has been prepared from a copy of the 4-vol. first edn, though for ease of reference all quotations are from James L. Clifford's OEN edn (1964), which reprints the 1751 text but without indicating the volume divisions.

11 Crabtree, who has made his appearance at the end of the preceding volume, is clearly a replacement for the commodore: Trunnion presides over the more carefree first half of the novel, the misanthrope over the darker second half.

12 Though he has already been 'almost persuaded, that so many unaccountable disappointments must have proceeded from some supernatural cause, of which the idiot Pallet was no more than the involuntary instrument' (ch. 61).

13 The notion, in connection with self-government, recurs in ch. 112, with its reference to Peregrine's 'stock of experience that would steer him clear of all those quicksands among which he had been formerly wrecked'.

14 In view of the allusion to Fielding in ch. 105 ('I might here, in imitation of some celebrated writers, furnish out a page or two, with the reflections [Peregrine] made upon the instability of human affairs. . .'), the balance, etc., in vol. IV might, in part, be a parody of the mid-point symbolism in *Tom Jones*; though Smollett is clearly more interested in its serious, iconographic, function.

15 Rufus Putney, 'The Plan of *Peregrine Pickle*', PMLA, 60 (1945), 1051–65.

16 The 'Memoirs' are discussed in detail by Howard S. Buck, *A Study in Smollett, Chiefly 'Peregrine Pickle'* (New Haven, Conn., 1925), ch. 2, and, together with MacKercher, by Lewis M. Knapp in *Tobias Smollett: Doctor of Men and Manners* (Princeton, N.J., 1949), pp. 121ff. See also Clifford's Introd., pp. xxvi–xxvii, and Boucé, *Les Romans de Smollett*, pp. 188–90 and 192. On the 'Memoirs' Boucé follows Putney, 'The Plan of *Peregrine Pickle*', p. 1064, to the effect that they confirm Smollett's 'thesis that the life of the upper classes was often vicious and immoral'.

17 His *A Study in Smollett* contains a collation of the first and second edns.

18 'That the mind might not be fatigued, nor the imagination disgusted by a succession of vitious objects, I have endeavoured to refresh the attention with occasional incidents of a different nature; and raised up a virtuous character, in opposition to the adventurer, with a view to amuse the fancy, engage the affection, and form a striking contrast which might heighten the expression, and give a *Relief* to the moral of the whole.' Quotations are from the OEN edn,

ed. Damian Grant (1971), which reproduces the text of the first edn, 2 vols, 1753.

19 Boucé analyses the novel in similar fashion, noting that Fathom enjoys his 'apogee' in ch. 35, from which he then declines (op. cit., p. 210, and cf. p. 239).

20 For a detailed discussion, see Ernst H. Kantorowicz, 'Oriens Augusti—Lever du Roi', *Dumbarton Oaks Papers*, 17 (1963), 117–77.

21 Compare the antithetical image in the first half of the novel, where we are told that Fathom 'surveyed the neighbouring coast of England, with fond and longing eyes, like another Moses reconnoitring the land of Canaan from the top of mount Pisgah' (ch. 27): and cf. also ch. 19, where England is alluded to as 'the Canaan of all able adventurers'.

22 Cf. ch. 61 ('Sure Providence hath still something in reserve for this unfortunate wretch. . .'; this is Don Diego speaking of himself), and ch. 62, Renaldo on Fathom's treatment of Monimia: 'Sacred heaven! why did providence wink at the triumph of such consummate perfidy?'

vii   Smollett: *Humphry Clinker*

Smollett's next novel, *Sir Launcelot Greaves*, appeared serially in *The British Magazine* between January 1760 and December 1761. The adoption of this mode of publication is sufficient in itself to indicate that Smollett conceived this work in a piecemeal, sequential fashion rather than, as is certainly the case with *Fathom*, in spatial terms. Not surprisingly, therefore, the symmetries in *Greaves* are of a minor order.[1] It wasn't until *Humphry Clinker* that the structural promise of the earlier novels was finally fulfilled, and in a manner as meaningful, if not as complex, as Fielding's in *Tom Jones*; for the assured architectonics here are the subtle formal complement to and embodiment of Smollett's Augustan themes. As a necessary preliminary I discuss these themes in some detail, even though what I say covers critical ground that has been trodden in part before.[2]

I

In *Humphry Clinker* the journey is at once geographical and metaphorical. As the travellers proceed through England to Scotland and back to England, the three women are in search of (and finally obtain) husbands, and their search parallels Matthew Bramble's own quest for physical, psychological, and moral health. Even Jery, for the most part the disengaged observer, is a changed man by the end of the novel as, realizing his own limitations, he sets up the young George Dennison 'as a model for imitation'.[3] Or, to put the novel's thematic concerns in a slightly different way—one which stresses the mature Smollett's Augustanism, but without, I hope, exaggerating or distorting it—it is about propriety and decorum, both within the individual and in the world around him. These concerns are expressed through certain key images. For example, noise is early on identified with disorder when Jery quotes Matthew Bramble on his arrival in Bath (letter of 24 April):

I wonder . . . what sort of sonata we are to expect from this
overture, in which the devil, that presides over horrid sounds,
hath given us such variations of discord—The trampling of
porters, the creaking and crashing of trunks, the snarling of
curs, the scolding of women, the squeaking and squalling of
fiddles and hautboys out of tune, the bouncing of the Irish
baronet over-head, and the bursting, belching, and brattling
of the French horns in the passage (not to mention the
harmonious peal that still thunders from the Abbey steeple). . . .

The 'harmonious peal' of bells, Jery has told us in the same letter, 'was
for the honour of Mr. Bullock, an eminent cow-keeper of Totten-
ham'; and this, together with the insolence of the Creole colonel's
servants, announces the theme of social break-down and the disruption of established hierarchies that is so important in *Humphry Clinker*. A
couple of pages later, and having made allowances for 'premature old
age' having coloured his view of the town, Bramble repeats his charge
that Bath 'is become the very center of racket and dissipation': 'here
we have nothing but noise, tumult, and hurry' (23 April). He then
goes on to introduce the subject of architecture, treating of it in a
characteristically Augustan way. One cannot help being reminded, as
one reads such passages, of Pope's *Epistle to Burlington*.[4] For Smollett as
for the earlier Augustans, virtue, literature, and architecture correspond analogically; and architecture also ideally expresses cosmic,
Providential, order:

one sees new houses starting up in every out-let and every corner
of Bath; contrived without judgment, executed without solidity,
and stuck together, with so little regard to plan and propriety,
that the different lines of the new rows and buildings interfere
with, and intersect one another in every different angle of
conjunction. They look like the wreck of streets and squares
disjointed by an earthquake . . . ; or, as if some Gothic devil had
stuffed them altogether in a bag, and left them to stand higgledy
piggledy, just as chance directed. What sort of a monster Bath
will become in a few years, with those growing excrescences, may
be easily conceived. . . . (23 April)

The phrase 'just as chance directed' is the important one; and note
that Bramble gives general, if qualified, approval to the Circus and
projected Crescent ('These, however fantastical, are still designs that

denote some ingenuity and knowledge in the architect'). Smollett's point is that John Wood the elder's work at Bath upheld the tradition of Palladian baroque architecture;[5] and the contrast of architectural modes is in part the subject of another of Bramble's letters (Scarborough, 4 July), in which this time it is the turn of York Minster to be condemned at the expense of the Assembly Rooms, which had been designed by Richard, Earl of Burlington:[6]

> There is nothing of this Arabic architecture in the Assembly Room, which seems to me to have been built upon a design of Palladio, and might be converted into an elegant place of worship; but it is indifferently contrived for that sort of idolatry which is performed in it at present: the grandeur of the fane gives a diminutive effect to the little painted divinities that are adored in it, and the company, on a ball-night, must look like an assembly of fantastic fairies, revelling by moon-light among the columns of a Grecian temple.

This is a key paragraph for our understanding of the novel. It invokes clearly enough the ultimately Vitruvian ideal of decorum that we are familiar with from the country-house poem of the seventeenth century and of which the *Epistle to Burlington* is a late example, according to which the building should echo the proportions of the human frame and should also be proportioned to the social standing of its owner.[7] Bramble also seems to allude to *A Midsummer Night's Dream*, II. i. 141, where Titania refers to the fairies' 'moonlight revels', though I suspect that the allusion might well have come via *Paradise Lost*, I. 775ff., the description of the entrance of the fallen angels into 'the spacious hall' of the newly-built Pandaemonium:[8]

> So thick the airy crowd
> Swarmed and were straitened; till the signal given,
> Behold a wonder! they but now who seemed
> In bigness to surpass Earth's giant sons
> Now less than smallest dwarfs, in narrow room
> Throng numberless, like that pygmean race
> Beyond the Indian mount, or faerie elves,
> Whose midnight revels, by a forest side
> Or fountain some belated peasant sees,
> Or dreams he sees, while overhead the moon
> Sits arbitress. . . .

The angels are suddenly reduced in scale and significance. So, too, are Pope's Timon, who undergoes a similar metamorphosis to become 'A puny insect' (*Epistle to Burlington*, l. 108), and Bramble's 'painted divinities', who, ironically, are unable to live up to the building they temporarily inhabit. Burlington's Palladian Assembly Rooms of 1730 already belong to a past age and so can be used as a symbolic reminder of contemporary physical and moral degeneracy: the present has the buildings it deserves, as exemplified in the ever-expanding Bath and London.

When Bramble, in his letter of 23 April, describes Bath as 'a monster', he is preparing the way for his later description of London, where the metaphor is worked out in more detail: 'the capital is become an overgrown monster; which, like a dropsical head, will in time leave the body and extremities without nourishment and support' (29 May). He closes the letter by repeating it with a significant extension: 'But I must . . . explore the depths of this chaos; this mishapen and monstrous capital, without head or tail, members or proportion.'

It is evident, then, that the meaning of the novel involves the traditional equations: body; building; body politic. Bramble's sickness is reflected in (and in part induced by) the sickness of 'luxury and corruption' (ibid.) in the body politic, and both have their analogue in houses 'contrived without judgment'. On the one hand, intemperance, disorder, chaos; on the other, virtue, decorum, propriety. Read in this way *Humphry Clinker* takes its place alongside such contemporary works as Goldsmith's *Traveller* and *Deserted Village*, and Langhorne's *Country Justice*, and this in itself should serve to indicate to the reader that Bramble's comments are not merely the subjective, embittered outpourings of an invalid who can define the external world only in terms of his illness. Tinged as they are with that melancholy so characteristic of late Augustan literature, there is every reason to believe that the nostalgia and the indignation are Smollett's as well as Bramble's.[9] With Bramble's words compare, for example, the following passage:[10]

It shou'd seem to me, from my (trivial) observations, that noblemen, and gentlemen have almost abandon'd the country. . . . London markets and London prices govern the whole kingdom; and as that increasing Wen, the metropolis, must be fed the body will gradually decay: all the canals, all the roads must be forced to supply it; and when they have brought all they can, and it shou'd by oversize, or particular seasons, want more—why then there will come a distress, a famine; and an insurrection. . . .

And if we may judge from the contrast between the Baynard and Dennison estates at the end of the novel, Smollett, like Byng and others, saw the answer to such problems in a renewed sense of responsibility among aristocrats and landowners. Only thus, they thought, could the dangerous imbalance caused by the new wealth and the influx of people into London be corrected and a harmonious equilibrium be restored.

Bramble even sees symptoms of luxury and the disruption of the social hierarchy in the pleasure gardens of Vauxhall and Ranelagh. To Lydia (as earlier to Fielding's Mrs Ellison),[11] they are paradisal; to Bramble, on the other hand, Vauxhall appears 'a composition of baubles, overcharged with paltry ornaments, ill conceived, and poorly executed; without any unity of design, or propriety of disposition' (29 May). Again, the key-note of breach of decorum is sounded, and even Lydia's praise is itself calculatedly double-edged: at Vauxhall she hears a celebrated female singer 'whose voice was so loud and so shrill, that it made my head ake through excess of pleasure' (31 May).

The excesses symbolized by the city and the artificial paradises of the pleasure gardens are counterbalanced by references to the felicity of the rural life. Lydia, for instance, in the letter just quoted, writes: 'I could gladly give up all these tumultuous pleasures, for country solitude, and a happy retreat with those we love. . . .' And yet *Humphry Clinker* does not resolve itself into what was obviously for Smollett the too easy traditional polarity of town versus country. For we have at this point to consider the role of Scotland, and particularly Edinburgh, in the scheme of the novel. Bath and London, as we have seen, express an extreme of disorder, and it is here that Bramble suffers his greatest ill health. But significantly, once in Edinburgh Bramble can comment: 'I now begin to feel the good effects of exercise—I eat like a farmer, sleep from mid-night till eight in the morning without interruption, and enjoy a constant tide of spirits, equally distant from inanition and excess . . .' (18 July): a passage which, incidentally, introduces the concept of the mean, the structural implications of which I examine later. The improvement in Bramble's health coincides with his arrival in Edinburgh, I suggest, because, while that city is far from representing an ideal (as the habit of voiding full chamber pots out of windows onto the streets below testifies), it is used by Smollett as an antithesis to

London and Bath to express a controlled disorder which is a comment on, and corrective to, their chaotic licence. The important episode here is the Saturnalian feast given by the cawdies for their masters and described by Jery in his letter of 8 August:

> In a large hall the cloth was laid on a long range of tables joined together, and here the company seated themselves, to the number of about fourscore, lords, and lairds, and other gentlemen, courtezans and cawdies mingled together, as the slaves and their masters were in the time of the Saturnalia in ancient Rome. . . . All [the] toasts being received with loud bursts of applause, Mr. Fraser called for pint glasses, and filled his own to the brim: then standing up, and all his brethren following his example, 'Ma lords and gentlemen (cried he), here is a cup of thanks for the great and undeserved honour you have done your poor errand-boys this day.'—So saying, he and they drank off their glasses in a trice, and, quitting their seats, took their station each behind one of the other guests;—exclaiming, 'Noo we're your honours' cawdies again.'

But Edinburgh marks only the beginning of the Scottish part of the company's tour, a tour in which they will subsequently encounter not only the progressivism of Glasgow ('a perfect bee-hive in point of industry'; Bramble, 28 August) but also the primitivism[12] of Dougal Campbell's house in the Western Highlands (Jery's letter of 3 September), where the hospitality received is of an almost Odysseyan simplicity: 'Our landlord's housekeeping is equally rough and hospitable, and savours much of the simplicity of ancient times. . . .' It is important to note, though, that Campbell himself regards his way of life as falling short of his ideal (for example, the forces of tradition work against him when he tries to do away with the household piper), and that Scottish primitivism has its dispiriting obverse side, as Bramble again reports in his letter of 28 August by commenting on the 'barren and moorish' ground of 'these north-western parts', and remarking on the 'meagre . . . looks' of the peasants. Once more the fault lies in part with the landowners: 'Agriculture cannot be expected to flourish where the farms are small, the leases short, and the husbandman begins upon a rack rent, without a sufficient stock to answer the purposes of improvement.' In short, Scotland itself, as Smollett presents it for the purposes of his argument, is a land of contrasting extremes, certainly no more than an ideal *in posse*.[13] The ideal *in esse*, combining industry and progress with primitive felicity, is found in Dennison's estate as highlighted by the barren estate belonging to Baynard. In them the larger objects of attack in the novel and the means of rectification are epitomized. Smollett's answer is offered in terms that are at once symbolic and strictly realistic, rather after the manner of Pope's life at Twickenham.[14] And it is here that the influence of the *Epistle to Burlington*, the ideals of which were never far from Smollett's mind as he penned *Humphry Clinker*, seems to come to the fore.

Of Baynard's estate Bramble tells us that 'As for the garden, which was well stocked with the best fruit which England could produce, there is not now the least vestige remaining of trees, walls, or hedges—Nothing appears but a naked circus of loose sand, with a dry bason and a leaden triton in the middle' (30 September). Mrs Baynard has appropriated a farm of 200 acres for walks and shrubberies; and the house, 'this *temple of cold reception*', corresponds to its grounds, since the chill without (the replanning of the grounds has exposed 'the east end . . . to the surly blasts that come from that quarter' (26 October)) is answered by the chill within: 'We dined in a large old Gothic parlour, which was formerly the hall. It was now paved with marble, and, notwithstanding the fire, which had been kindled about an hour, struck me with such a chill sensation, that when I entered it the teeth chattered in my jaws . . .' (30 September). Similarly, Pope, in the *Epistle to Burlington* (ll. 75–6, 111–12), condemns those whose rage for improvement leads them to open up large vistas only to find that they have exposed the house to a biting wind. And Timon's dining hall, too, is of marble, 'a Temple, and a Hecatomb' (156) where one sits 'In plenty starving, tantaliz'd in state' (163).

Baynard's wife, who 'had not taste enough to relish any rational enjoyment' and whose 'ruling passion was vanity' (30 September), is a specific instance exemplifying the spread and effects of emulative luxury in the kingdom at large. The antithesis and ideal is the fruitful estate created by Dennison and his wife from the neglected land and house inherited by them, and now described by Bramble as having 'attained to that pitch of rural felicity, at which I have been aspiring these twenty years in vain' (8 October). Here Bramble decides to stay, for a while at least, at the end of the novel, spending part of his time restoring Baynard's estate on the Dennison model, which, it is important to note, is an ideal not only for the landowner but also for the country as a whole. For Smollett, then, as for the earlier Augustans (and the overtones of the tradition of the country-house poem are also very strong here), true virtue is symbolized in the right management of the estate and garden, and—this is the burden of many of Bramble's remarks in the novel—in the right kind of architecture.

II

By concentrating almost exclusively on the significance of architecture, however, I have ignored much of the novel's thematic complexity and richness. And although it is not my intention to offer a full-scale interpretation, some of this complexity must be suggested before the way is clear for structural analysis. Sheridan Baker, for instance, has drawn attention to the scatological imagery and the related notion of the moral and physical purging and cleansing power of water. As he notes, 'even the dog is constipated.'[15] And the point is, surely, that Chowder's constipation, together with his bad temper, forges a symbolic link between him and the constipated and peevish Bramble; a link that is confirmed in Win's letter of 26 April when we learn that Chowder's disorders are increasing at Bath just as Bramble's are, and that 'The doctors think he is threatened with a dropsy—Parson Marrofat, who has got the same disorder, finds great benefit from the waters; but Chowder seems to like them no better than the squire. . . .' In addition, and more conventionally for a period in which the lady's lap-dog was often seen as a lover-substitute, Chowder is a projection of his mistress's frustrations, as Lydia hints in her letter of 6 May: 'what a pity it is, that a woman of her years and discretion, should place her affection upon such an ugly, ill-conditioned cur, that snarls and snaps at every body.' With his relation to Bramble and Tabitha thus established, it is important to notice when he disappears from the action of the novel. The crucial moment is recounted in Jery's letter of 24 May immediately after the appearance of Humphry on the scene. Humphry is waiting at dinner and accidentally treads on Chowder. Tabitha flies to the dog, picks him up, and, referring to Humphry, offers her brother the following ultimatum: 'am I to be affronted by every mangy hound that you pick up in the highway? I insist upon your sending this rascallion about his business immediately . . . you shall part with that rascal or me, upon the spot, without farther loss of time; and the world shall see whether you have more regard for your own flesh and blood, or for a beggarly foundling, taken from the dunghill——'.

The irony is splendid: Tabitha and her dog over against the 'mangy hound' Humphry—at least as much Bramble's 'flesh and blood', it turns out, as Tabitha herself. And Bramble offers his sister his own ultimatum: 'Either discard your four-footed favourite, or give me leave to bid you eternally adieu—For I am determined, that he and I shall live no longer under the same roof. . . .' The result is a promise to get rid of Chowder and a softening of Tabitha's temper ('My aunt seems to be much mended by the hint she received from her brother'); so that the disappearance of Chowder heralds the beginning of Tabitha's journey to fulfilment that is to culminate in her marriage to Lismahago, and coincides exactly with Bramble's formal adoption of Humphry Clinker as footman, which marks the first stage of his own journey to self-knowledge.

Humphry soon reveals himself as a methodist, and, significantly, as the centre of the novel's theme of moral reformation. Anti-methodist as the rational Bramble is, even he cannot help being affected by some of his footman's preaching. Thus, after seeing Humphry 'exalted upon a stool, . . . in the act of holding forth to' various servants at St James's, he asks him what he was saying to them, and Humphry replies: 'I distributed nothing . . . but a word of advice to my fellows in servitude and sin. . . . Concerning profane swearing. . . .' The dialogue continues:

> 'Nay, if thou can'st cure them of that disease, I shall think thee a wonderful doctor indeed—' 'Why not cure them, my good master? the hearts of those poor people are not so stubborn as your honour seems to think—Make them first sensible that you have nothing in view but their good, then they will listen with patience, and easily be convinced of the sin and folly of a practice that affords neither profit nor pleasure—' At this remark, our uncle changed colour, and looked round the company, conscious that his *own withers were not altogether unwrung.*   (Jery, 2 June)

Humphry, then, is both physical and spiritual doctor. As this passage indicates, it is his function to cure Bramble of his malaise, a function that is expressed symbolically in his attempts to save his master from drowning.

Water, in fact, is one of the novel's key images From Jery's dog Ponto who was drowned in the Isis (18 April), to the dropsical Chowder, the corrupted water of Bath and London, and Bramble's metaphorical allusions ('plung[ing] amidst the waves of excess'; 'I . . . enjoy a constant tide of spirits'; 'the tide of luxury'),[16] it permeates the novel, though nowhere are its symbolic implications so manifest as in

Humphry's rescue attempts, which appear to be Smollett's mature reconsideration of the drowning motif in *Roderick Random*, and which also introduce us to the most noticeable instances of repetitive patterning, present in *Humphry Clinker* as in the earlier novels.

The first rescue—an abortive one—occurs at Scarborough when Bramble is sea-bathing (Bramble, 4 July). Leaving Scarborough for Stockton, the party is immediately involved in a coach accident: 'In the afternoon, crossing a deep gutter, made by a torrent, the coach was so hard strained, that one of the irons, which connect the frame, snapt, and the leather sling on the same side, cracked in the middle...' (Jery, 10 July). The accident is again caused, if indirectly, by water; and once again Humphry comes to the rescue, this time through his skill as a blacksmith. The blacksmith who owned the forge they take the coach to has been dead some days, but Humphry is able to use his equipment; so that this incident, obviously connected to the preceding rescue at Scarborough, also looks even further back, to the coach accident which occurred on the way from Bath to London when Humphry, formerly apprenticed to a blacksmith who is now dead, was first employed by Bramble.

The drowning motif reappears with Tabitha's fears during a storm which springs up when the family are crossing from Kinghorn to Leith (Jery, 8 August), though a more important event from the present point of view takes place on the return journey from Scotland to England when, as Jery reports (12 September), Lismahago's drowned horse is discovered on the Solway sands, and its owner is presumed to have suffered the same fate. But 'one of the first persons we saw in Carlisle, was the lieutenant *in propria persona*. . . . Mrs. Bramble was the first that perceived him, and screamed as if she had seen a ghost. . . .'

The motif fuses here with a related one, that of the apparition, or the apparent return from the dead. It will reach its symbolic climax with the revelation of Humphry's identity; but in the meantime, and so that we don't miss the relevance of all this as part of a cumulative pattern, Smollett has the reappearance of Lismahago immediately follow the recognition scene involving the old man and his son who has just returned from the East Indies—an episode that is observed by Bramble and Jery only because they have been delayed by damage to their coach (ibid.). The recognition of the apothecary Grieve as Ferdinand Count Fathom, who saves Melvile's life when his coach is attacked by highwaymen (Bramble, 26 June), contributes to the pattern, as do the two 'ghost' stories recounted in Bramble's letters of 6 and 15 September.

But this emphasis on recognition is not solely directed at the identification of Humphry. It relates in addition to the analogous discovery of the identity of Lydia's lover, a discovery which involves Jery in an important moment of self-awareness. Wilson, indeed, is as meaningful for Jery as Humphry is for Bramble. It is now—that is, in Jery's letter of 4 October and the letter following—that the motifs just considered appear together. Jery and Lydia see Wilson riding by while they are standing at the window of an inn. Jery chases after him but is unable to find him, and asks: 'Am I to suppose that the horseman I saw was really a thing of flesh and blood, or a bubble that vanished into air?' As soon as this event is over, there occurs the coach accident in which Bramble, genuinely this time, comes close to death by drowning, and is rescued by Humphry:

> a great quantity of rain having fallen last night and this morning, there was such an accumulation of water, that a mill-head gave way, just as the coach was passing under it, and the flood rushed down with such impetuosity, as first floated, and then fairly overturned the carriage in the middle of the stream. . . .
> Humphry . . . flew like lightning to the coach, that was by this time filled with water, and, diving into it, brought up the poor 'squire, to all appearance, deprived of life. . . . Clinker perceiving . . . signs of life, immediately tied up his arm with a garter, and, pulling out a horse-fleam, let him blood in the farrier style. . . .

Ronald Paulson[17] has justly called this a 'baptism': Humphry has redeemed Bramble both physically and morally, taking him from the water to be reborn into a new awareness of himself and his responsibilities. (Jery actually describes Humphry as lifting Bramble 'as if he had been an infant of six months'.) For he is taken to an inn, where he recognizes his former undergraduate companion Dennison and identifies himself as 'Matthew Loyd of Glamorgan', at which point Humphry also announces himself as 'Matthew Loyd'. Bramble has regained consciousness to find himself, as it were, in the figure of his illegitimate son: 'Stand forth, Matthew Loyd—You see, gentlemen, how the sins of my youth rise up in judgment against me. . . .'

Only after this sudden awareness of himself in all his fallibility and imperfections can Bramble travel to the novel's ideal, the Dennison estate. And, as I have said, the revelation of Wilson's identity is no less crucial to Jery's moral development:

> When I weigh my own character with his, I am ashamed to find myself so light in the balance; but the comparison excites no envy—I propose him as a model for imitation—I have endeavoured to recommend myself to his friendship, and hope I have already found a place in his affection. I am, however, mortified to reflect what flagrant injustice we every day commit, and what absurd judgment we form, in viewing objects through the falsifying medium of prejudice and passion. Had you asked me a few days ago, the picture of Wilson the player, I should have drawn a portrait very unlike the real person and character of George Dennison—Without all doubt, the greatest advantage acquired in travelling and perusing mankind in the original, is that of dispelling those shameful clouds that darken the faculties of the mind, preventing it from judging with candour and precision. (14 October)

The balance-image, with its traditional implications, appears here as, indeed, we would expect it to. Wilson, together with Humphry, has been a symbolic figure throughout. He couldn't be recognized by Bramble at the beginning of the novel—even though he sold him a pair of spectacles!—because at this stage Bramble was just at the beginning of his pilgrimage 'to *unclog the wheels of life*' and achieve insight into self.[18] Similarly, from Edinburgh Jery reports that at a ball 'A young gentleman, the express image of that rascal Wilson, went up to ask [Lydia] to dance a minuet; and his sudden appearance shocked her so much, that she fainted away . . .' (8 August). The function of this false Wilson must be to suggest that with Edinburgh—and by implication Scotland as a whole—the novel's ideal has perhaps been hinted at, but not attained. And so the company return to England, and their journey comes to its close with the discovery of Wilson's and Humphry's identities somewhere in the midlands, the geographical mean between the extremes of Scotland and Bath and London.[19]

III

The subject-matter of *Humphry Clinker* as I have described it—the concern for decorum, propriety, and temperance over against various kinds of excess; in short, for that virtue which is self-knowledge—is mimed in the novel's structure. As we have seen, Smollett had been gradually feeling his way towards the iconographical implications of structure from *Roderick Random* to *Ferdinand Count Fathom*. In *Humphry Clinker* he achieves an almost perfect fusion of form and meaning.

The geographical symmetry of the journey, in which extremes achieve resolution in a mean, together with such explicit pointers as Bramble's remark that he 'enjoy[s] a constant tide of spirits, equally distant from inanition and excess' (18 July), encourage a description of the novel's moral ideal in Aristotelian terms; for, according to Aristotle,[20] virtue 'is a mean state between two vices, one of excess and one of defect. Furthermore, it is a mean state in that whereas the vices either fall short of or exceed what is right in feelings and in actions, virtue ascertains and adopts the mean.' We might compare Joseph Spence's notes of Pope's scheme for the *Epistles to Several Persons*:[21] 'We s^d not speak agst one large Vice, without speaking agst its contrary. —As to ye General Design of Providence ye two Extremes of a Vice, serve like two opposite biasses to keep up ye Ballance of things. . . . The middle ye point for Virtue. . . .'

The journey of Bramble and his company corresponds to a moral progression: Bath and London (luxury, corruption, disorder); 'the *Ultima Thule*' and Dougal Campbell's house (primitive simplicity; Jery's letter of 3 September discusses both together); Dennison (a rural ideal offering a temperate compromise between the other two). The pattern is clearly one of excess, defect, and mean, and Smollett underlines it by the novel's three-volume format: vol. I contains the whole of the stay at Bath and just under half the stay at London (seven letters out of a total of sixteen dated from London); vol. II concludes the London visit, contains the whole of the journey to Scotland, and sees the company's arrival in Edinburgh (it includes three letters out of the four dated from there); while the third volume sees the departure from Edinburgh, the remainder of the Scottish tour, and finally comes to rest at Dennison's estate. The symmetry is immediately intelligible: the extremes of Bath and London in the first volume are answered by the Scottish extreme at the beginning of the third volume (it is in the second letter that Jery announces: 'I am now little short of the *Ultima Thule* . . .'), with the transitional vol. II mediating between them, participating as it does both in the London visit (with which vol. I ends) and the stay in Scotland (with which vol. III opens):

Vol. I	Vol. II	Vol. III

London // London / Journey / Edinburgh // Edinburgh

Smollett could have left things at that, approximately miming the ideal of balance through this symmetrical disposition of the larger geographical units. But he appears to have gone considerably further, and, like Fielding before him, to have adopted a thoroughgoing Aristotelian approach by expressing the mean arithmetically. (Aristotle, we recall, had explained virtue as an arithmetic mean.)[22] The scheme of excess, defect, and mean, is enacted in *Humphry Clinker* by the number of letters in each volume: vol. I, thirty-five; vol. II, twenty; vol. III, twenty-eight.[23] For it will be observed that the mean between 35 and 20, the greatest and least totals, is $27\frac{1}{2}$, or, to the nearest whole number, 28, the total for vol. III.[24] So that this arithmetical pattern cuts across and yet counterpoints the geographical pattern just described, in which the second volume can be seen as a mean between the flanking extremes, I and III.

The importance of 28 lies in the fact that, arithmetically speaking, it is a perfect number since it is equal to the sum of its aliquot parts (1, 2, 4, 7, 14). And because it is perfect, it was regarded as symbolizing moral perfection and virtue.[25] Smollett is observing strict numerological decorum, therefore, in choosing it as the total for that volume in which the virtuous mean is attained. Moreover, I would now go on to suggest that the reason for Humphry's delayed appearance in the novel, which has caused so much critical speculation, is a numerological one which depends on our grasping the scheme I have outlined: if we exclude Wilson's letter dated 31 March (which this time we may legitimately do, because it disrupts the chronological sequence of the other letters) and count only the letters by Bramble and his family, we find that Humphry's arrival occurs in the twenty-eighth letter of vol. I.[26] We have only to recall Humphry's moral role in the novel to see that his association with the perfect and virtuous 28 is both fitting and just.[27]

There are, in addition, probably hints of mid-point symbolism in Humphry's release from prison (he has been wrongfully arrested as a highwayman) in the centre of the novel: Bramble's letter of 14 June announcing the release, which begins 'THANK Heaven! dear Lewis, the clouds are dispersed . . .', is the forty-second out of a total of eighty-three for the novel as a whole, and Jery's letter immediately preceding this, which tells of the arrest, actually describes Humphry in a position of centrality: 'I never saw any thing so strongly picturesque as this congregation of felons clanking their chains, in the midst of whom stood orator Clinker. . . .' It should also be noted that Wilson makes his reappearance, as Jery and Lydia stand by the window of an inn, at the centre of the final volume (Lydia's letter of 4 October; fifteenth of twenty-eight). It is again fitting that the two symbolically central characters should receive this kind of emphatic structural recognition.

With this, so far as I am aware, the numerological implications of *Humphry Clinker* are exhausted, though it is worth commenting in conclusion that Smollett might even have intended the three-volume format itself to carry symbolic weight; for in *The History and Adventures of an Atom* (1769) he had defined the number 3 as 'proportion'.[28] There can, I think, be little doubt that *Humphry Clinker* is the last work to be written in the main stream of that numerological tradition which certain eighteenth-century authors inherited from Renaissance humanism. Structurally and thematically it is a finely-wrought and moving monument to the ideals of English Augustanism.

NOTES

1 P.-G. Boucé, *Les Romans de Smollett*, pp. 225–40, notes that there are signs of haste in the novel, but argues valiantly for its structural coherence and, in doing so, offers the first good critical account of *Greaves*. There would be little point in trying to add here to what he says.

2 See especially Ronald Paulson, *Satire and the Novel in Eighteenth-Century England* (New Haven, Conn., 1967), pp. 196ff. and 206ff.; David L. Evans, '*Humphry Clinker*: Smollett's Tempered Augustanism', *Criticism*, 9 (1967), 257–74; Robert A. Donovan, *The Shaping Vision*, ch. 6; and Boucé, op. cit., Pt. II, ch. 4.

3 Jery's letter of 14 October. Quotations are from the first edn (3 vols, 1771) as edited by Lewis M. Knapp for OEN (1966). On Jery as observer see Boucé, op. cit., pp. 255–6.

4 David L. Evans has remarked on the affinities between *Humphry Clinker* and Pope's *Epistles*, art. cit., p. 271.

5 Emil Kaufmann, *Architecture in the Age of Reason*, pp. 32–4, and John Summerson, *Architecture in Britain: 1530–1830*, pp. 364, 366, and 386ff.

6 On the Assembly Rooms, see Summerson, pp. 338–9.

7 See Rudolf Wittkower, *Architectural Principles in the Age of Humanism*, Part IV; Christopher Butler, *Number Symbolism*, pp. 109ff.; and, on Pope's *Epistle*, William A. Gibson, 'Three Principles of Renaissance Architectural Theory in Pope's *Epistle to Burlington*', *SEL*, 11 (1971), 487–505.

8 Pandaemonium has risen a short time previously to 'the sound / Of dulcet symphonies' (ll. 711–12) because of the traditional relationship between musical and architectural proportions (see the note on ll. 710–12 in Fowler's edn of *Paradise Lost*).

9 See Lewis M. Knapp, 'Smollett's Self-Portrait in *The Expedition of Humphry Clinker*', in F. W. Hilles (ed.), *The Age of Johnson: Essays Presented to Chauncey Brewster Tinker*, pp. 149–58.

10 The Hon. John Byng, 'A Tour in the Midlands: 1789', 25 June; in *The Torrington*

Diaries, ed. C. Bruyn Andrews, abridged by Fanny Andrews, 1 vol. (1954), p. 200.

11 *Amelia*, VI. 5.

12 I use M. A. Goldberg's terms (*Smollett and the Scottish School*, ch. 6).

13 Goldberg, ibid., p. 165, comments on the general inadequacies of Scotland as depicted by Smollett, as does Paulson, *Satire and the Novel*, p. 206. Boucé, op. cit., p. 265, reminds us that *Humphry Clinker* describes a transitional Scotland which at once looks back to a traditional past and forward to an industrial future.

14 On which see Maynard Mack, *The Garden and The City*, ch. 1 and passim.

15 '*Humphry Clinker* as Comic Romance', in Robert D. Spector (ed.), *Essays on the Eighteenth-Century Novel* (Bloomington, Ind., 1965), p. 161.

16 Letters of 26 October, 18 July, and 29 May respectively.

17 *Satire and the Novel in Eighteenth-Century England*, p. 198.

18 The incident of the spectacles is recounted in Bramble's letter of 20 April and Lydia's of 21 April. Wilson actually reveals 'his name and family' here, significantly enough, but Win forgets what he has told her.

19 Knapp supplies a map in his edn. Note that Jery refers to the Hebrides as 'the *Ultima Thule*' at the beginning of his letter of 3 September.

20 *Nicomachean Ethics*, II. 6. 16 (1106 B). Loeb edn, tr. H. Rackham (1926), p. 95.

21 Transcribed in *Epistles to Several Persons*, ed. F. W. Bateson, p. xxi.

22 *Nicomachean Ethics*, II. 6. 4–17 (1106 A–B). Cf. ch. v above.

23 The count includes Wilson's letter of 31 March in vol. I. This is clearly intended to be regarded as separate because, in early edns of the novel, it was marked off, like the other letters, by a decorative printer's device. Contrast Martin's letter (included with Jery's of 23 June), which is not marked off in this way and is thus equally clearly not meant to be counted separately.

24 Alternatively, the mean is $27\frac{2}{3}$ (83, the total number of letters, divided by 3).

25 Bongo, *Numerorum mysteria*, pp. 464–5. This was the only perfect number available to Smollett, the first—6—being too small and the next—496—impossibly large.

26 It is significant that Wilson's letter should be so crucial to the overall count and yet not to this particular one: its structural function is thus similar to the function of Wilson himself, who is at once a part of the novel's action and yet, like Humphry, curiously outside it.

27 It should also be noted that Jery, the principal narrator, who is awakened to self-knowledge by young Dennison, writes 28 letters, while Bramble writes 27, which is also the total of letters written by the three women. Again, Wilson's letter is the odd man out, waiting, as it were, to increase one of the 27s to the perfect 28.

28 Shakespeare Head edn, 11 vols (Oxford, 1925–6), XI. 397. This work, with its references to Fr Athanasius Kircher (p. 393) and Agrippa's *Three Books* (p. 395), its pages on magic (pp. 392ff.), and its discussion of music according to Pythagorean principles ('he taught us how to express the octave by $\frac{1}{2}$, &c. &c.' (p. 439)), is sufficient and important evidence for Smollett's familiarity with numerological matters.

viii   Sterne: *Tristram Shandy*

In the thirty-sixth chapter of his *Life and Opinions*, vol. III,[1] Tristram
exhorts his 'unlearned reader' to

> Read, read, read, read, . . . or by the knowledge of the great saint
> *Paraleipomenon*—I tell you before-hand, you had better throw down
> the book at once; for without *much reading*, by which your
> reverence knows, I mean *much knowledge*, you will no more be able
> to penetrate the moral of the next marbled page (motly emblem
> of my work!) than the world with all its sagacity has been able to
> unraval [*sic*] the many opinions, transactions and truths which
> still lie mystically hid under the dark veil of the black one.

There is a corresponding passage in IV. 17: 'But mark, madam, we live
amongst riddles and mysteries—the most obvious things, which come
in our way, have dark sides, which the quickest sight cannot penetrate
into; and even the clearest and most exalted understandings amongst
us find ourselves puzzled and at a loss in almost every cranny of
nature's works. . . .' The act of 'penetrating' is analogous, Sterne
implies, to the act of 'unravelling': to 'unravel' is to glimpse, if only
for a moment, elusive Truth.[2] The untying of a knot has a similar
significance: in III. 8 Obadiah ties up Dr Slop's 'green bays bag' because
the clattering of the instruments inside it prevents him from hearing
himself whistle: 'he tied and cross-tied them all fast together from
one end to the other (as you would cord a trunk) with such a multiplicity of round-abouts and intricate cross turns, with a hard knot at
every intersection or point where the strings met,—that Dr *Slop* must
have had three fifths of *Job*'s patience at least to have unloosed
them. . . .' Slop, parodying Alexander, cuts the knots and also his
thumb, and the cutting of the thumb, we are meant to feel, is a just
punishment for presumption; for, as Sterne makes clear, the knots
and the mysteries they signify (which are the same as the mysteries of
the black and marbled pages) must be carefully untied:

In the case of these *knots* then, and of the several obstructions,
which, may it please your reverences, such knots cast in our way
in getting through life—every hasty man can whip out his pen-
knife and cut through them.—'Tis wrong. Believe me, Sirs, the
most virtuous way, and which both reason and conscience
dictate—is to take our teeth or our fingers to them. (III. 10)

A knot is an obstacle but also, as Eithne Wilkins[3] has reminded us, 'a
node . . . , a focal point'. To untie the knot or unravel the web, then,
is to achieve insight into those 'riddles and mysteries' which are so
manifestly Sterne's subject in *Tristram Shandy*; to cut the knot is a
destructive and hubristic action implying that the slow and painful
journey to the centre, the node, is not worth while. Paradoxically,
weaving signifies the same thing as unravelling. If we weave, we
create. Hence of the *Tristrapaedia* we are told: 'My father spun his
[knowledge], every thread of it, out of his own brain,—or reeled and
cross-twisted what all other spinners and spinsters had spun before
him, that 'twas pretty near the same torture to him' (V. 16).[4] Now the
Tristrapaedia, in its turn, parallels *Tristram Shandy* itself, and both are
echoed in Toby's campaigns and bowling green.[5] In other words, they
are all attempts to come to terms with, to encapsulate, the mysteries
of the external world and, ultimately, of the universe. Hence, too,
Walter's theories, which are in one way laughable, but in another
way not. Faced with the ineffable, I think Sterne is asking, who are we
to dismiss out of hand the belief in astrology, the power of names,
and—I would submit—symbolic numbers?

For there can be no doubt that *Tristram Shandy*'s structure is to a large
extent numerological and that Sterne sees number symbolism as a
still valid way of describing the structure of the universe. At the same
time he shares in the scepticism of his age, so that the numbers in
Tristram Shandy are also a hitherto unexplored aspect of Sterne's 'learned
wit'[6] and—because they are pursued in such elaborate detail—of
his deliberate (one might say perverse) eccentricity. Moreover, the
numerological structure supports recent critical speculations about
the spatial organization of *Tristram Shandy*.[7] If, as F. W. Bateson originally
suggested, such devices as the wavy line illustrating the flourish of
Corporal Trim's stick in IX. 4 are parodies of pattern-poems,[8]
then we might say that, ultimately, the novel itself is one vast
pattern-poem. Conceived by a writer who was also a painter and
musician, its structural harmonies are, literally, the harmonies of the

161

cosmos itself, and Tristram-Sterne writes unambiguously as an *alter deus*.

The first volume opens, significantly, on a Sunday night: the beginning of *a* week; but also, surely, the beginning of *the* Week of Creation, since Walter's exasperated reference to '*the creation of the world*' at the end of chapter 1 hints that the creation of Tristram and of the novel recapitulate the primal act of creation. Support for the notion comes from Tristram's insistence in I. 4 that he is going 'to go on tracing every thing . . . , as *Horace* says, *ab Ovo*', a remark that is usually regarded as a flippant rejection of classical precept (Tristram continues: '*Horace*, I know, does not recommend this fashion altogether: But that gentleman is speaking only of an epic poem or a tragedy;—(I forget which) . . .'). But is it not also something more? For Horace, in the *Ars poetica*, is talking of the Trojan war, and the egg he is thinking of is the egg of Leda from which Helen was born. In neo-Platonic readings of the myth Helen (with or without her twin Clytemnestra) symbolized discord, and was complemented by the offspring of Leda's second egg, the twins Castor and Pollux (concord). Together they expressed the *discordia concors* of the created universe; so that the eggs of Leda became identified with the cosmic egg, or egg of the world.[9] Sterne may imply all or only part of this. At any rate, there can be little doubt as to the initiatory nature of his first volume, and to his implied exploitation of the traditional analogy between the author (of a literary work) and God, the Supreme Creator.[10]

If we examine the traditional associations of the monad, we find that it is identified with the originative principle: it is, to quote Agrippa,[11] 'the one beginning, and end of all things. . . . And as all things proceeded of one into many things, so all things endeavour to return to that one, from which they proceeded. . . . One therefore is referred to the high God. . . .' And, too, the circular nature of the monad means that the thematic links between the first and last (ninth) volumes of *Tristram Shandy*—which have been convincingly traced by Wayne Booth[12]—take on an added significance: the novel itself completes a circle.[13] It is also relevant that the subject-matter of vol. I should be so inclusive, containing as it does Tristram's conception and Yorick's death.[14] For in these two extremes is the whole story of man's mortal life, and, as we have seen, the meaning of the monad. Sterne emphasizes their thematic importance in a way that is by now familiar: the black page[15] commemorating Yorick's death is placed in the centre of the volume (between chapters 12 and 13; the total for the volume is twenty-five) and it is surrounded by images of birth, since the Yorick chapters are preceded by the introduction of the village midwife (ch. 7) and by the dedication of all but the hobby-horsical chapters of the first volume to the moon (the planet which traditionally governed birth and growth),[16] and the black page is immediately succeeded (ch. 13) by the reintroduction of the midwife.

Not content with utilizing the monad in the way I have suggested, Sterne reinforced its symbolic implications and, at the same time, the parallel between the creation of his microcosmic novel and the macrocosm, by the structural exploitation of another creative number, 25. This, the total number of chapters in vol. I, is the number specifically associated with the creation of the world:[17] 'The yeere of our Lorde beginneth the .xxv. day of March, the same day supposed to be the first day upon which the worlde was created . . .'—an association that would still have been alive for Sterne and his readers since the year was reckoned from Lady Day (25 March) until 1752.[18]

Even this is not all. Sterne is very careful to locate the date of Tristram's conception in a passage which follows two paragraphs after the reference to the Horatian egg: 'I was begot in the night, betwixt the first *Sunday* and the first *Monday* in the month of *March* . . .' (I. 4). And the end of the same chapter refers us explicitly to '*Lady-Day*. . . , the 25th of the same month in which I date my geniture . . .'. The clues are obviously being laid so thickly that we should scarcely be surprised to encounter the occasional substantive allusion to 25 as well.[19] And just as Tristram and the world were begotten in March, so was the novel: Tristram-Sterne reminds us in I. 18 that 'this very day, in which I am now writing this book for the edification of the world, —. . . is *March* 9, 1759 . . .'; while in chapter 21 he comments: 'that observation is my own;—and was struck out by me this very rainy day, *March* 26, 1759. . . .'

If we now turn to vol. IX with the above discussion of vol. I in mind, we find that there is a relationship between them that has passed unnoticed by Booth, namely, the curious hiatus in the ninth volume which occurs between chapters 17 and 20 and the corresponding inclusion of the missing chapters (18 and 19) in the *twenty-fifth chapter*: 'how was it possible [that the reader] should foresee the necessity I was under of writing the 25th chapter of my book, before the 18th, &c', asks Sterne in IX. 25. The answer is that he could foresee it if he had grasped Sterne's plan: the circularity of the work on the one hand and the thematic significance of the creative number, 25, on the other.

(As it is, we now find that IX. 25 is about creation, since it contains—in chapters 18 and 19—the beginning of the interview between Toby and widow Wadman, including a statement to the effect that the begetting of children is 'a principal end . . . of the institution [of marriage]'.)

Once again the clues are there. In chapter 17, just before the hiatus, Tristram declares that he owes his tailor 'some five and twenty pounds at least'; and chapter 25 itself contains a reference to 'the cake-bakers of Lerné'—whom we will encounter, if we pursue the allusion, in *Gargantua and Pantagruel*, I. 25. Not that the first and last volumes afford the only instances of Sterne's juggling with 25: the fourth volume—which really announces a new beginning, since Bobby's death makes Tristram 'heir-apparent to the *Shandy* family—and it is from this point properly, that the story of my LIFE and my OPINIONS sets out' (IV. 32)—plays the same trick as the ninth except that here it is the twenty-fourth chapter that is missing and is, in effect, embodied in the twenty-fifth. IV. 27, by the way, mentions the 'twenty or five and twenty seconds' it took the hot chestnut to impart its 'genial warmth' to Phutatorius's cod-piece.

Allusions to 25 are also present in other volumes: III. 14, for example ('twenty or five and twenty yards' of cloth); and III. 20, 'The Author's Preface' ('five and twenty minutes') and VI. 6 ('five and twenty years': compare V. 38, 'five and twenty days the flux was upon us'). We might say that, together with the 'creation of the world' phrase and its variants (IV. 13; VIII. 19; VIII. 22, etc.), it becomes a running motif, substantive and structural, the function of which is to keep Sterne's great theme—the mystery of creation in all its manifestations (cosmic, human, artistic)—continually before us.

II

Because it breaks away from unity, the dyad is traditionally evil, the number of the fallen, material world. Du Bartas's *Devine Weekes and Workes* (of which Sterne seems to have possessed a copy)[20] could have told him that 2 is the 'first Number, and the Parent / Of Female Payres'; hence it is *fœmina nuncupatus* and associated with generation, and, in addition, was regarded as symbolizing opposing entities, particularly man in his twin aspects of body and soul, corporeal and spiritual.[21]

Each of these meanings appears to be exploited by Sterne in vol. II. The feminine character of 2, for instance, is adequately brought out by the fact that it is in this volume that Mrs Shandy goes into labour and by Walter's and Toby's discourse on the nature of women, a discourse that begins in chapter 7 as Walter tries to elucidate for his brother the difference between the right end and the wrong end 'of that animal, call'd Woman'. Furthermore, the significance of 2 as the number of the duality of body and soul surely explains why Sterne should reserve the end of this volume for Walter Shandy's theory about the seat of the soul, and his emphasis on the intimate relationship between the soul and the body (ch. 19). But Walter is concerned for the salvation of the soul in a purely practical sense: it all depends on the manner of one's birth. John M. Stedmond has rightly commented:[22] 'He has no apparent concern with moral conduct as a revelation of the quality of soul, the main subject of the sermon so artfully juxtaposed with Walter's theory.' So that even the sermon in chapter 17 becomes relevant to the associations of the dyad, reminding us as it does that man is not only corporeal and mutable, but that he partakes in addition of the divine and eternal.

There are too many substantive occurrences of 2 in the volume as a whole for us to regard them as anything other than explicit numerological pointers. Thus, in chapter 7, Walter's pipe snaps in two; Toby is described as 'muttering the two words [right end] low to himself, and fixing his two eyes insensibly as he muttered them, upon a small crevice, form'd by a bad joint in the chimney-piece'; and Walter informs him that 'every thing in this earthly world . . . has two handles . . . [or] at least . . . every one has two hands,—which comes to the same thing.' Chapter 17 contains Trim's introduction of two sentinels and Yorick's reminder (in the sermon) of 'the duties of religion . . . [and] of morality, which are so inseparably connected together, that you cannot divide these two *tables*, even in imagination, (tho' the attempt is often made in practice) without breaking and mutually destroying them both'. Yorick deduces two rules from his sermon, with which he concludes it, and the sermon itself was lost twice and printed 'two years and three months after *Yorick's* death'—information which Tristram offers us 'two reasons' for imparting (ch. 17). Obadiah receives 'two crowns' for fetching Slop's bag (ch. 18); in the following chapter Walter holds that 'Knowledge, like matter, . . . [is] divisible *in infinitum*', and bases the theory embodied in the chapter on 'two . . . axioms' which are enumerated for us, and so on.

The unfortunate associations of 2 ('the number of discord, and confusion, [and] misfortune'),[23] moreover, perhaps explain the emphasis on misfortune in vol. II. Chapter 7—which contains so many allusions to the number—ends with the remark that 'the confusion and distresses of our domestic misadventures . . . are now coming thick one upon the back of another'; and it is this meaning of 2 that connects with and explains the 19 of the volume's chapter-total. For 19 is traditionally *infaustus* and disharmonious, possessing no redeeming features.[24] Fittingly, therefore, the nineteenth chapter carries Walter's 'lament . . . that so many things in this world were out of joint;—that the political arch was giving way; and that . . . we are a ruined, undone people . . .'; and the whole chapter is about the destruction of the soul.

But since, as I have tried to indicate already, Sterne draws attention to his symbolic numbers either by exploiting their most obvious associations or by reiterating the number itself until we cannot but be aware of it (the 2s in vol. II), it should be no surprise to discover that this is not the only instance of the symbolic use of 19 in the novel. Indeed, vol. I has already prepared us for its appearance in the second volume; for its nineteenth chapter (which contains Walter's theory of Christian names and thus complements II. 19, containing his other theory) is to a large extent a lament on the name Tristram: Walter 'had the lowest and most contemptible opinion of it of any thing in the world,—thinking it could possibly produce nothing in *rerum naturâ*, but what was extreamly mean and pitiful'. It is, we are told at the end of the chapter, a 'melancholy dissyllable of sound!' And IV. 19 clinches the matter: here we find 'My FATHER's LAMENTATION' on the evils that have befallen his son. *Tristram Shandy*, too, has its elements of repetitive structuring, and they function clearly enough to reinforce the novel's numerology.

III

Tristram isn't born until the third volume. This delay has caused a certain amount of amusement to readers, and justifiably so. Nevertheless, the joke seems to be a pointedly numerological one rather than anything else. The first three volumes form an integrated narrative unit covering the period from Tristram's conception to his birth.[25] I suggest that this is so because Sterne had in mind, and wished structurally to exemplify as closely as it was possible to do, the Pythagorean notion of the three stages of creation: (1) undifferentiated unity; (2) the separation into two opposite powers to create the world order; (3) the reunion or 'marriage' of the opposites to generate life.[26] Hence 3 had a special generative significance and became known as the first of the marriage numbers, and also as completion (because it possesses beginning, middle, and end). Thus Agrippa reminds us that 'By three (as *Tresmegistus* saith) the world is perfected' (II. 6, p. 180).

Once again Sterne was determined to insist substantively on 3 in this volume as he insisted on 2 in vol. II. It would be tedious as well as unnecessary to list all of these references; here it is sufficient to mention that Obadiah has 'three children' (ch. 7); that 'three drops of oyl' would have cured the hinge on the parlour door (ch. 21); that Tristram refers to 'three several roads' in chapter 23; that Walter pays 'three half crowns' for Bruscambille on noses, of which 'there are not three . . . in *Christendom*' (ch. 35); and that 'one winter's night' Walter had spent 'three hours [in] painful translation of *Slawkenbergius*' (ch. 41).[27]

The climax comes in chapter 32, however, with Tristram's great-grandfather's nose, which, we are told (following Rabelais), 'was shaped . . . like an ace of clubs'—an explicit directive, surely, to another meaning of 3, this time as the first male number (in the Pythagorean system, we recall, odd numbers were regarded as being male, even as female): a significance that barely conceals its probable biological origins in the threefold nature of the male genitals, and one that also reinforces its generative power as outlined above.[28]

In addition, Sterne's recommendation to turn to the island of Ennasin episode in *Gargantua and Pantagruel*, IV. 9—'if you would know the strange way of getting a-kin amongst so flat nosed a people,—you must read the book'—is probably another oblique way of directing us to the number: Pantagruel arrives at the 'triangular island' 'on the third day . . . some two or three hours after [sunrise]'; and Ennasin boasts 300,000 inhabitants who are able to march out and defend it if necessary.[29]

It remains only to ask why vol. III should possess forty-two chapters. There are, I think, two equally plausible reasons. First, in view of the insistence in chapter 33 on Tristram's genealogy, which traces his family back to 'king *Harry* the VIIIth's time', Sterne probably alludes to 42 as a genealogical number, an interpretation deriving from the forty-two generations from Abraham to Christ as recounted in Matthew 1. (The number 3 is involved here, too, since the generations were divided into three sets of fourteen; ibid., verse 17.) And second, we know from I. 19 of Walter's veneration for Hermes Trismegistus, and in vol. IV we encounter his attempt to have his son named

Trismegistus. Now since Hermes Trismegistus was the mythical author of the forty-two books containing all knowledge of cosmography, astrology, religion, geography, medicine, and so forth,[30] it is quite possible that Sterne wanted to bring out in the formal structure of his novel this further connection between 3 (Trismegistus, or thrice-great) and 42.

IV

Volumes V and VII must be taken together for reasons that will become apparent later on. They also require rather detailed treatment, and so it is more convenient to discuss the numerological implications of the remaining volumes—IV, VI, VIII, and IX—first.

Four is the number of justice and of cosmic harmony (the interlocking of the 4 elements to create the world order). Microcosmically, it is the number of the body, composed of the four humours and governed by their corresponding temperaments.[31] Significantly, therefore, Walter refers to the elements in chapter 16: 'we shall have a devilish month of it, brother *Toby* . . . fire, water, women, wind—brother *Toby*!—'Tis some misfortune, quoth my uncle *Toby*—That it is, cried my father,—to have so many jarring elements breaking loose, and riding triumph in every corner of a gentleman's house . . .'; a remark which should be read in conjunction with Tristram's reference to the harmonizing of the four humours right at the end of the volume:[32]

> And as the bilious and more saturnine passions, by creating
> disorders in the blood and humours, have as bad an influence,
> I see, upon the body politick as body natural—and as nothing
> but a habit of virtue can fully govern those passions, and subject
> them to reason—I should add to my prayer—that God would
> give my subjects grace to be as WISE as they were MERRY. . . .
> (ch. 32)

While 4 as divisive justice, together with the chapter-total of 32 (because of its divisibility another number of justice),[33] perhaps explain the allusions to balances—the emblems of justice—in this volume: in chapter 25, for instance, where Tristram writes of the 'necessary equipoise and balance, (whether of good or bad) betwixt chapter and chapter, from whence the just proportions and harmony of the whole work results', and chapter 31, which ends with elaborate balance-imagery as Walter weighs in his mind the respective merits of the conflicting and opposed projects, whether to enclose the Ox-moor or send Bobby on his travels. The reasons in favour of both schemes, says Tristram, are 'equally balanced by each other'; 'nothing . . . appeared so strongly in behalf of the one, which was not either strictly applicable to the other, or at least so far counterbalanced by some consideration of equal weight, as to keep the scales even'; 'No body, but he who has felt it, can conceive what a plaguing thing it is to have a man's mind torn asunder by two projects of equal strength, both obstinately pulling in a contrary direction at the same time. . . .'

Substantive references to 6 in the sixth volume are sufficiently numerous to indicate that Sterne is pursuing the same policy of clue-laying as in the earlier volumes;[34] and it seems to me that the symbolic meanings of the hexad dictated his change in subject-matter here to Toby's amours, since 6, the number of harmony and of marriage, is dedicated to Venus. If we should doubt the accessibility of these meanings to Sterne, it is worth reminding ourselves of their relevance to Rabelais's Abbey of Thelema, which M. A. Screech has explored in some detail.[35]

Volume VI, then, is to a large extent about love and marriage, particularly from chapter 30 until the end. If we ask, Why 30?, the answer lies, I suspect, in its significance as another Pythagorean marriage number, deriving in part from the digital gesture for 30;[36] while the chapter-total for the volume as a whole, forty, is also appropriate; for 40 is a nuptial number with important harmonic and generative properties.[37] But the most interesting chapter of all is the thirty-fifth, where we actually see Toby moving from the patronage of Mars to that of Venus: '—Softer visions,—gentler vibrations stole sweetly in upon his slumbers;—the trumpet of war fell out of his hands,—he took up the lute, sweet instrument! of all others the most delicate! the most difficult!—how wilt thou touch it, my dear uncle *Toby*?' The iconographical relevance of trumpet and lute at this point is clear enough;[38] and so, too, is the significance of 35. Again, we might say that just as Sterne had to delay the birth of Tristram until vol. III to fulfil his preordained numerological plan, so did he have to delay the precise moment when Toby's amours began until this stage in his narrative because only 6 and 35 in combination possessed exactly the right meanings: 35 is known as 'harmony' (because it is the sum of the first feminine cube (8) and the first masculine cube (27)) and, most relevant of all to Toby's situation, it is Plato's upper limit for the male marriage age.[39]

The associations of 7 (which bear no relation to love, harmony, or marriage) fairly obviously dictated the postponement of the next instalment of the amours until vol. VIII, because 8 is the female number *par excellence*. It is, as we have just seen, the female cube in the Platonic *lambda* series and was also dedicated to Cybele, mother of the gods.[40] Even more relevantly, it was sacred to Juno (goddess of marriage) and Hymen.[41] Fittingly, therefore, widow Wadman takes the stage here; and fittingly, too, the narrative proper doesn't begin until the eighth chapter, when we are told that the widow is '*a perfect woman*'.

The narrative and thematic links between the sixth and eighth volumes are self-evident; and the numerical links are no less evident. For the number 35—the symbolic and structural importance of which for vol. VI I have just examined—is echoed in vol. VIII in the most emphatic manner possible: it is the total number of chapters in that volume. The meanings of 35 already adduced are more than sufficient to account for its appearance here.

Volume IX continues and concludes Toby's amours, and thus completes the triad of volumes (VI, VIII, and IX) concerned with Toby and love. The fact that 9 is the square of 3 and that the ninth volume has 33 chapters is sufficient to hint that some kind of numerological scheme is still operating, and it seems likely, bearing in mind the emphasis in this volume on the widow's interest in Toby's generative organs, that Sterne wants us to recall his almost too explicit use of the male 3 in vol. III.[42]

Nine is also an unfortunate number, connected with melancholy, misfortune, and death. And it is only just that the novel, so full of misfortunes of various kinds, should end on an elegiac note; a note that does, in fact, accord with an important meaning of 33 as a number of suffering and sorrow.[43] We might, in addition, suspect an element of self-referring symbolism in connection with 9; for the novel contains several references to nine-month periods (e.g., III. 20; III. 24; and IV. 19), and begins with Tristram's (supposed) nine-months' gestation, and ends with Toby's amours—which last exactly nine months![44]

There is, however, a final suggestion I should like to make as to the relevance of 33. If we turn to IX. 33, we find that the sterile bull provides the climax to a discourse on the begetting of children ('—THAT provision should be made for continuing the race of so great, so exalted and godlike a Being as man—I am far from denying', etc.). Similarly, VI. 33 quotes Cardan on the care that should be taken in begetting children, and in VIII. 33 Walter tries to distinguish between the 'two different and distinct kinds of *love*', the rational and the natural, 'the first ancient—without mother—where Venus had nothing to do: the second, begotten of Jupiter and Dione . . . [which] partakes wholly of the nature of Venus.' But Toby, as ever, is not interested in distinctions: 'What signifies it, brother Shandy, . . . which of the two it is, provided it will but make a man marry, and love his wife, and get a few children.'

The associations that 33 possessed for Sterne in *Tristram Shandy* appear, then, to be indisputable; and the reason for them emerges from the penultimate paragraph of IX. 33 where Walter describes his bull as being 'as good a Bull as ever p–ss'd, and might have done for Europa herself in purer times. . . .' The novel ends, as it begins, with a Jovian metamorphosis; and just as Leda's egg had a symbolic significance for vol. I, so does the bull in vol. IX. I suspect, in fact, that Sterne might want us to recall that the Jovian bull was stellified as the constellation Taurus, a zodiacal house of Venus, and that the principal star-total for Taurus as given in Ptolemy's *Almagest* is 33. So that the number is connected specifically with Venus and all her attributes as a planetary deity—the subject-matter, indeed, of VIII. 33, IX. 33, and so on.[45] Obviously, one is chary of suggesting a sudden shift from Pythagorean-Platonic-Biblical number symbolism (which predominates in the novel as a whole) to astronomical numbers in one instance only. Nevertheless, the evidence seems to me to be strong, supported as it is by astrological allusions throughout the novel; and I present it for what the reader may think it is worth.

V

I want to turn now to the fifth and seventh volumes, which I consider together because they are linked in several ways: for example, vol. V begins with Walter planning Bobby's route through France, and vol. VII contains Tristram's journey through France; in V. 9 Trim, looking at Susannah, asks: 'are we not like a flower in the field . . . is not all flesh grass?', and in VII. 9 Tristram apostrophizes Janatone: 'thou carriest the principles of change within thy frame; . . . e'er twice twelve months are pass'd and gone, . . . thou mayest go off like a flower, and lose thy beauty . . .'; in both V. 26 and VII. 26 the main narrative is resumed after a digression; and both volumes have forty-three chapters.

The main theme of the opening chapters of vol. V—which are heavily indebted to Burton's *Anatomy*[46]—is mutability. Bobby's death provokes from his father a lament that reaches out to embrace the cosmos itself: 'Where is *Troy* and *Mycenæ*, and *Thebes* and *Delos*, and *Persepolis*, and *Agrigentum*? . . . What is become, brother *Toby*, of *Nineveh* and *Babylon*, of *Cizicum* and *Mitylenæ*? The fairest towns that ever the sun rose upon, are now no more . . .' (V. 3). Along with creation, mutability is, of course, central to the whole novel: just how central I hope to show when I discuss vol. VII. But it is a prominent theme in the fifth volume because of the intimate connection between 5 and the mutable world;[47] though it is characteristic of Sterne's desire for inclusiveness in utilizing symbolic numbers that he should allude to at least two other important meanings of the pentad: marriage and health. Sir Thomas Browne expresses the nuptial significance of 5 in the fifth chapter of his *Garden of Cyrus* as follows:[48] it is 'the Conjugall Number, which ancient Numerists made out by two and three, the first parity and imparity, the active and passive digits, the materiall and formall principles in generative Societies'. Compare *Tristram Shandy*, V. 31, where Walter tells us that the opening pages of his *Tristrapaedia* are 'a prefatory introduction, . . . or an introductory preface . . . upon political or civil government; the foundation of which being laid in the first conjunction betwixt male and female, for procreation of the species—I was insensibly led into it'. And so he continues for the whole chapter, following it (but not until we have had a substantive reference to 5 as Trim recites the first five commandments)[49] with a discourse on 'Blessed health' (chaps 33ff.).

But this by no means exhausts the significance of the number for the novel. It has, indeed, a very special place in Sterne's scheme, since it is embodied in Tristram's birth date, 5 November (I. 5). And if we wonder why Sterne should have chosen that particular date for the birth of his melancholy (*tristis*) hero with his crushed nose and his maimed genitals, then the reason is not far to seek. The date has obvious unfortunate associations in English history;[50] while even more important, if we recall the novel's themes of sterility and misfortune, is the maleficent nature of 5 in ancient thought. Bongo, for instance, quotes[51] Virgil's *quintam fuge* from the first *Georgic*; notes that the fifth day after the new moon (*quinta luna*) is disapproved of by Hesiod, and remarks: 'Antiquis .n. creditum est, quidquid Luna quinta nasceretur, sterile atq. damnosum fore.' Little wonder, if the number is thus associated with sterility, that Tristram, born on the fifth, should be violently circumcised in vol. V when he is five years old (ch. 17)!

Circumcision is traditionally associated with the number 8 (Leviticus 12:3), and Tristram is circumcised in chapter 17 rather than (as we might expect) the eighth chapter. Again, however, there is a reason for this. What Tristram suffers is, after all, an accident, not a planned ritual, and the 17 appears to have been deliberately chosen: like 19, it is *infaustus* and symbolizes misfortune. More specifically, it is associated with the death of Osiris (17 November), the point about which, surely, is his dismemberment and the fact that Isis was able to recover all the bodily fragments but one: his phallus.[52] Once again, by the way, we should note the cumulative sequence: Tristram's circumcision occurs in V. 17; in IV. 17 Tristram has mentioned 'the misfortune of my NOSE [falling] so heavily upon my father's head'; and in III. 17 Dr Slop has remarked to Walter that, when the child is being born, 'if the hip is mistaken for the head,—there is a possibility (if it is a boy) that the forceps *'.

VI

Many critics have seen the epigraph to vol. VII—'Non enim excursus hic eius, sed opus ipsum est'—as merely another joke at the long-suffering reader's expense. I should like to argue, on the contrary, that Sterne means what he says, and that here we have the real core of the novel.[53] Misfortune and the preoccupation with time are ubiquitous in *Tristram Shandy*; Burton's *Anatomy* was one of its main inspirations. Now these things are connected, it seems to me, and have a common centre in the name 'Tristram' itself, which immediately places Sterne's hero under the patronage of Saturn—lord of *tristitia* (melancholy), of time, and of mutability. Well might Tristram have said, with Burton at the beginning of the *Anatomy*, '*Saturn* was the Lord of my geniture'; and well might we regard *Tristram Shandy* as the English eighteenth-century's supreme expression of the temperamental, psychological, and cosmic influence of Saturn.

The fifth volume, I have said, is important for this aspect of the novel, as it had to be because of the associations of 5 with the mutable world (it is significant that this volume contains the largest number of borrowings from Burton). And yet the full development of the theme had to wait until vol. VII, because 7 alone is Saturn's number.[54]

It is first necessary to establish just how Saturnian Tristram is.

Saturn is, in addition to the attributes listed above, the god of old age and death, of misfortune and consumption. His colour is black. Astrologers agree that the child of Saturn is lean, withered, and pale.[55] Could we find a more apt description of Tristram-Sterne as he portrays himself in the seventh volume[56]—'very thin' (ch. 13); 'a man with pale face, and clad in black' (ch. 17)? In chapter 34 his black clothes are mentioned again, together with his 'face as pale as ashes', and a priest thinks he is dying. The volume begins with Tristram's 'vile cough'—a consumptive one; and chapter 30 tells us that 'milk coffee . . . is excellently good for a consumption.' Moreover, Saturn dominates Tristram's birth date in a way which many have noticed but not accounted for. The influence reveals itself in Tristram's *actual* gestation period: he is conceived in early March and born in early November: 'as near nine kalendar months as any husband could in reason have expected' (I. 5). Ignoring the 'as near', readers have complained that Sterne couldn't count, since Tristram is an eight-months', not a nine-months', child. But this is exactly his point, and shows again how essential numerological and astrological lore is to the very meaning of the novel. For each month of the gestation period was traditionally dedicated to one of the planetary deities; and the eighth month was ruled over by Saturn.[57]

Tristram, then, confronts us with the uniquely human problem of the awareness of time, of mutability, and death. This is the whole theme of vol. VII, which opens with Death knocking at the door. And the motif is pursued (as Death pursues Tristram) through the sickness of chapter 2 ('Sick! sick! sick! sick!'), the apostrophe to mutable Janatone in chapter 9 and the decay of Christianity in chapter 14, to the symbolically disordered chimes of chapter 15 (matched by Lippius's clock in chapter 39, which is 'all out of joints, and had not gone for some years . . .'), and all the other manifestations of disorder in which the volume abounds.

Tristram has reminded us in the novel's Dedication (which first appeared in the second edition of vols I and II) that 'I live in a constant endeavour to fence against the infirmities of ill health, and other evils of life, by mirth'; in IV. 22 he has told us that he writes 'against the spleen'; and that same volume ends, as we have seen, with his vision of an ideal kingdom in which 'the bilious and more saturnine passions' are kept under control. In fact, the whole novel is cathartic, and the seventh volume in particular epitomizes the flight from Saturn that *Tristram Shandy* is, in a very real sense, about. (For, as the interruption of Tristram's begetting by the question about the winding of the clock reminds us, to come into existence is to be immediately subject to Saturn (time, mortality); so that there is more than one meaning—as the novel implies—that can be attached to the pseudo-Aristotelian observation 'Quod omne animal post coitum est triste', quoted in V. 36.)

It epitomizes the flight from Saturn by embodying the traditional modes of purging melancholy, as any devotee of Burton will have noticed: travel, sociability (Tristram's plain becomes peopled in chapter 43) and, above all, venery—for Venus, goddess of love, music, and the dance, is antithetic to Saturn.[58] The modulation from the dance of death to the festive dance begins in VII. 38, where 'the whole world was going out a May-poling. . . .'And it is finally accomplished in the magnificent forty-third chapter where, just for a second—for in the mutable world such insights can only be evanescent—Tristram attains to the vision of universal harmony, of unity in a world of multiplicity, that he—in part through the structure of the novel itself—has been seeking all along. It is expressed, as all such visions must be,[59] in a circular dance to the accompaniment of music, primeval symbols both of the ordered motion of the cosmos:[60]

They are running at the ring of pleasure. . . . I'll take a dance, said I. . . .

A sun-burnt daughter of Labour rose up from the groupe to meet me as I advanced towards them; her hair, which was a dark chesnut, approaching rather to black, was tied up in a knot, all but a single tress. . . .

A lame youth, whom Apollo had recompenced with a pipe, and to which he had added a tabourin of his own accord, ran sweetly over the prelude, as he sat upon the bank—Tie me up this tress instantly, said Nannette, putting a piece of string into my hand—It taught me to forget I was a stranger—The whole knot fell down—We had been seven years acquainted.

The youth struck the note upon the tabourin—his pipe followed, and off we bounded. . . .

The sister of the youth who had stolen her voice from heaven, sung alternately with her brother—'twas a Gascoigne roundelay.

VIVA LA JOIA!
FIDON LA TRISTESSA!

The nymphs join'd in unison, and their swains an octave below them—

At such a moment is the knot untied: we have modulated with Tristram from the key of Saturn to the key of Venus and of love; from mutable 7 (mentioned explicitly in the passage) to harmonious 8 ('The nymphs join'd in unison, and their swains an octave below them'). So that Toby's amours must inevitably follow in the eighth volume, in an attempt to sustain the new key.

The attempt will fail, but the moment of victory over *la tristessa* has been real, and all the more convincing because it has occurred in Saturn's volume bearing a Saturnian chapter-total; for as the Tristram who declares in VII. 14 that he 'must be cut short in the midst of [his] days' doubtless knew, he who has Saturn as the 'Lord of [his] Geniture' will, 'if he be meanly dignified', live only forty-three years.[61]

VII

I am not arguing that Sterne had the end of his novel—which was, after all, to lie eight volumes and some seven years ahead—clearly in view when he was penning the first volume. But it does seem to me that number symbolism did give him some kind of scheme or formula to work to by suggesting associations and themes. And it would, as I implied at the beginning of this chapter, be too easy to see the novel's numerology merely as a further instance of Sterne's jests at the expense of 'exploded opinions, and forsaken fooleries'.[62] For as Arthur H. Cash has shown,[63] Sterne had strong affinities with the rational Christianity of the Cambridge Platonists and such followers of theirs as Samuel Clarke who believed that 'the moral law . . . can be discovered *a priori* by reason alone, much as mathematical truths are found.' There is an example in the sermon in II. 17, where Sterne refers to 'calm reason and the unchangeable obligations of justice and truth . . .' and reminds us that 'to govern our actions by the eternal measures of right and wrong . . . will comprehend the duties . . . of morality. . . .' We must suppose, then, that these beliefs fostered in Sterne an attitude to symbolic numbers that was rather like Fielding's as I have discussed it in connection with *Tom Jones*—that on the one hand he regarded them with detached amusement as a form of false wit; and that on the other he saw them (with more than a hint of nostalgia and to an extent that we inevitably, I suppose, find it difficult to accept) as retaining considerable validity as expressions of eternal moral truths.

NOTES

1 Quotations are from the first edn, 9 vols (1760–7).
2 Cf. VII. 27 ('But this rich bale is not to be open'd now; except a thread or two of it, merely to unravel the mystery of my father's stay at AUXERRE') and 28 ('Now this is the most puzzled skein of all. . .').
3 *The Rose-Garden Game: The Symbolic Background to the European Prayer-Beads* (1969), p. 204.
4 Cf. J. E. Cirlot, *A Dictionary of Symbols*, tr. J. Sage (1967), s.v. Weaving, and Pope's *Epistle to Dr Arbuthnot*, ll. 89–94, where the metaphor, used satirically, implies that the cobweb (i.e., poem) is a microcosm, and the poet-spider a parody of God.
5 See, for example, John M. Stedmond, *The Comic Art of Laurence Sterne* (Toronto, 1967), pp. 119–20.
6 See Douglas Jefferson's '*Tristram Shandy* and the Tradition of Learned Wit', *EC*, 1 (1951), 225–48. In this connection it should be noted that Sterne's specific numerological antecedents are likely to be *Gargantua and Pantagruel* and the Scriblerus Club's *Memoirs of the Extraordinary Life, Works, and Discoveries of Martinus Scriblerus*. Rabelais refers to symbolic numbers in II. 18; III. 11; III. 17; III. 20; III. 49; and V. 36, etc.; while the *Memoirs*, ch. 7, indulge in the familiar speculation as to whether 'the Creation was finish'd in six days, because six is the most perfect number; or if six be the most perfect number because the Creation was finished in six days?' (ed. Charles Kerby-Miller (New York, 1966), pp. 123–4). See, in addition, the 1723 *Memoirs*, with their insistence on 7s (ibid., Appendix 6, pp. 379, 381). The influence of Rabelais and the *Memoirs* on *Tristram Shandy* is discussed by, among others, John Ferriar, *Illustrations of Sterne*, 2 vols (1812), I. 41ff. and 93; Henri Fluchère, *Laurence Sterne: From Tristram to Yorick*, tr. and abridged Barbara Bray (1965), pp. 174–6 and 200–2; and John M. Stedmond, op. cit., pp. 49–54 and Appendix.
7 The latest and most sustained account, which relates the novel to the doctrine *ut pictura poesis*, is William V. Holtz, *Image and Immortality: A Study of 'Tristram Shandy'* (Providence, R.I., 1970), passim.
8 See Jefferson, '*Tristram Shandy* and the Tradition of Learned Wit', p. 237n.
9 See Edgar Wind, *Pagan Mysteries in the Renaissance* (rev. edn, 1967), pp. 167ff. and notes, and Macrobius, *Saturnalia*, VII. 16. 8: in the rites of Liber 'the egg is so revered and worshiped that (by reason of its rounded and almost spherical shape and as completely encased and containing life) it is called the image of the universe, which by general consent is held to be the first beginning of all things'; tr. Percival Vaughan Davies (New York, 1969), p. 513. A 1694 edn of Macrobius's *Works* is listed as item 1837 in *A Catalogue of a Curious and Valuable Collection of Books, among which are included the Entire Library of the late Reverend and Learned Laurence Sterne* (facsimile, 1930). The Macrobius, and the other works which I cite below as being in the catalogue, seem likely to have been Sterne's.
10 As Christopher Ricks notes, in connection with IV. 32, in his Introd. to the Penguin English Library *Tristram Shandy*, ed. Graham Petrie (Harmondsworth, 1967), p. 20.
11 *Three Books of Occult Philosophy*, II. 4 (p. 174).
12 Wayne Booth, 'Did Sterne Complete *Tristram Shandy*?', *MP*, 48 (1950–1), 172–83, citing, among other instances, an echo of I. 6 in IX. 25 and of I. 3 in IX. 1.

13 Nine is also circular because it always reproduces itself: $2 \times 9 = 18$; $1 + 8 = 9$, etc., and because it completes the initial series of integers. The novel thus appears to form a complete cycle as it stands; but this doesn't necessarily mean that it is finished: Sterne could have continued with another cycle (10–19), and so on. Perhaps the best comment as to whether the novel is completed or not (because it leaves the question teasingly open) is made by the concluding phrase 'cock and bull', i.e., a story with neither beginning nor end (*OED*, Cock-and-bull 2, citing a 1714 transln of Thomas à Kempis; the same meaning is given in Francis Grose, *A Classical Dictionary of the Vulgar Tongue* (1785)).

14 Cf. John Traugott, *Tristram Shandy's World: Sterne's Philosophical Rhetoric* (Berkeley and Los Angeles, Calif., 1954), p. 43.

15 Ferriar, *Illustrations*, II. 37–9, hints that the origin of the black page might lie in Robert Fludd's partly numerological *Utriusque cosmi historia*, where a black page 'is emblematic of the chaos' (on Fludd, see Frances A. Yates, *Theatre of the World* (1969), especially ch. 3). Other instances of the novel's preoccupation with the mid-point may be noted here: in the centre of vol. III (chaps 21, 22 of a total of forty-two) we have 'the affair of *hinges*' (cf. 'the well-balanced world on hinges hung' at the central line (122 of a total of 244) of Milton's *Nativity Ode*, mentioned in Fowler, *Triumphal Forms*, pp. 115–16n); the forty chapters of vol. VI are evenly divided (ch. 20 announces 'WE are now going to enter upon a new scene of events', and in it Tristram takes leave of all that has preceded; the narrative resumes with ch. 21); the middle of vol. VII (ch. 21 of a total of forty-three) sees the abbess and the novice stranded half-way up a hill; in VIII. 18 (central out of thirty-five) the fortifications are demolished; and in IX. 17 (central out of thirty-three) Toby finally enters the widow's house.

16 Lucina, goddess of childbirth, is, of course, a moon goddess. The connection between the moon and generation is discussed by, e.g., Agrippa, II. 32 (p. 283). IX. 33—the last chapter of the novel—also juxtaposes death and birth.

17 *New Calendar of 1561*, cit. Alexander Dunlop, 'The Unity of Spenser's *Amoretti*', in Fowler (ed.), *Silent Poetry*, p. 167, n. 5.

18 R. L. Poole, 'The Beginning of the Year in the Middle Ages', *Proceedings of the British Academy*, 10 (1921–3), p. 125.

19 E.g., ch. 16 ('twenty or five-and-twenty miles'), ch. 18 ('a silk of five-and-twenty shillings a yard'), and ch. 21 ('some twenty or five-and-twenty years').

20 Library sale catalogue, item 256. Numbers are discussed in *The Columnes*, second day, second week; 1605 edn, pp. 472–3.

21 See Bongo, p. 251; Agrippa, II. 5 (pp. 177–8); and Vincent F. Hopper, *Medieval Number Symbolism* (1938), pp. 39–40.

22 *The Comic Art of Laurence Sterne*, p. 88.

23 Agrippa, p. 177.

24 Bongo, p. 423.

25 The unity of the three volumes is apparent in several ways: III. 1 begins where II. 18 left off; there is a distinct break at the end of vol. III, where Tristram tells us 'we have leisure enough upon our hands'; and the volume also contains 'The Author's Preface' (between chaps 20 and 21) which should have appeared at the beginning of vol. I. As I see it, the numerological structure cuts across, and was conceived independently of, the two-volume blocks in which the novel was originally published: i.e., vols. I and II, Dec. 1759; III and IV, Jan.

1761; V and VI, Dec. 1761; VII and VIII, Jan. 1765. Vol. IX appeared separately in Jan. 1767.

26 See F. M. Cornford, *Plato's Cosmology* (1937), pp. 3–4, and, in addition, Hopper, p. 6, and Cirlot, *Dictionary*, s.v. Ternary: 'Undoubtedly, the vital, human significance of the number three and the ternary embraces the multi-secular origins of biological evolution. The existence of two (father and mother) must almost inevitably be followed by three (the son).'

27 Compare III. 38: 'a thousand distresses and domestic misadventures crouding in upon me thick and three-fold. . . .'

28 The relationship between nose and genitals is perhaps too commonplace to need documentation: for example, W. C. Curry, *Chaucer and the Mediæval Sciences* (1968), p. 87, and *Humphry Clinker*, Jery's letter of 18 April.

29 Tr. Urquhart and Motteux, Everyman edn, 2 vols (1949), II. 123.

30 See G. R. S. Mead, *Thrice-Great Hermes: Studies in Hellenistic Theosophy and Gnosis*, 3 vols (1906), III. 224–5; see also Hopper, *Medieval Number Symbolism*, p. 53. Marvin K. Singleton attempts to trace Trismegistic influences on the novel in two articles: 'Trismegistic Tenor and Vehicle in Sterne's *Tristram Shandy*', *Papers in Language and Literature*, 4 (1968), 158–69; and 'Deuced Knowledge as Shandean Nub: Paracelsian Hermetic as Metaphoric Bridge in *Tristram Shandy*', *Zeitschrift für Anglistik und Amerikanistik*, 16 (1968), 274–84.

31 *Timaeus*, 32 B–C, tr. R. G. Bury, Loeb edn, pp. 59–61; F. M. Cornford, 'Mysticism and Science in the Pythagorean Tradition', *Classical Quarterly*, 17 (1923), 4; and Macrobius, *Commentary on the Dream of Scipio*, I. 6. 24–33.

32 As we have seen (ch. iv), 4 also symbolizes reason and virtue. I suspect, incidentally, that the *tetractys* (10 as the sum of $1+2+3+4$; see *Gargantua and Pantagruel*, V. 36, 'the Tetradic steps') accounts for the large number of references to 10 in vol. IV, in chaps 19, 25, 26, and 28.

33 Bongo, p. 486, and Agrippa, II. 15 (p. 223). Cf. p. 118, n. 23 above.

34 E.g., chaps 2 ('half a dozen pages'); 11 (six musical terms applied to six of Yorick's sermons); 13 ('six weeks'), etc.

35 On 6, see Bongo, pp. 266–8, and Agrippa, II. 9 (Venus is guardian of the sixth day of the planetary week). All these and other relevant meanings are discussed in M. A. Screech, *The Rabelaisian Marriage* (1958), pp. 29–34. On Sterne and John Hall-Stevenson's Demoniacs (imitating the Monks of Medmenham, who modelled themselves on the Abbey of Thelema), see W. L. Cross, *The Life and Times of Laurence Sterne* (New Haven, Conn., 1929), pp. 130ff.

36 *Gargantua and Pantagruel*, III. 20 could well have been Sterne's source: 'Goatsnose . . . lifted up into the air his left hand, the whole fingers whereof he retained fist ways closed together, except the thumb and the fore-finger, whose nails he softly joined and coupled to one another. I understand, quoth Pantagruel, what he meaneth by that sign. It denotes marriage, and withal the number thirty, according to the profession of the Pythagoreans' (Everyman edn, I. 325).

37 Bongo, p. 501, in connection with Isaac's marriage to Rebecca when he was forty (Genesis 25:20). Burton draws attention to this marriage in his discussion of marriage ages in *Anatomy*, III. 2. 5. 5. See also Agrippa, II. 15 (p. 223), and Plutarch's *De animae procreatione*, 14 (*Moralia*, tr. Philemon Holland (1657), pp. 849–50. This is the edn of Holland's transln listed as item 177 in the library sale catalogue).

The 40s in VII. 1 are presumably intended as a retrospective pointer to the previous volume's chapter-total.

38 The one was an attribute of Mars, the other of Venus. See, e.g., Claudian's *Epithalamium* X, 195ff. (Loeb edn, tr. M. Platnauer, 2 vols (1922), I. 257); and, for the lute and love, the frontispiece to Burton's *Anatomy*.

39 Plutarch, *Moralia*, ed. cit., p. 849, and Hopper, op. cit., p. 45 (35 as harmony); and Plato, *Laws*, VI, 785 B, reported in Burton, III. 2. 5. 5: 'he that marrieth not before 35 years of his age, must be compelled. . .': *Anatomy*, ed. A. R. Shilleto, introd. A. H. Bullen, 3 vols (1893), III. 284.

40 Bongo, p. 324 (following Martianus Capella: Capella is mentioned, by the way, in VI. 2.). Macrobius, *Commentary on the Dream of Scipio*, I. 6. 15–16, discusses the female 8 in connection with 35.

41 See Fowler, *Triumphal Forms*, pp. 151–4, citing especially Jonson's *Hymenaei*.

42 This is perhaps confirmed by the number of references to 3 in the ninth volume: e.g., chaps 16 ('three steps'); 20 ('three pages'; 'rub your hands thrice across your foreheads'); 31 ('two or three times together', 'middle [i.e., third] finger', 'three words'), etc.

43 On these meanings of 9, see Bongo, pp. 334, 344, 351, etc. The connection between 33 and suffering derives in part from the belief that Christ was crucified when he was 33; though, as Gunnar Qvarnström has also pointed out in a discussion of Milton's use of 33, 'it is the sum of the numbers constituted by the letters in the name of Abel' (=sorrow, mourning): *The Enchanted Palace: Some Structural Aspects of 'Paradise Lost'*, p. 114.

44 Henri Fluchère, *Laurence Sterne*, p. 106.

45 Ptolemy's star-totals had been fairly well known in the sixteenth and early seventeenth centuries, as Fowler indicates in *Spenser and the Numbers of Time*, pp. 114–15, 199–200, and 237–8. But to use a star-total in the mid-eighteenth century is to be very obscure indeed! In Leviticus 12:4, incidentally, it is stated that thirty-three days are required for the purification of a woman after bearing a male child; yet another way in which Sterne might have connected the number with the begetting of children.

46 Stedmond, *The Comic Art of Laurence Sterne*, Appendix, p. 167, noting echoes and excerpts in V. 1, 2, and 3.

47 Plutarch, *De E apud Delphos*, 388 C–F, relates the arithmetical circularity of 5 to the universal cycle of generation and decay. See also Hopper, op. cit., p. 43, citing Martianus Capella's *De nuptiis* on 5 as 'the number of this world'.

48 *Works*, ed. Geoffrey Keynes, 4 vols (1928), IV. 120. Five is associated directly with health, since the pentacle or five-pointed star was the emblem of Hygea (goddess of health). The symbolism was common up to, and including, the eighteenth century.

49 One of many allusions to the number in this volume, needless to say. The two most important are in ch. 15, where Tristram tunes his fiddle—'They should be *fifths*'—and mentions borrowing 'five guineas', and ch. 21, in which Trim actually counts round the thumb and fingers of one hand.

50 For the importance of the 5 November celebrations in the early eighteenth century, see the *Memoirs of Martinus Scriblerus*, ed. cit., p. 240, n. 41. In *Tom Jones*, XVI. 5, Partridge mentions 'the Gunpowder-Treason Service' which remained in *The Book of Common Prayer* until the mid-nineteenth century.

51 Bongo, pp. 452–3. In Dryden's 1697 transln the Virgil passage reads as follows: 'The lucky Days, in each revolving Moon, / For Labour chuse: The Fifth be sure to shun; / That gave the Furies and pale *Pluto* Birth, / And arm'd, against the Skies, the Sons of Earth. . .'; *Georgics*, I. 371–4, in *The Poems of John Dryden*, ed. James Kinsley, 4 vols (Oxford, 1958), II. 928.

52 Bongo discusses the unfortunate implications of 17 on pp. 416–17. For Osiris and 17, see Plutarch, *De Iside et Osiride*, 367 E–F (*Moralia* (1657), p. 1061: 'of all other numbers [the Pythagoreans] most abhor and detest it').

53 William V. Holtz, *Image and Immortality*, also regards vol. VII as being important, interpreting it as 'an exorcism of . . . death' which enables Tristram to resume the story in his 'normal manner' (pp. 133–4).

54 In the Ptolemaic system Saturn is the seventh planet, counting outwards from the earth; he is also guardian of the seventh day of the planetary week: the two reasons given by Agrippa (II. 10 (p. 195)) for associating the number with Saturn. Macrobius, *Commentary*, 1. 6. 62–82, demonstrates exhaustively how 7 governs man's earthly life. Harold Love, in his ingenious note 'A Shandean Number Game', *Notes and Queries*, n.s. 18 (1971), 339, shows how Sterne alludes to the number 7 in VII. 7: the chapter contains seven paragraphs and seven speakers; Tristram christens the tall man and the short man '*Size-Ace*' (i.e., $6+1$), and his debts are estimated to be £7,000. He also points out that the chapter contains 343 English words; i.e., 7^3. But Love sees this merely as an isolated phenomenon in the novel rather than as belonging to a larger numerological context.

55 Burton, I. 3. 1. 1; Ptolemy, *Tetrabiblos*, II. 8 and III. 12 (Loeb edn, tr. F. E. Robbins (1940), pp. 181, 327); and Raymond Klibansky, Erwin Panofsky, and Fritz Saxl, *Saturn and Melancholy* (1964), passim.

56 Cross, *Life and Times*, p. 382, however, mentions the fashionable black attire worn by Sterne once he became 'a man of the world'. Its significance is obviously not solely emblematic.

57 Lynn Thorndike, *A History of Magic and Experimental Science*, 8 vols (New York, 1923–58), IV (1934), 209–10. See also Agrippa, II. 21 (p. 238), and William Lilly, *Christian Astrology* (1647), I. 8 (p. 60). Note that when, in IV. 19, Walter speculates whether 'due attention . . . to [Mrs Shandy's] evacuations and repletions—and the rest of her non-naturals, might not, in a course of nine months gestation, have set all things to rights.—My child was bereft of these!', he means that Tristram was 'bereft of' a 'nine months gestation', as well as everything else.

58 Burton, II. 2. 3 and II. 2. 4, and Lilly, op. cit., p. 61. Sterne recommended love as a cure in a letter of 23 [August?] 1765: 'I am glad that you are in love—'twill cure you (at least) of the spleen, which has a bad effect on both man and woman'; *Letters*, ed. L. P. Curtis (Oxford, 1965), p. 256.

59 See Eithne Wilkins, *The Rose-Garden Game*, passim.

60 Compare the sacramental dance on the top of mount Taurira in *A Sentimental Journey*, ed. Gardner D. Stout, Jr (Berkeley and Los Angeles, Calif., 1967), pp. 283–4 and notes, and *Roderick Random*, ch. 43, where Roderick's Saturnian misanthropy is transformed to 'mirth and social joy' by the dancing of soldiers and their wives.

61 Lilly, op. cit., p. 61. The number is the mean between Saturn's greatest and least years (57 and 30). Lilly gives $43\frac{1}{2}$ in a table, but rounds it down to 43 in his

text. The emphasis on mutability in vol. V is sufficient to account for its chapter-total of 43. I suspect in the case of vol. VII, however, that Sterne might in addition have intended 43 to be understood as a number of release, in allusion to the 430 years of Exodus 12:40–1. In his sermon 'National Mercies considered. On the Inauguration of his present Majesty', Sterne recounts how God had delivered the Israelites after 'the chains of their captivity had been fixed and rivetted by a succession of four hundred and thirty years . . .'; in *The Sermons of Mr. Yorick*, 7th edn, 4 vols (1765–6), III (1766), 173. Tristram's liberation from death and crossing of the plain in VII. 43 could well carry such typological overtones.

62 Ferriar, *Illustrations of Sterne*, II. 53.
63 *Sterne's Comedy of Moral Sentiments: The Ethical Dimension of the 'Journey'*, Duquesne Studies, Philological Series, 6 (Pittsburgh, Pa., 1966), p. 109; and cf. ch. v above.

Appendix

Prefatory Table from *The Holy Bible, with Practical Observations on each Chapter*. By the Late Rev. Mr Ostervald, 2 vols (Newcastle upon Tyne, 1793).

The OLD and NEW TESTAMENTS contain,

Books in the Old	39	The New	27	Total	66
Chapters	929		260		1,189
Verses	23,214		7,959		31,173
Words	592,439		181,253		773,692
Letters	2,728,100		838,380		3,566,480

APOCRYPHA

Chapters	183
Verses	6,081
Words	152,185

The middle chapter, and the least in the Bible, is Psalm cxvii..
The middle verse is the 8th of Psalm cxviii.
The middle time 2 Chronicles, chap. iv. verse 16.
The word AND occurs in the Old Testament 35,543 times..
The same in the New Testament, occurs 10,684 times.
The word JEHOVAH occurs 6,855 times.

OLD TESTAMENT

The middle book is Proverbs.
The middle chapter is Job xxix.
The middle verse is 2 Chron. chap. xx. between the 17th and 18th verses.
The least verse is 1 Chron. chap. i. and 1st verse.

NEW TESTAMENT

The middle book is 2 Thessalonians.
The middle chapter is between Romans xiii. and xiv.

The middle verse is Acts, chap. xvii. verse 17.
The least verse is John chap. xi. verse 35.
The 21st verse of Ezra vii. has all the letters of the Alphabet.
The 2d of Kings, chap. xix. and Isaiah xxxvii. are alike.

Select Bibliography

List of editions cited on more than one occasion.

AGRIPPA, HENRY CORNELIUS, *Three Books of Occult Philosophy*, tr. J. F. London, 1651.

AITKEN, *see under* DEFOE.

ALTER, ROBERT, *Fielding and the Nature of the Novel*. Cambridge, Mass., 1968.

ARISTOTLE, *Nicomachean Ethics*, tr. H. Rackham. Loeb Classical Library. London, 1926.

BATESON, F. W., *see under* POPE.

BATTESTIN, M. C., 'Fielding's Definition of Wisdom: Some Functions of Ambiguity and Emblem in *Tom Jones*'. *ELH*, 35, 1968.

—— *The Moral Basis of Fielding's Art*. Middletown, Conn., 1959.

—— '*Tom Jones*: The Argument of Design', in H. K. Miller, E. Rothstein, and G. S. Rousseau (eds), *The Augustan Milieu: Essays Presented to Louis A. Landa*. Oxford, 1970. *See also under* FIELDING.

BLUME, FRIEDRICH, *Renaissance and Baroque Music: A Comprehensive Survey*, tr. M. D. Herter Norton. London, 1968.

BOND, *see under* Spectator.

BONGO, PIETRO, *Numerorum mysteria*. Bergamo, 1599.

BOUCÉ, PAUL-GABRIEL, *Les Romans de Smollett: Étude Critique*. Publications de la Sorbonne; Littératures, I. Paris, 1971.

BOULTON, *see under* BURKE, EDMUND.

BROOKS, DOUGLAS, 'The Interpolated Tales in *Joseph Andrews* Again'. *MP*, 65, 1968.

—— 'Richardson's *Pamela* and Fielding's *Joseph Andrews*'. *EC*, 17, 1967.

—— and FOWLER, ALASTAIR, 'The Structure of Dryden's *A Song for St. Cecilia's Day, 1687*', in A. Fowler (ed.), *Silent Poetry*. London, 1970. *See also under* FIELDING.

BROWN, E. K., *Rhythm in the Novel*. Toronto, 1967.

BROWN, HOMER O., 'The Displaced Self in the Novels of Daniel Defoe'. *ELH*, 38, 1971.

BUCK, H. S., *A Study in Smollett, Chiefly 'Peregrine Pickle'*. New Haven, Conn., 1925.

BUKOFZER, MANFRED F., *Music in the Baroque Era*. London, 1948.

BURKE, EDMUND, *A Philosophical Enquiry into the Origin of our Ideas of the Sublime and Beautiful*, ed. J. T. Boulton. London, 1958.

BURKE, JOSEPH, *see under* HOGARTH.

BURTON, ROBERT, *The Anatomy of Melancholy*, ed. A. R. Shilleto, introd. A. H. Bullen. 3 vols. London, 1893.

BUTLER, CHRISTOPHER, *Number Symbolism*. London, 1970.

CIRLOT, J. E., *A Dictionary of Symbols*, tr. J. Sage. London, 1967.

CLIFFORD, *see under* SMOLLETT.

COOPER, ANTHONY ASHLEY, THIRD EARL OF SHAFTESBURY, *Characteristics, of Men, Manners, Opinions, Times*, ed. J. M. Robertson. 2 vols. London, 1900.

CORNFORD, F. M., 'Mysticism and Science in the Pythagorean Tradition'. *Classical Quarterly*, 17, 1923.

CROSS, W. L., *The History of Henry Fielding*. 3 vols. New Haven, Conn., 1918.

——*The Life and Times of Laurence Sterne*. New Haven, Conn., 1929.

DEFOE, DANIEL, *Captain Singleton*, ed. Shiv K. Kumar. Oxford English Novels. London, 1969.

—— *Colonel Jack*, ed. S. H. Monk. Oxford English Novels. London, 1965.

—— *Conjugal Lewdness; or, Matrimonial Whoredom. A Treatise Concerning the Use and Abuse of the Marriage Bed*, introd. M. E. Novak. Gainesville, Fla., 1967.

—— *Moll Flanders*, introd. Bonamy Dobrée. The World's Classics. London, 1961.

—— *Robinson Crusoe*, introd. Austin Dobson. London, 1883.

—— *Romances and Narratives by Daniel Defoe*, ed. G. A. Aitken. 16 vols. London, 1895.

—— *Roxana*, ed. Jane Jack. Oxford English Novels. London, 1964.

DONOVAN, ROBERT, *The Shaping Vision: Imagination in the English Novel from Defoe to Dickens*. Ithaca, N.Y., 1966.

EHRENPREIS, IRVIN, *Fielding: Tom Jones*. Studies in English Literature, 23. London, 1964.

EVANS, DAVID L., '*Humphry Clinker*: Smollett's Tempered Augustanism'. *Criticism*, 9, 1967.

FERRIAR, JOHN, *Illustrations of Sterne*. 2 vols. London, 1812.

FIELDING, HENRY, *Amelia*. 4 vols. London, 1752.

—— *Joseph Andrews*, ed. M. C. Battestin. Oxford, 1967.

—— '*Joseph Andrews*' and '*Shamela*', ed. Douglas Brooks. Oxford English Novels. London, 1970.

—— *Tom Jones*. 4 vols. London, 1749.

FLUCHÈRE, HENRI, *Laurence Sterne: From Tristram to Yorick*, tr. and abridged Barbara Bray. London, 1965.

FOWLER, ALASTAIR (ed.), *Silent Poetry: Essays in Numerological Analysis*. London, 1970.

FOWLER, ALASTAIR, *Spenser and the Numbers of Time*. London, 1964.

—— *Triumphal Forms: Structural Patterns in Elizabethan Poetry*. Cambridge, 1970. *See also under* BROOKS and MILTON.

FUSSELL, PAUL, *The Rhetorical World of Augustan Humanism*. London, 1969.

GEIRINGER, IRENE and GEIRINGER, KARL, *Johann Sebastian Bach: The Culmination of an Era*. London, 1967.

GOLDBERG, M. A., *Smollett and the Scottish School*. Albuquerque, New Mexico, 1959.

GRANT, *see under* SMOLLETT.

GREIF, MARTIN J., 'The Conversion of Robinson Crusoe'. *SEL*, 6, 1966.

GUTHKELCH, *see under* SWIFT.

HILLES, F. W., 'Art and Artifice in *Tom Jones*', in Maynard Mack and Ian Gregor (eds), *Imagined Worlds: Essays on Some English Novels and Novelists in Honour of John Butt*. London, 1968.

—— 'The Plan of *Clarissa*'. *PQ*, 45, 1966.

HOGARTH, WILLIAM, *The Analysis of Beauty*, ed. Joseph Burke. Oxford, 1955.

—— *Hogarth's Graphic Works*, ed. Ronald Paulson. 2 vols. New Haven, Conn., and London, 1965.

HOLTZ, WILLIAM V., *Image and Immortality: A Study of 'Tristram Shandy'*. Providence, R.I., 1970.

HOPPER, VINCENT F., *Medieval Number Symbolism*. New York, 1938.

HUME, ROBERT D., 'The Conclusion of Defoe's *Roxana*: Fiasco or Tour de Force?' *ECS*, 3, 1969–70.

HUNTER, J. PAUL, *The Reluctant Pilgrim: Defoe's Emblematic Method and Quest for Form in 'Robinson Crusoe'*. Baltimore, Md., 1966.

JACK, *see under* DEFOE.

JEFFERSON, DOUGLAS, '*Tristram Shandy* and the Tradition of Learned Wit'. *EC*, 1, 1951.

KANTOROWICZ, ERNST H., 'Oriens Augusti—Lever du Roi'. *Dumbarton Oaks Papers*, 17, 1963.

KAUFMANN, EMIL, *Architecture in the Age of Reason*. New York, 1968.

KLIBANSKY, RAYMOND, PANOFSKY, ERWIN, and SAXL, FRITZ, *Saturn and Melancholy: Studies in the History of Natural Philosophy, Religion, and Art*. London, 1964.

KNAPP, *see under* SMOLLETT.

KUMAR, *see under* DEFOE.

LEWALSKI, BARBARA, *Milton's Brief Epic: The Genre, Meaning, and Art of 'Paradise Regained'*. Providence, R.I., 1966.

LILLY, WILLIAM, *Christian Astrology*. London, 1647.

MCBURNEY, W. H., '*Colonel Jacque*: Defoe's Definition of the Complete English Gentleman'. *SEL*, 2, 1962.

187

MACK, MAYNARD, *The Garden and The City: Retirement and Politics in the Later Poetry of Pope 1731–1743*. Toronto, Buffalo, and London, 1969.

MALINS, EDWARD, *English Landscaping and Literature 1660–1840*. London, 1966.

MILLER, CHARLES KERBY, *see under* SCRIBLERUS.

MILNE, JAMES LEES, *Earls of Creation: Five Great Patrons of Eighteenth-Century Art*. London, 1962.

MILTON, JOHN, *The Poems of John Milton*, ed. John Carey and Alastair Fowler. London, 1968.

MONK, *see under* DEFOE.

NOVAK, MAXIMILLIAN E., 'Crime and Punishment in Defoe's *Roxana*'. *JEGP*, 65, 1966.

—— *Defoe and the Nature of Man*. London, 1963.

—— 'Defoe's "Indifferent Monitor": The Complexity of *Moll Flanders*'. *ECS*, 3, 1969–70.

PANOFSKY, ERWIN, *Meaning in the Visual Arts: Papers in and on Art History*. Garden City, N.Y., 1955. *See also under* KLIBANSKY.

PAULSON, RONALD, *Hogarth: His Life, Art, and Times*. 2 vols. New Haven, Conn., and London, 1971.

—— *Satire and the Novel in Eighteenth-Century England*. New Haven, Conn., and London, 1967. *See also under* HOGARTH.

PETERSON, SPIRO, 'The Matrimonial Theme of Defoe's *Roxana*'. *PMLA*, 70, 1955.

PLATO, *Timaeus*, tr. R. G. Bury. Loeb Classical Library. London, 1929.

PLUTARCH, *The Morals*, tr. Philemon Holland. London, 1657.

POPE, ALEXANDER, *Epistles to Several Persons*, ed. F. W. Bateson, Twickenham edn, vol. III. ii. London, 1961.

PUTNEY, RUFUS, 'The Plan of *Peregrine Pickle*'. *PMLA*, 60, 1945.

QVARNSTRÖM, GUNNAR, *The Enchanted Palace: Some Structural Aspects of 'Paradise Lost'*. Stockholm, 1967.

RABELAIS, FRANÇOIS, *Gargantua and Pantagruel*, tr. Sir Thomas Urquhart and Peter le Motteux. Everyman's Library. 2 vols. London, 1949–50.

RICHARDSON, SAMUEL, *Pamela*, ed. M. Kinkead-Weekes. Everyman's Library. 2 vols. London, 1962–3.

RICHETTI, JOHN J., *Popular Fiction Before Richardson: Narrative Patterns 1700–1739*. Oxford, 1969.

RØSTVIG, MAREN-SOFIE, 'The Hidden Sense: Milton and the Neo-platonic Method of Numerical Composition', in *The Hidden Sense*. Norwegian Studies in English, 9, 1963.

—— 'Structure as Prophecy: The Influence of Biblical Exegesis upon Theories of Literary Structure', in Alastair Fowler (ed.), *Silent Poetry*. London, 1970.

RUTHVEN, K. K., 'Fielding, Square, and the Fitness of Things'. *ECS*, 5, 1971–2.

SAXL, *see under* KLIBANSKY.

SCRIBLERUS, *Memoirs of the Extraordinary Life, Works, and Discoveries of Martinus Scriblerus*, ed. Charles Kerby-Miller. New York, 1966.

SCRIMGEOUR, GARY J., 'The Problem of Realism in Defoe's *Captain Singleton*'. *HLQ*, 27, 1963–4.

SHAFTESBURY, *see under* COOPER.

SMITH, D. NICHOL, *see under* SWIFT.

SMOLLETT, TOBIAS, *Ferdinand Count Fathom*, ed. Damian Grant. Oxford English Novels. London, 1971.

—— *Humphry Clinker*, ed. Lewis M. Knapp. Oxford English Novels. London, 1966.

—— *Peregrine Pickle*, ed. James L. Clifford. Oxford English Novels. London, 1964.

—— *Roderick Random*. 2 vols. London, 1748.

Spectator, The, ed. D. F. Bond. 5 vols. Oxford, 1965.

STARR, G. A., *Defoe and Spiritual Autobiography*. Princeton, N.J., 1965.

STEDMOND, JOHN M., *The Comic Art of Laurence Sterne*. Toronto, 1967.

STERNE, LAURENCE, *A Catalogue of a Curious and Valuable Collection of Books, among which are included the Entire Library of the late Reverend and Learned Laurence Sterne*. Under the title *A Facsimile Reproduction of a Unique Catalogue of Laurence Sterne's Library*, introd. Charles Whibley. London and New York, 1930.

—— *Tristram Shandy*. 9 vols. London, 1760–7.

SUMMERSON, JOHN, *Architecture in Britain: 1530–1830*. The Pelican History of Art. Harmondsworth, 1970.

SWEDENBERG, H. T., *The Theory of the Epic in England 1650–1800*. Berkeley and Los Angeles, Calif., 1944.

SWIFT, JONATHAN, *A Tale of a Tub*, ed. A. C. Guthkelch and D. Nichol Smith. Oxford, 1958.

UPTON, JOHN, *Spenser's 'Faerie Queene'. A New Edition with a Glossary, and Notes Explanatory and Critical*. 2 vols. London, 1758.

WEEKES, M. KINKEAD, *see under* RICHARDSON.

WILKINS, EITHNE, *The Rose-Garden Game: The Symbolic Background to the European Prayer-Beads*. London, 1969.

WITTKOWER, RUDOLF, *Architectural Principles in the Age of Humanism*. London, 1962.

WRIGHT, ANDREW, *Henry Fielding: Mask and Feast*. London, 1965.

Index